DATE DUE

MAR 29 1996	
OCT 16 1996	
OCT 30 1996	
NOV 14 1996	
NOV 28 1996	
JAN 20 1997	
FEB - 8 1997	
FEB 24 1997	
MAR 26 1997	
FEB 19 1999	
NOV - 1 1999	
OCT 25 2000	
APR 11 2003	

BRODART.   Cat. No. 23-221

Addiction Psychiatry

Addiction Psychiatry

Current Diagnosis and Treatment

Norman S. Miller, M.D.
The University of Illinois at Chicago
Department of Psychiatry
Chicago, Illinois

WILEY-LISS

A John Wiley & Sons, Inc., Publication

New York / Chichester / Brisbane / Toronto / Singapore

Miller, Norman S.
    Addiction psychiatry: current diagnosis and treatment / Norman
S. Miller.
      p. cm.
    Includes index.
    ISBN 0-471-56201-7 (cloth : alk. paper)
    1. Dual diagnosis.   2. Substance abuse.   I. Title.
    [DNLM: 1. Behavior, Addictive—psychology.   2. Behavior,
Addictive—diagnosis.   3. Behavior, Addictive—therapy.   4. Mental
Disorders.   WM 176 M647c 1994]
    RC564.68.M55 1994
    616.86—dc20
    DNLM/DLC
    for Library of Congress   94-32386

To my mother and father

Contents

Preface

Addiction psychiatry is a new field. I am writing as a clinician, teacher, and researcher in this developing area. These are exciting times for those who are dedicated to the diagnosis and treatment of addictive disorders. Moreover, the field offers hope and enthusiasm to all psychiatrists who diagnose and treat patients with addictive disorders. Other professionals can also benefit from this work.

Competency in this field has been defined by the American Board of Psychiatry and Neurology in its Added Qualifications for Addiction Psychiatry. Board certification is based on a body of clinical skills and research knowledge that exists in the field of addiction psychiatry. We now have a commitment to set standards for the field.

This book offers clinical psychiatrists and other physicians and professionals a synthesis of the current diagnosis and treatment in addiction psychiatry. It contains clinical and practical information to guide the clinician, based on a critical review of the standards of care. The contents of the book are based on current clinical and basic research from allied fields relevant to addiction psychiatry.

Residents have inspired me to write this book. Residents in psychiatry and other specialties are the future of addiction psychiatry. They challenge us to find new ways of teaching addiction psychiatry.

I am not the originator of the field of addiction psychiatry. I thank those important leaders who have been instrumental in creating the field of addiction psychiatry, particularly Drs. Richard Frances and Sheldon Miller. I wish also to thank Dr. R. Jeffrey Goldsmith for his review of the manuscript and Mrs. Tracey L. France for her editorial and technical assistance.

PART 1

Introduction and Concepts

1

Brief History of Addiction Psychiatry

HISTORY

The field of addiction psychiatry arose from clinical experience and a large body of research knowledge pertaining to the substance related disorders. As exemplified by the recent addition of addiction psychiatry as an Added Qualification to the American Board of Psychiatry and Neurology, psychiatrists are assuming substantial responsibilities regarding the diagnosis and treatment of addictions. This new interest in addictions is attributable to the inclusion of independent and exclusionary criteria for substance use disorders in DSM-III and DSM-III-R, the explosion of substance use problems in psychiatric populations, and the competition for reimbursement for psychiatric disorders.

The growth of the addiction treatment establishment was shaped by the Alcoholics Anonymous (AA) movement and selected psychiatrists who diagnosed and treated addictive disorders. A substantial minority of the psychiatrists who strongly supported the treatment of addictive disorders formed the organization that is called the American Academy of Psychiatrists in Alcoholism and Addictions (AAPAA).

Heretofore, "psychiatric methods" were employed by psychiatrists in the diagnosis and treatment of addictive disorders. These traditional methods met with limited success, and considerable untoward results. The practice of assigning an underlying cause to abnormal drinking and drug use was advanced by psychoanalysts.[1] More recently, addictions have been considered as independent disorders by psychiatrists, equal in importance to other psychiatric disorders. Putative neurochemical models have been proposed for addictive disorders, similar to other psychiatric disorders such as schizophrenia and affective disorders. The "biological basis" has replaced the "psychological explanation" for addictive use of alcohol and drugs. Genetic studies also support a "brain" substrate for addictive use of both alcohol and drugs.

It is predicted that addiction psychiatry will assume a leadership role in the field of Psychiatry. The major impetus for the establishment and growth of addiction psychiatry is the patients who suffer from addictive disorders. The future of addiction psychiatry belongs to them.

TREATMENT

The origins of addiction treatment can be traced to the psychiatric profession, namely, Drs. William Silkworth, Harry Tiebout, and Ruth Fox. These psychiatrists understood the addiction process and made clinical, organizational, and literary contributions to the addictions treatment field. Dr. Silkworth treated Bill W., who later became a cofounder of Alcoholics Anonymous. Dr. Tiebout wrote several seminal articles to the dynamics of the treatment response. Dr. Ruth Fox began regular meetings with other physicians at the New York Academy of Medicine who were interested in alcoholism and its treatment.

The Alcoholics Anonymous movement has provided an accurate depiction of the addictive behaviors and psyche of the person addicted to alcohol and other drugs.[2] Cofounded by a physician (surgeon) alcoholic, AA uses a type of "medical model" of addiction. Drug addiction is also viewed as being similar to alcoholism not only because the majority of contemporary alcoholics are addicted to other drugs, but also because it fits the medical model and is supported by similar research. Currently, millions of alcoholics and drug addicts are recovering in AA throughout the world. Other organizations that have adapted the principles of AA, such as Narcotics Anonymous and Cocaine Anonymous, have proven to be successful in supporting recovery from drug addiction.

As addiction psychiatry moves into the addiction field, it emphasizes the traditional psychiatric methods less less increasingly incorporates specific addiction treatment methods. The focus shifts from the diagnosis and treatment of "psychiatric disorders" as causes of drinking and drug use in alcoholics and drug addicts to the addictive disease itself as an independent disorder. What is being added to and incorporated in the psychiatric approach is the adoption of the clinical skills and techniques of addiction treatment and addiction research that developed outside of, and in, traditional psychiatry over the past 50 years. Addiction psychiatry represents a change in psychiatry's view of and approach to addictive disorders towards a willingness to provide effective diagnosis and treatment in all settings where they exist.

FOCUS

An Integration of Addictive and Psychiatric Disorders

Studies have clearly shown that addiction to alcohol and other drugs can generate psychiatric symptoms that resolve with abstinence and specific treatment of the addiction, thereby establishing addiction as an independent disorder.[3,4] Research has not demonstrated that psychiatric symptoms or underlying disorders cause addiction to alcohol and drugs.

Although studies are lacking, clinical experience strongly suggests that concomitant treatment of independent psychiatric disorders will improve the prognosis of the addictive disorder. On the other hand, studies have shown that the prognosis for treatment of independent psychiatric disorders remains poor without specific treatment of the independent addictive disorders.

What we have learned over the past 50 years is that treatment of addiction as an independent disorder carries the best prognosis whether or not another psychiatric disorder is present.[5] Cooccurring psychiatric and addictive disorders are best treated concurrently with the traditional tools of psychiatry, coupled with the innovated techniques developed in addiction treatment. This book is aimed at the link between these two traditions and their ultimate integration for the benefit of the addicted patient.[6,7]

REFERENCES

1. Ries RK & Samson H (1987). Substance abuse among inpatient psychiatric patients. *Substance Abuse* 8:28–34.

2. *Alcoholics Anonymous Membership 1989 Survey.* New York: Alcoholics Anonymous World Services, Inc.
3. Miller NS, Mahler JC, Belkin BM & Bold MS (1990). Psychiatric diagnosis in alcohol and drug dependence. *Ann Clin Psych* 3(1):79–89.
4. Blankfield A (1986). Psychiatric symptoms in alcohol dependence. Diagnosis and treatment implications. *J Substance Abuse Treat* 3:275–278.
5. Harrison A, Hoffman NG & Sneed SG (1991). Treatment outcome. In Miller NS (ed.), *Comprehensive Handbook of Drug and Alcohol Addiction.* New York: Marcel-Dekker.
6. Hoffmann NG & Miller NS (1992). Treatment outcomes for abstinence-based programs. *Psych Ann* 22(8):402–408.
7. Miller NS & Gold MS (1992). The psychiatrist's role in integrating pharmacological and nonpharmacological treatments for addictive disorders. *Psych Ann* 22(8):436–440.

2

DSM I–IV and Exclusionary Criteria for Addictive Disorders

HISTORY

The DSM for Substance Use Disorders

DSM-I. The progression from the first edition of the *Diagnostic and Statistical Manual of Mental Disorders* (DSM-I, 1952) to the DSM-III-R (1985) and DSM-IV (1994) (draft) illustrates many of the key elements in the context of nosology for addictive disorders. What is initially striking is the change in diagnostic labels in recent decades. The term "alcoholism" was coined in 1849 by the French physician Gabriel in his doctoral dissertation, *Essai su l'alcolisme,* and was first used in its modern sense in 1866. Alcoholism then, as now, meant an addiction to alcohol, among many other connotations that it has acquired with usage over the years. Unfortunately, in a perhaps misguided attempt to find an empirically neutral term, alcoholism was dropped from the recent nomenclatures, apparently because of the moral stigmata of addictive drinking and desire.

Originally, alcoholism was retain in DSM-I, published in 1952, but was subsumed under Personality Disorders. Specifically, addiction was considered a subcategory of sociopathic personality disturbance. There were separate codes for alcoholism and for drug addiction. The implication was clear that addiction was considered a derangement of personality that arose because of a pattern of sociopathic traits. This categorization scheme prohibited alcoholism or drug addiction from being separately diagnosed and implied dependence on causality of an "underlying" disorder.[1]

DSM-II. In DSM-II (1968), alcoholism and drug dependence were separated incompletely under Personality Disorders and Certain Other Non-psychotic Mental Disorders. References were retained to the secondary status of addiction and its association with other psychiatric disorders—"if the alcoholism is due to another mental disorder, both diagnoses should be made." The term "alcoholism" was kept but "addiction" was dropped to provide what was thought to be a more comprehensive diagnosis: "drug dependence."

The intention was that drug dependence would not require the presence of physiological addiction, but merely "evidence of habitual use or a clear sense of need for the drug." Already, there was confusion over the meaning of the terms "addiction" and "dependence" in formal usage, as the former is a behavioral term and the latter a pharmacological term. In the psychiatric categorization, the meanings appear to have been inadvertently reversed and not rooted in proper use of language and scientific and medical history for these terms. Although the break was not clear, DSM-II did advance the conceptualization of alcoholism and drug addiction toward independent status, apart from an "underlying" disorder.[2]

DSM-III. DSM-III (1985) was different from DSM-II in that the independent status of addiction moved toward more explicit recognition, and more specific definitions were included. The institution of newer terminology helped to promote recognition of independent addictive disorders. However, by attempting to maintain bridges with earlier versions of the manual, DSM-III created new ambiguities of classification.

The principal source of confusion was the adoption of the terms "abuse" and "pharmacologic dependence" as diagnostic entities. The emphasis on pharmacological dependence refueled the notion that physiological tolerance and dependence were somehow essential to the diagnosis of a drug or alcohol disorder. Perhaps it was more important that the term "addiction," which for so long had denoted a loss of control, was deleted. This powerful label had apparently acquired the baggage of stigma, and lost its scientific appeal. "Abuse," a term that historically implied volition and invited value judgments, was substituted for "addiction" to describe a pattern of pathological use. This arbitrary semantic shift, which curiously departs from neutrality, continues to have dangerous social and conceptual implications.[3,4] The use of "abuse" also harkens back to the earlier notion that abnormal alcohol and other drug use arises out of personality factors that are under volitional control. Perhaps the most serious mistake is that "abuse" is a pejoritive term.

Another arbitrary alteration from the reality of the drug and alcohol culture was the adoption of the term "substance." Other terms, such as "chemical," could have been used that are more specific, but the intent to divest the nomenclature from old attitudes actually divorced it from its rich clinical and research traditions. Many addiction researchers and clinicians have argued that the use of the overinclusive term "substance" has done more to dilute the cause of a primary role for alcohol and drug addiction than to enhance its status as an accepted diagnosis.[3-6]

DSM-III-R. The revision of DSM-III (DSM-III-R, 1985) included a de-emphasizing of the importance of tolerance and dependence as criteria necessary to diagnose addiction. The DSM-III-R acknowledged that the behavioral dependence elements more accurately defined the loss of control over drinking. The behavioral loss of control over alcohol and other

---

TABLE 2.1. DSM-III-R Criteria for Diagnosis of Psychoactive Substance Dependence

1. Repeated effort or persistent desire to cut down or control substance use.

2. Often intoxicated or impaired by substance use when expected to fulfill social or occupational obligations when substance use is a hazard (e.g., does not go to work because hung over or high, drives when drunk).

3. *Tolerance:* need for increased amounts of substance to achieve intoxication or desired effect, or diminished effect with continued use of same amount.

4. *Withdrawal:* substance-specific syndrome following cessation or reduction of intake of substance.

5. Frequent *preoccupation* with seeking or taking the substance.

6. Has given up some important social, occupational, or recreational activity to seek or take the substance.

7. Often uses a psychoactive substance to relieve or avoid withdrawal symptoms (e.g., takes a drink or diazepam to relieve morning shakes).

8. Often takes the substance in larger doses or over a longer period than he or she intended.

9. Continuation of substance use despite a physical or mental disorder or a significant social or legal problem that the individual knows to be exacerbated by the use of the substance.

---

drugs appeared to be central to "dependence syndrome" as the principal clinical feature of its chronic, relapsing nature (see Table 2.1).

The "dependence syndrome" was an extension of the concerted work done by the World Health Organization, led by Edwards, in their formation of the alcohol dependence syndrome. Ironically, by incorporating the pharmacologically based term "dependence," the dependence syndrome did much to enhance the emphasis on the physiological connotations. In fact, a diagnosis of dependence syndrome can be made with only the three criteria for tolerance and dependence, without a single criterion for addictive use.

If the DSM-III-R classification system were applied literally, the rate of false positive diagnosis for alcohol dependence would be enormous, because tolerance and physical dependence are associated with regular alcohol use in many individuals that does necessarily involve addiction.[3,6]

In actual practice, clinicians have been reluctant to use the pharmacological term "dependence" for what is addictive behavior, opting for the term "abuse." As discussed earlier, abuse does not really mean addiction, and implies willful, improper, or unethical use due to an underlying disorder or a quest for hedonistic or immoral pleasure. What is clear from the garbled use of terms in the evolution of nosology is that alcoholism and drug addiction lack acceptance as primary disorders on the same level with other diseases. The lack of clarity in concepts, frank neglect of correct language, as well as a disregard of an abundance of relevant research data have led to our present state of confusion. The good news is that Substance Use Disorders still occupies a logistically separate section in DSM-III-R, for now.

DSM-IV. DSM-IV (1994) does not represent a significant departure from DSM-III-R. Most of the essential features that established Substance Use Disorders as independent disorders are secured. Notable changes include reducing the criteria to seven from nine by collapsing three criteria for tolerance and withdrawal into two criteria and the six criteria for addictive behaviors into five criteria. A requirement of a minimum of three criteria to establish a substance dependence was retained.

A significant addition was a return to a distinction for physiological withdrawal with or without physiological dependence. Physiological dependence is defined by criteria (1) and (2) (see Table 2.2). Because physiological tolerance and dependence (withdrawal) are almost always present, even in naive users, meeting the criteria for tolerance, i.e., markedly

TABLE 2.2. DSM-IV Criteria for Diagnosis of Psychoactive Substance Abuse

A maladaptive pattern of substance use, leading to clinically significant impairment or distress, as manifested by three or more of the following occurring at any time in the same twelve month period.

(1) Tolerance, as defined by either of the following:
    (a) need for markedly increased amounts of the substance to achieve intoxication or desired effect;
    (b) markedly diminished effect with continued use of the same amount of the substance.

(2) Withdrawal, as manifested by either of the following:
    (a) the characteristic Withdrawal syndrome for the substance (refer to criteria A and B of the criteria sets for Withdrawal from the specific substances);
    (b) the same (or closely related) substance is taken to relieve or avoid withdrawal symptoms.

(3) The substance is often taken in larger amounts or over a longer period than was intended.

(4) A persistent desire or unsuccessful efforts to cut down or control substance use.

(5) A great deal of time is spent in activities necessary to obtain the substance (e.g., visiting multiple doctors or driving long distances), use the substance (e.g., chain-smoking), or recover from its effects.

(6) Important social, occupational, or recreational activities given up or reduced because of substance use.

(7) Continued substance use despite knowledge of having had a persistent or recurrent physical or psychological problem that was likely to have been caused or exacerbated by the substance (e.g., current cocaine use despite recognition of cocaine-induced depression, or continued drinking despite recognition that an ulcer was made worse by alcohol consumption).

Specify if:
    With Physiological Dependence: Evidence of tolerance or withdrawal (i.e., either item (1) or (2) is present)
    Without Physiological Dependence: No evidence of tolerance or withdrawal (i.e., neither item (1) nor (2) is present)

increased amounts of the substance and identifying a withdrawal specific for the substance, will continue to be a source of confusion to clinicians. Also, the significance of the presence or absence of tolerance or dependence in cases of addictive use of a substance is minimal beyond treatment of detoxification. The majority of those who are addicted to alcohol do not show marked withdrawal symptoms. Moreover, many highly addicting drugs, such as stimulants, show limited withdrawal symptoms and signs.

DIAGNOSIS

Exclusionary Criteria

Of critical importance is the retention of the exclusionary criteria for substance use disorders before making other psychiatric diagnoses. Accurate diagnoses of either addictive or other psychiatric disorders are possible when the criteria are correctly applied.

The various diagnostic categories used to describe alcoholism and drug addiction have changed in the various revisions of the DSM. However, the behaviors of addiction have remained essentially the same, whether the terms have been alcoholism, alcohol abuse, or alcohol dependence. An addiction is defined as a preoccupation with acquiring a substance, the compulsive use of that substance in spite of adverse consequences, and a pattern of relapse after abstinence. The changes in labels have led to confusion in both clinical practice and research, but alcoholism and other drug addictions have remained independent disorders.[7]

There are several Axis I diagnoses in DSM-III-R that require the exclusion of alcohol and drug use diagnoses before they can be made. These diagnoses include the residual phase of schizophrenia, primary insomnia, Tourette's disorder, chronic motor or vocal tic disorder, and transient tic disorder. In addition, the intoxication or withdrawal from drugs or alcohol cannot be used to explain symptoms of panic disorder or generalized anxiety disorder, psychogenic amnesia, or hypersomnia.[7]

For unclear reasons, the DSM-III-R exclusionary criteria for organic factors do not make specific mention of the need to consider alcohol or other drugs. The need to exclude alcohol and drugs as organic factors is evident for many forms of psychotic disorders, affective disorders, anxiety disorders, and psychogenic fugue states.[7]

Perhaps the most compelling reason to give exclusionary status to alcohol and drug diagnoses is for purposes of prognosis and treatment. The psychiatric syndromes induced by alcohol and drugs will more closely follow the course of an addictive disorder, i.e., the psychiatric symptoms and physiological parameters will lessen or resolve with abstinence over days, weeks, or perhaps months in protracted withdrawal.[8–11] Effective treatments will usually address the alcohol- and drug-induced disorders, rather than independent psychiatric disorders. Because clinical diagnoses are principally used to determine prognosis and treatment, it is important to make precise diagnostic assessments. For example, when patients are evaluated at one point in time without urinalysis to exclude current drug use and without blood analysis to exclude drug intoxication (being "under-the-influence"), the risk for misdiagnosis is high.[12]

REFERENCES

1. Baldessarini RJ (1985). *Chemother Psych.* Cambridge: Harvard University Press.
2. Dackis CA & Gold MS (1985). Pharmacological approaches to cocaine addiction. *J Subst Abuse Treat* 2:139–145.
3. Schuckit MA, Zisook S & Mortola J (1985). Clinical implications of DSM-III diagnosis of alcohol abuse and alcohol dependence. *Am J Psych* 142:12.
4. Edwards G, Arif A & Hodgson R (1981). Nomenclature and classification of drug and alcohol related problems. *Bull WHO* 59:225–242.
5. Jaffe JH (1983). Drug addiction and drug abuse. In Gilman AG, Goodman LS, Rall TW & Murad F (eds.). *The Pharmacological Basis of Therapeutics,* 6th ed. New York: Macmillan.
6. Robins LD (1984). The diagnosis of alcoholism after DSM-III. In Grinspoon L (ed.) Washington, DC: American Psychiatric Press.
7. *Diagnostic and Statistical Manual of Mental Disorders, 3rd ed. rev.* (1985). Washington, DC: American Psychiatric Press.
8. Liskow B, Mayfield D & Thiele J (1982). Alcohol and affective disorder: Assessment and treatment. *J Clin Psych* 34:144–147.
9. Zern MA, Halbreich U, Bacon K, Galanter M, Kang BJ & Gasparini F (1986). Relationship between serum cortisol, liver function, and depression in detoxified alcoholics. *Alcoholism Clin Exp Res* 10:320–329.
10. Burch EA, Goldschmidt TJ & Schwartz BD (1986). Drug intake and the dexamethasone suppression test. *J Clin Psych* 47:144–146.
11. Willenbring ML, Morley JE, Niewoehner CB, Heilman, RO, Carlson CH & Shafer RB (1984). Adrenocortical hyperactivity in newly admitted alcoholics: Prevalence, course and associated variables. *Psychoneuroendrocinology* 9:415–422.
12. Miller NS, Gold MS & Belkin BM (1989). Clinical laboratory testing in drug abuse and addiction. *Ann Clin Psych* 4:227–236.

3

Classification for Diagnosis in Addiction Psychiatry

DIAGNOSIS

Nosology

Nosology for the addictive disorders is a constant source of confusion for both clinicians and researchers. Several errors in basic definitions are responsible for some of the abstruseness in clinical concepts and research criteria. The class name of "dependence" is misleading and inaccurate, and the use of the term "abuse" for pathological use is unscientific. The effort to disguise an old disease in a more fashionable and less offensive name of "dependence" instead of "addiction" not only avoids the truth, but also hampers addiction treatment research. Future research, particularly biological investigations of neurochemical correlates, and clinical accuracy both depend on valid definitions.[1,2]

The current criteria do not clearly define addictive behavior and are written in a cumbersome style that is not easily appreciated by nonspecialists. Furthermore, there is no simplified scheme to direct the clinician to search for a diagnosis and provide the researcher with operational constructs.

The DSM-III-R and the proposed DSM-IV do not thoroughly address important considerations in diagnoses of addiction, including denial of drug use by the addict and by those surrounding him or her, polysubstance use, and psychological states affected by drug addiction such as personality, mood, cognition, and attitude. Areas for future research to test the diagnostic criteria in addiction to alcohol and other drugs include natural history, relationship between other psychiatric disorders and alcohol/drug dependence, symptoms and dynamics of drug addiction, biological markers, and neurochemical correlates of drug addiction.

Abuse versus Dependence

The term "abuse," as originally defined for pharmacological and behavioral purposes, differs from the various popular meanings it has acquired. Abuse means improper use or misuse outside the norm or standard for a given social structure in which the drug is used.[3] The term implies use that is voluntary, unethical, and morally wrong. Abuse is also used frequently (but not necessarily) to connote unfavorable or untoward consequences of drug use.

The diagnosis of abuse as presented in DSM-III, DSM-III-R, and DSM-IV contains definitions that are really not different from the diagnostic category of "dependence" as is described in the respective DSMs. "A pattern of pathological use" is required for the diagnosis of abuse in DSM-III and implicit in this definition is "loss of control," that is, an inability to cut down or stop drinking. This loss of control clearly falls outside the original intent of the term abuse and more in the domain of addiction and dependence as defined in DSM-III-R.[5] Other definitions of abuse stated in the diagnostic criteria in DSM-III imply tolerance and dependence, that is, "need for daily use of alcohol for adequate functioning," that again are not usually contained in the meaning of abuse. The term abuse cannot correctly indicate a description of an entire medical/psychiatric disorder for which a diagnosis, treatment, and clinical course exist.[3,5]

The differentiation between abuse and dependence on physiological grounds, as operationally defined in DSM-III, was eventually eliminated in DSM-III-R and DSM-IV.[4] The difference between abuse and dependence based on tolerance and withdrawal (dependence) does not appear to be clinically relevant. Schuckit et al.[6] concluded that there was no prognostic implication for the division between alcohol abuse and dependence in 403 male primary alcoholic patients. The two diagnostic groups differed in that subjects with alcohol dependence drank more per day but did not differ in the number of days spent drinking, compared to the patients with alcohol abuse. The two groups were demographically virtually identical, and this similarity extended to presence of early life antisocial problems, drug-use patterns, psychiatric histories, and family histories of psychiatric disorder.[6]

The term abuse was retained as a diagnostic category in DSM-III-R and DSM-IV (Table 3.1).[2] The intention was to preserve a diagnostic category for milder and recent-onset cases of alcohol-drug abuse. However, "loss of control" was pervasive in the criteria for abuse: (1) continued use despite a persistent (preoccupation) social, occupational, psychological, or physical problem that is caused or exacerbated by use of the alcohol/drug (compulsive use), and (2) recurrent use (relapse) in situations when use is hazardous (e.g., driving while intoxicated).

Abuse is differentiated from dependence in DSM-III-R and DSM-IV by the inclusion of the physiological states of tolerance and dependence in the latter diagnostic category. Most, if not all, of the individuals who demonstrate "loss of control" as in alcohol abuse will qualify for the diagnosis of "dependence" by DSM-III-R (Table 2.1) and DSM-IV criteria (Table 2.2). The loss of control in "dependence syndrome" implies an involuntary state consistent with a primary addictive disorder. The criteria 1, 2, 5, 6, and 9 in the diagnosis of dependence in DSM-III-R are found in the diagnosis of abuse in DSM-III-R and DSM-IV. Inaccurately, abuse is defined as "mild dependence," without a clear distinction in definition between abuse and dependence in DSM-III-R and DSM-IV. The remaining criteria—3, 4, 7, and 8—for "substance dependence," are largely physiological, and the old DSM-III distinction between pattern of pathological use (abuse) and tolerance (dependence) is actually retained.

The broadening of the definition of "dependence" to include clinically relevant behaviors, cognition, and symptoms that indicate a significant

---

TABLE 3.1. DSM-III-R Criteria for Diagnosis of Psychoactive Substance Abuse*

A. A maladaptive pattern of substance use is indicated by at least one of the following:
    1. *Continued use* despite a persistent social, occupational, psychological, or physical problem that is caused or exacerbated by use of the substance.
    2. *Recurrent use* in situations in which use is hazardous (e.g., driving while intoxicated).
B. Some symptoms of disturbance have persisted for at least 1 month or have occurred repeatedly over a longer period of time.
C. Patient has never met the criteria for psychoactive substance dependence for this substance.

---

*See DSM-IV.

degree of involvement with a psychoactive substance, as done in DSM-III-R, does not serve to clarify diagnostic terminology. The diagnostic designation of "clinical dependence syndrome" to describe pathological drug use with characteristic symptoms and course is to overstate the original pharmacological meaning of dependence and to further add to the accumulated confusion.[1,3,7] The pharmacological definition of dependence is the onset of a predictable, stereotypical set of signs and symptoms on the cessation of the use of a drug and the suppression of those signs and symptoms by further drug use. In short, definition of the term addiction includes behaviors, cognition, and symptoms that indicate a significant degree of involvement with a psychoactive substance, whereas the term dependence does not.

The use of the diagnosis "addiction" instead of "dependence disorder" is operationally valid and less ambiguous. In clinical practice, as with the term "abuse," the term "dependence" has evolved to denote a variety of conditions that have little theoretical and empirical basis.

Salient Concepts

1. The self-medication hypothesis has been advanced to explain a pattern of escalating drug use in an effort to relieve symptoms of any underlying psychiatric or medical disorder. Although individuals may use a drug to temporarily relieve distressing symptoms, this behavior does not necessarily lead to addictive use. Indeed, the reverse may be true. Studies indicate that alcoholics use alcohol despite depression from continued alcohol use that worsens rather than lessens depression. The depression that results from cocaine use is frequently worse than any depression that may appear to promote its use.

2. The concept of hedonism as a goal of drug use is outdated. Pleasure may be a factor for early drug use, but subsequent drug use frequently leads to adverse symptoms such as anxiety and depression that more than neutralize any pleasure derived originally. Evidence for this line of reasoning can be obtained from clinical histories from addicts and inferred from high suicide rates among addicts.

3. The severity of withdrawal symptoms correlated with relative addictive liability of drugs is misleading. Cocaine and marijuana are two of the most addicting drugs known, yet neither produces a "dramatic

and physiologically evident withdrawal" such as can be seen with morphine and alcohol.

4. Dependence or withdrawal symptoms as an explanation for compulsive use is a common misconception. Addiction frequently occurs in the absence of measurable "withdrawal symptoms." Severe dependency occurs in the absence of measurable "withdrawal symptoms." Severe dependency may in fact motivate discontinuation of the drug because further use only worsens the withdrawal symptoms and abstinence will alleviate them eventually. Compulsive use appears to occur in spite of the severity of dependence. Dependence or withdrawal symptoms do not account for relapse or reinstatement or addiction in detoxified or abstinent individuals. Several drugs that cause physical dependence are refused in self-administration experiments in animals despite the ability of the drugs to relieve withdrawal.

5. The "need" to use or to be dependent on a drug is an erroneous use of the term dependence (withdrawal). To be dependent on a drug in the sense of "needs" is not the same as to be addicted to a drug. An example of being "dependent on a drug" in the sense of need is digitalis in the treatment of congestive heart failure. An individual who discontinues digitalis will suffer from a relapse of the symptoms of congestive heart failure. A usual situation of an addiction to digitalis would suppose that the individual uses digitalis with loss of control that results in toxicity. An addiction to a drug is the use of the drug to the point of development of toxicity, particularly with chronic use. Addiction to drugs and alcohol is a primary disorder that is positive, self-sustaining, self-perpetuating, and automatic, and probably is not dependent on negative withdrawal effects for expression.

Addiction

A convenient approach to understanding the criteria for substance-dependence disorder is to group them according to the three principles of addiction as suggested by Jaffe.[3] Preoccupation, compulsive use and relapse constitute a behavioral strategy for identifying addictive behavior.[1,2,3,8] The criteria themselves are perhaps difficult to discriminate from each other because of the similarity and overlap and the ultimate adverse consequences attendant on any of them. All indicate loss of control with a substance that is clearly evident in a pattern of use in which the substance or drug occupies a high priority in the individual's repertoire of choices. The distinguishing feature of these criteria of addiction is the pursuit of the substance or drug. The substance or drug is the object of the pathological use. The antecedent condition is drug-seeking behavior from which consequences, positive or negative, may follow. The reverse in which the consequences are given an etiological placement is often an incorrect interpretation of addictive use, that is, the addict uses *addictively* because of depression, whereas depression is more likely to be a consequence of addictive use. The confusion in the sequence of cause and effect is important in determining the presence of addictive behavior.

Preoccupation with the acquisition is illustrated by criteria 5 and 6, DSM-III-R and DSM-IV. These criteria require a judgment as to what is meant by preoccupation with acquisition. In simple terms, the addict clearly assigns a high priority to acquiring the substance, for example, he frequently chooses recreational and social activities in which alcohol is present or spends hundreds of dollars to purchase cocaine on a salary that does not support that cost. Family or occupational considerations are sacrificed for the time and energy to use substances, for example, choosing to be with drinking friends rather than with spouse or children, or consistently working at a job with a hangover or actually missing time by arriving late or leaving early.

Compulsive use is a misunderstood and misapplied concept. Compulsivity is the continued use of a substance in spite of (not because of) adverse consequences. Regular or frequent use is implied by not necessarily required. Episodic or binge drinking or drug use may involve a few hours or days, but if repeated in a pattern of pathological use over time it constitutes addictive use by virtue of recurrent loss of control. The major difficulties with these criteria are similar to those discussed with criteria for preoccupation that pertain to social or occupational consequences. Again, the emphasis should be placed on the compulsive drug use despite the adverse social or occupational consequences. The antecedent position of drug use that results in adverse consequences must be identified. Too often other consequences of drug use are attributed to the causal role incorrectly; that is, someone is drinking abnormally because of employment problems, whereas the reverse may more likely to be true. A rule of thumb in clinical practice is that if drugs or alcohol are abnormally used (i.e., with adverse consequences), then an addiction is responsible for adverse consequences. It is important to remember that the addict will frequently unconsciously deny that substances are causing physical, mental, legal, or employment problems.

Relapse is the sine qua non of diagnosing addictive behavior. An individual may have one or a few bad experiences with alcohol and drugs—a few instances of loss of control over time with a substance that may lead to adverse consequences is confirmatory. It is a misconception that addicts cannot stop drug use: many do, although usually not indefinitely; and an addict who returns to a drug inevitably exhibits the earlier abnormal use eventually. Again, denial and faulty recollection make obtaining a true history of relapse difficult, so that corroborative history by others who observe the addict is often necessary. Even then denial may be present in some who know the addict. The antecedent condition of drug seeking must be established because often a "reason" other than drugs is given for the return for their use, such as depression, anxiety, and interpersonal difficulties, whereas the reverse is often the actual sequence. The addict will frequently deny "loss of control" unconsciously or consciously so that it must be inferred at times.

The message is clear that alcohol or drugs have assumed a central position in the addict's life and the expense to the addict to acquire substances may be great, as measured by time, interpersonal relationships, and money. These social and occupational consequences may vary and, because of denial, be difficult to assess.

A reduction in the primary emphasis in these important areas was made in DSM-III-R because the emphasis is on the drug-seeking behavior and not the consequences in determining whether a given criterion is met. The criteria required for social and occupational impairment may be subject to changing laws, social customs, and practices, and are therefore difficult to judge in a universal way. Addiction, by its definition, is difficult to conceive without envisioning some degree of impairment in social or occupational function.[8] The critical and fundamental component of drug addiction is "loss of control," which would appear to inevitably result in social and occupational consequences, depending on the definition, disclosure, and measurement of impairment. More sensitive indicators for consequences should be developed for accurate identification of social and occupational impairment. The emphasis by DSM-III-R and DSM-IV criteria on the drug-seeking behavior is refreshing and needed, nonetheless.

Tolerance and Dependence

Tolerance and dependence (withdrawal) are important but may be confusing and misleading concepts to use as criteria for "dependence syndrome" or "addiction." Tolerance and dependence do accompany addiction although their presence depends on definition. Tolerance and dependence can also occur in the absence of "loss of control" of the use of a drug. Frequently, potent analgesics that are prescribed for legitimate indications for pain produce tolerance and dependence without a concurrent or consequent pattern of pathological use. The many forms of tolerance include dispositional, pharmacodynamic, behavioral, and genetic mechanisms. The presence or absence of any of these forms does not necessarily confirm or refute the diagnosis of addiction or dependence, nor does a college student who has increased his or her capacity for alcohol by regular use without developing ostensible signs of addiction meet the criteria for a drug-use disorder. Because tolerance develops at different rates and degrees to various classes of drugs—for example, dramatically to opiates and subtly to alcohol (ethanol) and THC (marijuana)—the addiction to the drug may or may not be obvious before the onset of definable and measurable tolerance. Individual differences can pose problems in interpreting a given case.[3,5] Tolerance to certain drugs such as alcohol may be more inherited than acquired. Early increased tolerance may be indicative of a predisposition to alcohol addiction.

The criteria for tolerance in DSM-III-R and DSM-IV are:

1. Develops a need for increased amounts of substance to achieve intoxication or desired effect
2. Diminished effect with continued use of same amount.
3. Often takes the substance in larger doses or over a longer period than person intended.

The criteria for dependence are:

1. Substance-specific syndrome following cessation or reduction of intake of substance.
2. Often uses a psychoactive substance to relieve or avoid withdrawal symptoms (e.g., takes a drink or diazepam to relieve morning shakes).

Generally, tolerance and dependence often accompany chronic and regular use of many drugs, so that the effect is less on a constant dose or increasing amounts of a drug are required to achieve the same desired effect or to offset incipient withdrawal symptoms.[5]

Development of tolerance and dependence may be considered expected pharmacological accompaniments of drug use—a general physiological adaptation by the cellular components of the body, whether or not addiction occurs. The development of tolerance and dependence occurs with continued use of either cocaine or antidepressants regardless of the addictive potential, which is clearly different for these two drugs. Tolerance to the sedative effect and perhaps even the antidepressant effect may develop with continued use of antidepressants.[9] A dependence syndrome (withdrawal symptoms) may develop with antidepressants, as manifested by anxiety, malaise, bradycardia, and restlessness.[9] The addictive potential of these therapeutic drugs is considered low. Tolerance to euphoria, alertness, hypertension, and tachycardia and a dependence syndrome (withdrawal) of intense depression, somnolence, and hyperphagia may occur in response to repeated cocaine use.[10,11] The addictive potential of cocaine is very high.

The time-honored concepts that long and heavy or even regular use are necessary for the development of tolerance and dependence may also be inaccurate. Tolerance to alcohol and opiates may develop to a single dose.[12] Also, dependence or withdrawal symptoms may occur after a single dose of alcohol or opiates.[5,12] The common hangover from alcohol is a form of dependence yet does not necessarily imply addiction. The criteria specified for dependence will determine their presence or absence. For instance, if depression, hypersomnolence, and delusions are attributed to a physiological basis (as they should be), then the symptoms of cocaine withdrawal will be considered physiological and not psychological or pharmacological. The use of only the "gold standard" of alcohol and morphine withdrawal for physiological dependence is outdated and exclusive. There are many valid symptoms of dependence that indicate physiological withdrawal and occurrence of seizures. Delirium tremens includes hallucinations, delusion, anxiety, agitation, and hypervigilance, which are psychological manifestations of underlying neurophysiological aberrations.[13] The most striking feature of opiate withdrawal is the "craving" and drug-seeking behavior. Physiological symptoms of nausea, vomiting, cramps, and piloerection, although significant, are subjective and sometimes barely behavioral manifestations.

Perhaps the concepts of tolerance and dependence should be deemphasized as criteria for "drug-use disorder" because of problems such as greater correlations with drug use than with addictive behavior, and frequent misattributions and misconceptions of the significance of tolerance and dependence to addiction. Inclusion of these physiological markers may still be useful if the implication is restricted to use, or regular use, of the drug. The nonspecific symptoms of tolerance and dependence and their lack of close relationship with a time course for all drugs suggest an accurate and chronic generalized neurochemical adaptation of the brain to the pharmacological effects of drug use.[14] Nausea, malaise, anxiety, depression, irritability, and tremor occur as withdrawal symptoms from acute or chronic use of a wide variety of drugs, both stimulants and depressants, and often differ quantitatively and not qualitatively.[14]

Substance

The replacement of the word "substance" by "drug" in the DSM-III-R and DSM-IV diagnosis of "substance-use disorders" would provide a more definitive term. A valid and contemporary "class name" might be "drug-use disorder." The term "substance" is overly inclusive and not specific enough to denote important characteristics peculiar to drugs. "Substance" is a generic word that is defined as an essence, spirit, form, or property, physical or otherwise.[15] The term drug is a species-specific designation for pharmacologically active substances that are chemical agents affecting living processes.[15] Agents such as vapors, solvents, and residues are clearly chemicals that fit the definition of a drug, as is alcohol (ethanol).

Disorders that arise from the use of drugs may be defined as a "drug-use disorder."[1] Confusion can arise from the modern usage of the term "drug" to refer to medications; this only misleads and restricts important implications. Abuse, addiction, tolerance, and dependence do occur to a variety of medications, and to emphasize these aspects of drugs is to encourage a more complete understanding and knowledge of the assets and liabilities of the usage of medications.[5,16] Furthermore, many of the drugs of abuse and addictive potential are pharmacologically and neurochemically similar to drugs used for medicinal and therapeutic purposes. Some antidepressants affect the same neurotransmitter systems in the brain as does cocaine—both drugs block the reuptake mechanism in the presynaptic neuron for the termination of the neurotransmitters dopamine and norepinephrine.[9] The neuropharmacological similarities do not necessarily imply that all or most therapeutic drugs have significant abuse and addictive potential. The use of the term "drug" would emphasize the commonality between drugs of abuse and medication effects, rather than create artificial and confusing differences, as does the use of the term "substance."

The term "substance" allows for the inclusion of a wide variety of disorders that have similarities to and often overlap with drug-use disorders but are not states of intoxication that pharmacologically affect the brain, as do drugs. Food is a substance that is not foreign biochemically but can be used in a nonpharmacological fashion, resulting a variety of addictive behaviors. Drug-use disorders possess important psychological, social, medical, and cultural differences from these nondrug disorders. Although addiction to a substance such as food may share with drug addiction common neurophysiological and neurochemical basis that is located in the limbic system, diluting the importance of foreign, pharmacological effects on the brain and behavior by drugs in drug addiction or dependence should be avoided. Drug and brain–receptor interactions represent distinct neurochemical processes that produce stereotypical and predictable responses in mood, cognition, and behavior.[5,17]

Denial of Substance Use

Denial regarding drug use and consequences from alcohol and other drugs is undoubtedly a common and prevalent problem that is inherent in a drug-use disorder. Because of the denial that is imminent in the addiction process, self-report by an addict is often unsatisfactory and misleading, and makes obtaining a history of a drug use difficult. The denial that is both intentional and unintentional is present in the user and often in those persons associated with the user. The denial may be severe enough to persist in spite of overwhelming medical, psychiatric, social, and occupational evidence in support of a drug-use disorder. The network of denial is pervasive, firmly rooted, and resistant to confrontation with facts in a manner similar to that of delusion. Recognition of these rather critical obstacles is important to making a clinical diagnosis that is dependent on available clinical data. A diagnosis based on empirical observations of addictive behavior such as preoccupation, compulsive use, and relapse can be made without full cooperation of the addict, and other corroborative historical sources can be used. The power of the denial can be of delusional proportions and not responsive to persuasive logic.

Laboratory testing can be an important method to detect drug use, especially in the drug-use disorders in which loss of control of drug use is operative. Drugs may be found in a variety of "body fluids," even in the presence of emphatic and unequivocal denial of actual drug use. Conversely, a positive test for the presence of drugs does not confirm a drug-use disorder but only suggests or supports the diagnosis. The danger of accepting a false sense of security by a negative result in drug testing is important. For a variety of reasons, a negative result for drugs can occur in the presence of a highly active addiction. Many drugs of addiction have short half-lives, some instruments routinely used to measure drugs have low sensitivities, and close observations must be made in the specimen collections to avoid deceptive exchanges.[18] Finally, the addict may not be using the drug(s) at the particular time of laboratory testing.

The Duration Criteria

Once the pattern of pathological use has been established and the criteria for addiction have been identified, the duration of use is essentially irrelevant for the purpose of establishing a diagnosis. Each class of drugs has a predictable constellation of signs and symptoms to make it possible to identify a general course and prognosis for that class.[5,19] Each individual has a characteristic pattern of addiction to drugs, contributing personality factors, life stressors, and biophysiological predispositions to the addiction. The properties of the drug and characteristics of the individual in concert will determine the time required to develop an active addiction. Considerable variability exists across classes of drugs and types of individuals; that is, cocaine addiction may take weeks and alcohol addiction may take months or years to develop. The diagnosis of a drug-use disorder may be made by recognizing the essential core of addiction, that is, "loss of control" manifested by preoccupation, compulsivity, and relapse to any drug, in any individual, and in any time course.

Polysubstance Diagnosis in DSM-III-R

The use of more than one drug simultaneously or at least regularly and interchangeably by those who have a drug-use disorder is more the rule than the exception. However, the addict, as most do, may have a "drug of choice," so that to require equal use of drugs is not realistic. Therefore, the terms "multiple," and "poly" should be used for accuracy. Eighty percent of those under the age of 30 years who qualify for the diagnosis of alcohol dependence have an addiction to another drug in addition to alcohol.[20] The possible clusters of drugs are numerous, and to assign diagnostic categories that are meaningful and valid to cover all combinations is difficult. This multiple drug use implies a commonality of vulnerability to drugs across classes of drugs by those who are addicted. Although a drug addict may often have a priority or hierarchy of drugs used, addiction to a large number of drugs may often exist. The era of the single-drug user is rapidly passing. This increasingly common fact necessitates use of a more diagnostic category such as drug-use disorder that includes the polydrug user and the alcoholic.

INTERACTIONS

Other States Affected by Drug Addiction (Consequences)

Other possible addictions or revisions to or clarifications of the DSM-III-R criteria might include states such as mood, affect, cognition, interpersonal relationships, attitudes, values (individuals), and standards (social). Because denial is so pervasive and central to drug addiction, many of the criteria listed in DSM-III-R are often difficult to ascertain. Often the addicted individual presents initially with complaints regarding mood, affect, interpersonal relationships, and attitude before the addiction is apparent and detected. Moreover, these states suffer substantial deterioration as a result of a drug addiction and should be considered in the evaluation of a drug-use disorder. Because alcohol and drugs have profound neurochemical effects on the brain that are translated into subjective and behavior manifestations, an aid to identifying alcohol and drugs as an etiology is to understand the derivation of disturbances in these functions.

Anxiety and depression are frequent consequences of chronic drug use that may motivate the user to seek treatment for these symptoms but not for the original addiction.[15,21] The presence of these symptoms may suggest further investigation for drug and alcohol use and an addiction. Alcohol is a significant depressant of mood, and withdrawal from alcohol is often associated with anxiety.[12] Cocaine intoxication elevates mood and produces anxiety, and withdrawal from cocaine often produces depression and agitation.[6,10] A common error is to attribute addictive drug use as a contingent on disturbances in mood states such as anxiety and depression and to treat these symptoms without addressing the addiction, which is self-perpetuating and automatic.

Furthermore, symptoms such as mood disturbances occur as part of and originate from the addictive process in the abstinent state. Treatment of only the symptoms often will not alleviate the anxiety and depression because the addiction is allowed to continue unabated.[22] The hopelessness, pathos, and worthlessness felt by the addict are products of the mood disturbances derived from the addiction. Psychiatric treatment will not correct the symptoms of anxiety and depression caused by addiction. The basis for this contention is the common location of mood disturbance and addiction, which may be in the limbic system.[23]

As previously noted, interpersonal relationships are often affected by abnormal drug use. Eventually, some disturbance with either family, friends, employer, or the legal system is present in virtually all drug disorders as preoccupation and compulsive drug use leads to adversely altered interpersonal relationships. Finally, attitudes, values, and standards often become distorted and sacrificed in drug addiction. Addicts will resort to crime, prostitution, and other acts of poor judgment to support acquisition of expensive drugs and to compensate for the financially costly consequences of drug use and addiction. Although these subjective and personal entities are difficult to measure and assess, some consideration and enumeration of the impact of the addiction by other than an intuitive basis may be desirable.[24]

Special Considerations in Diagnosis

Research Areas. Research investigations are urgently needed in many areas of drug-use disorders, particularly in diagnosis. The magnitude and severity of drug and alcohol use cannot be accurately assessed without proper criteria for incidence and prevalence estimation. The underlying neurochemical correlates will not be definitely identified without a clear diagnostic formulation. Other psychiatric disorders that are often confused with addiction cannot be separated from addiction without correct assignment of symptoms to diagnostic categories.

The natural history of drug-use disorders is virtually unknown for many drugs. Important epidemiological, psychiatric, and biological studies depend heavily on diagnostic criteria that are valid and reliable. More emphasis might be placed on the commonalities rather than differences of drug or alcohol addictions to arrive at more generalized concepts that fit today's practices.

Both longitudinal and cross-sectional studies need to be done to test the validity and reliability of these criteria for diagnosis of substance-use disorders (addictions). Basic assumptions regarding addiction and traditional psychiatry can be challenged. Presently, an opposing "philosophy" exists between the two. Traditional psychiatry that requires a reason or etiology for alcohol or drug use based on antiquated notions of dependence or need should be reexamined. New investigations in addiction as a primary disorder aided by neurochemical formulations may provide a clearer understanding for treatments to be developed and applied.[23]

REFERENCES

1. Rounsaville BM, Spitzer RL & Williams JBW (1986). Proposed changes in DSM-III substance abuse disorders: Description and rationale. *Am J Psych* 143:463–468.
2. Rounsaville BJ, Kosten TR, Williams JBW & Spitzer RI (1987). A field trial of DSM-III-R psychoactive substance dependence disorders. *Am J Psych* 144:3.
3. Jaffe JH (1983). Drug addiction and drug abuse. In Gilman AG, Goodman LS, Rall TW & Murad F (eds.) *The Pharmacological Basis of Therapeutics,* 6th ed. New York: Macmillan.
4. Robins LD (1984). The diagnosis of alcoholism after DSM-III. In Grinspoon L, (ed.), *Psychiatry Update: The American Psychiatric Association Annual Review, vol. III,* Washington, DC: American Psychiatric Press.
5. Hoffman FG (1983). *A Handbook on Drug and Alcohol Abuse,* 2nd ed. New York: Oxford University Press.
6. Schuckit MA, Zisook S & Mortola J (1985). Clinical implications of DSM-III diagnosis of alcohol abuse and alcohol dependence. *Am J Psych* 142:12.
7. Edwards G, Arif A & Hodgson R (1981). Nomenclature and classification of drug and alcohol related problems. *Bull WHO* 59:225–242.
8. Milam JR & Ketchum K (1981). *Under the Influence.* Kirkland, WA: Madrona Publishers.
9. Baldessarini RJ (1985). *Chemother Psych.* Cambridge: Harvard University Press.
10. Gold MS & Vereby K (1984). The psychopharmacology of cocaine. *Psych Ann* 14(10):714–722.
11. Mule SJ (1984). The pharmacodynamics of cocaine. *Psych Ann* 14(10):724–727.

12. Ritchie JM (1985). The aliphatic alcohols. In Gilman AG, Goodman LS, Rall TW & Murad F (eds.), *The Pharmacological Basis of Therapeutics.* New York: Macmillan.

13. Lieber CS (1982). *Medical Disorders of Alcoholism: Pathogenesis and Treatment.* Philadelphia: Saunders.

14. Hill MA & Bangham AD (1975). General depressant drug dependency: A biophysical hypothesis. *Adv Exp Med Biol* 59:1–9.

15. Benet LZ & Sheiner LB (1985). Introduction. In Gilman AG, Goodman LS, Rall TW & Murad F (eds.), *The Pharmacological Basis of Therapeutics,* 7th ed., pp. 1–2. New York: Macmillan.

16. Schuckit MA (1984). *Drugs and Alcohol Abuse.* New York: Plenum.

17. Dackis CA & Gold MS (1985). Pharmacological approaches to cocaine addiction. *J Subst Abuse Treat* 2:139–145.

18. Gold MS & Dackis CA (1986). Role of the laboratory in the evaluation of suspected drug abuse. *J Clin Psych* 47:1 (Suppl.).

19. Gilman AG, Goodman LS, Rall TW & Murad F (eds.) (1985). *The Pharmacological Basis of Therapeutics,* 7th ed., pp. 532–581. New York: Macmillan.

20. Galizio M & Maish SA (1985). *Determinants of Substance Abuse,* pp. 383–424. New York: Plenum.

21. Miller NS & Gold MS (1987). The medical diagnosis and treatment of alcohol dependence. *Medical Times* 115(9):109–112.

22. Miller NS (1987). A primer of a treatment process for alcoholism and drug abuse. *Psych Lett* 5(7):30–37.

23. Miller NS, Dackis CA & Gold MS (1987). The neurochemistry of addiction, tolerance and dependence. *J Subst Abuse Treat* (in press)

24. Vaillant GE (1983). *The Natural History of Alcoholism.* Cambridge: Harvard University Press.

PART II

Association of Psychiatric and Addictive Disorders: Core of Addiction Psychiatry

4

Relationship of Psychiatric and Addictive Disorders: An Overview

OVERVIEW

The comorbidity of psychiatric symptoms and substance-related disorders is common because intoxication and withdrawal from alcohol and other drugs can produce psychiatric symptoms and syndromes.[1–11] Moreover, a high rate exists for both classes of disorders, so that the two are likely to occur together as random events. This comorbidity tends to result in a more problematic course of treatment, frequently arousing the interest of clinicians and researchers.[12–17]

The acute and chronic pharmacological actions of alcohol and drugs can induce many of the known psychiatric syndromes, for example, depression, anxiety, personality disturbances, and psychoses.[1–4,17–19] On the other hand, patients with certain psychiatric disorders appear to be particularly prone to develop substance-use disorders, such as antisocial personality disorders and schizophrenic disorders.[20,21] Surprisingly, only a few studies have examined the "interaction" between these psychiatric and substance-use disorders.

Controlled studies to not confirm an etiologic role of psychiatric disorders in the development of substance-use disorders. Instead, they suggest that the effect of alcohol and drugs play a causal role in the production of psychiatric symptoms.[22,23]

ETIOLOGY

The Pharmacological Effects of Alcohol and Drugs

There is considerable evidence that alcohol and other drugs can produce psychiatric syndromes through several pharmacological mechanisms. Acute and chronic intoxication with stimulants as well as withdrawal from depressants can cause many symptoms of anxiety disorders that mimic phobic, obsessive–compulsive, panic, and generalized anxiety disorders.[1,2,24,25] Conversely, acute and chronic intoxication with depressants or withdrawal from stimulants can cause a severe and incapacitating depression similar in quality to major depression.[1,2,26,27] Psychotic symptoms are produced during intoxication with stimulants and during withdrawal from depressants. For example, prolonged cocaine or amphetamine administration may result in hallucinations and delusions during intoxication. In contrast, alcohol and sedative–hypnotic administration can result in these symptoms during withdrawal.[28,29]

PREVALENCE

Comorbidity

Patient Populations.   There have been several studies of both inpatient and outpatient populations that have assessed the prevalence of cooccurring psychiatric and substance-use disorders. Because these studies are naturally biased toward more severely affected patient populations, they tend to report high rates of comorbidity. One explanation for this is that such comorbidity acts to motivate the alcoholic to seek diagnosis and treatment. Another explanation, supported by the finding of some studies, is that comorbid patients tend to have more problematic courses, more severe psychopathology, and more medical, psychological, and social consequences.[30–32]

As noted, the cooccurrence of alcohol with other drug dependence is particularly common in younger populations. More than 80% of alcoholics under the age of 30 are addicted to another drug—most commonly marijuana, followed by cocaine, sedative–hypnotics (benzodiazepines and barbiturates), and opiates. Using drug dependence as an index, studies of inpatient and outpatient populations have found that 70–90% of cocaine addicts, 50–60% of marijuana addicts, 50–75% of opiate addicts, and

25–50% of benzodiazepine addicts are alcohol dependent.[33,34] In both research and clinical practice, this comorbidity of multiple drug dependence and alcohol dependence is readily apparent.

Several studies have found a 25%–50% prevalence rate of substance-use disorders in general medical populations. For general psychiatric populations the rate was 50–75%. In both groups, rates were higher in inpatients than outpatients.[35-42] Unfortunately, in actual clinical practice, the diagnosis of addiction is underestimated in all populations. The same may be true of the converse situation, i.e., the presence of psychiatric disorders among people with substance-use disorders. This situation, although less prevalent, remains significant according to several studies.[1,2,43-45]

FOCUS

Depression

Most of the research on the relationship of psychiatric and addictive disorders has pertained to depression and anxiety disorders. Many studies have found a relatively high incidence of depression among people with substance-use disorders.[1,2,30] However, there are several limitations of many of these studies because they assessed subjects' affective states in cross-sectional interviews. For example, Schuckit has reported that depressive symptoms occur in 98% of alcoholics at some point in their life histories and that one-third meet criteria for persistent depression interfering with functioning over a period of 2 weeks or longer. After 2–4 weeks, 5–10% of male and 15% of female alcoholics may show evidence of severe depression.[1,2]

Administration of low to moderate doses (three to five drinks) of alcohol can produce sadness and irritability under controlled experimental conditions in normal, healthy subjects. Tamerin and Mendelson reported the development of severe suicidal depression after 2 weeks of experimental intoxication, providing support for the notion that alcoholics experience increasing anxiety and depression secondary to chronic heavy drinking.[46] Other investigators have studied the intake of higher doses of alcohol over longer periods of time, finding elevations in depression rating scale scores and clinical pictures that resemble major depressive episodes.[47,48] Such alcohol administration in healthy women has been shown to produce mood disruptions that can still be measured days after the experiment.[49] In sum, continuous heavy drinking produces what can be called "a depressive syndrome" of chronic intoxication. This type of mood disturbance is also commonly associated with cannabis intoxication.[50]

Schuckit reviewed the relationship between alcoholism and affective disorders, delineating five possible types of interactions that may also be applied to drug dependence.

1. Alcohol can cause depressive symptoms in anyone.
2. Signs of transient serious depression can follow prolonged drinking.
3. Drinking may escalate during primary affective episodes in some patients, typically during mania.
4. Depressive symptoms secondary to alcohol use can occur coincidentally in other psychiatric disorders.
5. A small proportion of patients have independent alcoholism and affective disorder.[1,2,51]

In light of these complex interactions, it is not surprising that the prevalence rates of affective disorders in alcoholic and drug-addicted populations are highly variable, ranging from 5–59% in some studies.[10,12,52–54] In addition, the rates are somewhat higher for females, varying as much as two- or threefold. Rates were frequently associated with the methods of assessment and nature of the controlled variables.[55]

Cooccurrence of depressive and other psychiatric symptoms is high in individuals on methadone maintenance and those with other opiate intoxications. For example, Rounsaville et al.[56] found that 90% of 533 opiate addicts met Research Diagnostic Criteria (RDC) for a psychiatric syndrome at some time during their lives.

These included major depression in 74%, alcoholism in 34%, and antisocial personality in 27%.[56] Khantzian and Teece found that 60% of 133 narcotic addicts met DSM-III criteria for an affective disorder.[57] Gawin and Kleber also found high rates of affective disorders in cocaine addicts, with 50% meeting DSM-III criteria.[58]

Anxiety

The association of anxiety disorders with substance-use disorders is high. However, most studies have assessed prevalence rates of anxiety disorders in patients who are in the active state of alcohol and drug dependence or who are in the early stages of detoxification. The prevalence of phobic states, particularly agoraphobia, is relatively high in these populations compared with other psychiatric disorders.[17,18,24,59,60] These findings were confirmed by the Epidemiological Catchment Area (ECA) study.

Other surveys have recently shown that the one-year prevalence rate of major anxiety disorders is as high as 8% in the general population, with 6% fulfilling criteria for agoraphobia, 5% generalized anxiety disorder, and 1–3% panic or obsessive–compulsive disease.[59] Winokur and Holemon, using criteria similar to that for DSM-III Panic Disorder, found that five of 31 (16%) panic patients showed signs of excessive drinking at the time of the interview.[61] Woodruff et al. found that nine of 61 (15%) anxiety-disorder patients in a psychiatric clinic were alcoholic.[6] Conversely, Mullaney and Trippett reported that one-third of their inpatient alcoholic populations had clinically disabling agoraphobia or social phobia.[24] Similarly, Hesselbrock et al. found a lifetime history of phobia in 27% and of panic disorder in 10% of a hospitalized alcoholic population.[23]

Small, Stockwell and colleagues have published several studies of the cooccurrence of psychiatric and substance-use disorders.[17,18] In one, they reported that 32 of 40 male alcoholic inpatients (80%) had agoraphobia and/or social phobia when last drinking. The more severely phobic males were found to be the most dependent on alcohol, whereas those with no phobias were the least alcohol dependent.[17] In another retrospective study, Stockwell et al.[18] found that dependence on alcohol and periods of heavy drinking were associated with an exacerbation of agoraphobia and social phobias.

Furthermore, subsequent periods of abstinence were associated with substantial improvement in these phobic anxiety states. In this study, 19 of 84 (22.6%) of alcoholics admitted for detoxification met DSM-III criteria for one or more anxiety disorders.[18] Another study found that approximately 44% of 48 inpatient alcoholics were suffering from anxiety disorders, particularly phobias.[4] Finally, 173 abstinent patients were screened for phobias and avoidant personality disorder using DSM-III criteria. More than half met criteria for one of these disorders, with 8.5% suffering from agoraphobia, 7.8% from social phobia, and 35.1% from avoidant personality disorder.[63]

Alcohol generates anxiety via its effects on the autonomic nervous system. For example, alcohol withdrawal is characterized by sympathetic nervous system discharge. This release of catecholamines by the adrenergic neurons produces excitatory responses that are indistinguishable from certain signs and symptoms of anxiety disorders. In general, the sympathetic nervous system is considered to be "biologic basis" of panic attacks. It is interesting to note that the lactate infusion test precipitates panic attacks in alcoholics as well as in those with an apparent innate vulnerability to panic attacks.[64] In addition, alcoholics tend to have high lactate blood levels during periods of intoxication, providing further evidence that chronic alcohol intake may play an etiologic role in the production of anxiety.[65]

Cocaine, in particular, stimulates the sympathetic nervous system during intoxication. It does this by enhancing the effects of catecholamines on the postsynaptic neurons. Cocaine administration, especially in chronic use, produces intense anxiety as well as physiological manifestations of anxiety. In addition, chronic cocaine intoxication commonly produces suspiciousness, phobic fears, and paranoid delusions.[66,67]

The consumption of stimulants and depressants can intensify preexisting major psychiatric disorders. Most patients actually refrain from using alcohol and drugs in order to avoid a worsening of their anxiety disorder. In most instances, abstinence results in an amelioration or elimination of many of the symptoms of anxiety, including panic attacks, phobias, generalized anxiety, and obsessive–compulsive rituals. However, it may take days, weeks, or even months before many of the autonomic and electrophysiological changes secondary to alcohol and drugs revert back to normal.[68,69] Finally, when data are generated before the onset of severe alcohol and drug problems or well beyond the syndrome, there is little evidence of elevated rates of major anxiety syndromes.[60]

INTERACTIONS

Psychiatric Syndromes and Addiction

Several studies have looked at "interaction" between alcohol (and other drugs) and affect (mood). Mayfield and colleagues selected three groups of subjects: depressed alcoholics, depressed nonalcoholics, and nondepressed nonalcoholics, measuring their mood and affective responses to ingested alcohol. The results were unexpected and contrary to the long-held belief that alcoholics drink to feel better. However, they provided insight into the motivation behind "normal" or nonaddictive use of alcohol. Findings showed that the depressed nonalcoholics experienced the greatest improvement in mood and affect, followed by the nondepressed nonalcoholics (normals). The least benefit was provided to depressed alcoholics, who tended to drink in spite of an alcohol-induced depressed.[70,71]

Mayfield and Coleman also performed a prospective and retrospective study of cyclic manic depressives.[71] They followed 59 patients for 2 years and also examined 41 cases in review of records. Excessive drinking was noted in 20% of the patients with cyclic affective disorder. Only half of the patients who drank had a change in drinking behavior during episodes of affective disorder, particularly mania. During depressive episodes, patients tended to reduce or not change their drinking behavior. In general, drinking behavior was positively correlated with elated mood, but negatively or inconsistently correlated with depression.[71]

Other studies have supported the finding that depressed mood is associated with a decrease in amount of alcoholic consumption. For example, Pauleikhoff examined almost 900 "cyclic depressives" and found only two cases of excessive drinking related to depression.[72] Campanella and Fossi reported four out of five alcoholics ceased drinking during depressives episodes.[73] In contrast, excessive drinking in mania seems to occur together with other signs of euphoria, overactivity, and poor judgment.[74]

There have been several studies that have examined the effects of cocaine in humans under laboratory conditions. In one study, intravenous cocaine was administered to cocaine addicts who reported sensations of euphoria, followed by paranoia and depression.[67] In another study, cocaine addicts who inhaled cocaine reported paranoia.[68] In a National Institute on Drug Abuse (NIDA) sponsored survey, depression and suicidal thoughts were the most common psychiatric symptoms induced by cocaine, followed by paranoia.[75]

In animal studies, cocaine is self-administered in spite of serious, often fatal adverse consequences. Monkeys and rats have been reported to continue to press a bar in order to receive injections of cocaine to the point of convulsions, inanition, exhaustion, and death.[76,77] In these animals, the pursuit of the cocaine itself, not underlying psychological factors, motivated this extraordinary addictive cocaine use. The animals seem to be pursuing some pharmacological effects of cocaine which have yet to be fully elucidated, although studies to dates suggest involvement of the reward center in the hypothalamus.[78] Other theories incorporate the drive states, describing an autonomous urge for cocaine as in other drives such as eating and sex.[78]

METHODOLOGY

Methodological Bias

Most of the investigations of psychiatric diagnosis in alcohol and other drug addiction have had a built-in methodological bias in that they focused on patient groups who are generally from more severely affected populations. Therefore, most prevalence rates for anxiety and depression among alcoholics are based on populations that may not represent the true frequency in the native state. The ECA data support this notion with the finding that the rate of affective disorder in alcoholics in the general population is similar to the overall rate of affective disorder in the general population.[10,12]

Drug Effects

The use of drugs is associated with prevalence rates of anxiety and affective symptoms similar to those for alcoholics. Several studies have documented significant anxiety and affective symptoms resulting from the pharmacological effects of intoxication and withdrawal from both sedative and stimulant drugs.[70] The drugs may be prescribed or used illicitly, and the effects may continue over time.

Alcohol Effects

The relationship between severity of psychiatric symptoms and time after drinking and drug use tends to vary from study to study. Weissman found that 59% alcoholics interviewed shortly after their last drink had a depressive syndrome with symptom patterns similar to major depression. Other studies have found similarly high rates of depression among recently intoxicated or detoxified alcoholics. Many studies have clearly demonstrated that the depressive syndrome diminishes rapidly over days in the majority of the alcoholics and drug addicts, persisting in only a small minority.[1,2,19,79,80]

Measurements

The instruments used to diagnose anxiety and depression in alcoholics and drug addicts are important sources of methodological variance. There are differences in sensitivity and specificity among the various objective and subjective tests used to measure depression. DSM-III diagnosis by clinical interview and the Hamilton Depression Scale show higher sensitivity and specificity than the Beck Depression Inventory and the Depression Scale of the Minnesota Multiphasic Personality Inventory. However, all measures do show improvement of depression in alcoholics and drug addicts with abstinence.[49,81]

Predictors of Prognoses

Finally, although the anxiety and depressions occurring in conjunction with alcohol or drug intoxication are indistinguishable on sectional analyses from their independently occurring counterparts, the sociodemography, family history, early life course, and prognosis in alcoholics more closely resemble those observed for alcoholics with mood disorders than for those with anxiety or major depression.[1,2,82–84]

REFERENCES

1. Schuckit MA (1982). The history of psychotic symptoms in alcoholics. *J Clin Psych* 43:53–57.
2. Schuckit MA (1983). Alcoholism and other psychiatric disorders. *Hosp Commun Psych* 34:1022–1027.
3. Blankfield A (1986). Psychiatric symptoms in alcohol dependence: Diagnostic and treatment implications. *J Subst Abuse Treat* 3:275–278.
4. Bowen RE, Cipywynk CM, D'Arcy C & Keegan D (1984). Alcoholism, anxiety disorders and agoraphobia. *Alcoholism Clin Exp Res* 8:48–50.
5. Dorus W, Kennedy J, Gibbons RD & Ravi S (1987). Symptoms of diagnosis of depression in alcoholics. *Alcoholism Clin Exp Res* 11:1150–1154.
6. Rounsaville B, Dolinsky ZS, Babor TE & Meyer RE (1987). Psychopathology as a predictor of treatment outcome in alcoholics. *Arch Gen Psych* 44:505–513.
7. McLellan T, MacGahan J & Druley K (1980). Psychopathology and substance abuse. In Gottheil E, McLellan T & Druley K (eds.). Substance Abuse and Psychiatric Illness, pp. 3–26. New York: Pergamon Press.
8. Attia R (1988). Dual diagnosis: Definition and treatment. Alcohol Treat A 5:53–63.
9. Bukstein OG, Brent DA, Kaminen Y (1989). Comorbidity of substance abuse

and other psychiatric disorders in adolescents. *Am J Psych* 145(6):1131–1141.

10. Helzer JE & Przybeck TR (1988). The co-occurrence of alcoholism with other psychiatric disorders in the general population and its impact on treatment. *J Stud Alcohol* 49:219–224.

11. Diagnostic and Statistical Manual of Mental Disorders, 3rd ed rev. (1985). Washington, DC: American Psychiatric Press.

12. Robins LN, Helzer JE, Przybeck TR, Regier DA (1988). Alcohol disorders in the community: A report from the epidemiologic catchment area. In Rose R & Barrett J (eds.), Alcoholism: Origins and Outcome, pp. 15–28. New York: Raven.

13. Mirin SM & Weiss RD (1986). Affective illness in substance abusers. *Psych Clin N Am* 3:503–514.

14. Mirin SM & Weiss RD (1986). Psychopathology in chronic cocaine abusers. *Am J Drug Alc Abuse* 12:17–29.

15. Weiss KJ, Rosenberg DJ & Sollogub AC (1985). Prevalence of anxiety disorder among alcoholics. *J Clin Psych* 46:3–5.

16. Weiss Rd, Mirin SM & Michael JL, et al. (1986). Psychopathology in chronic cocaine abusers. *Am J Drug Alc Abuse* 12:17–29.

17. Small P, Stockwell T, Cantar S & Hodgson R (1984). Alcohol dependence and phobic anxiety states. I. A prevalence study. *Br J Psych* 144:54–57.

18. Stockwell T, Small P, Hodgson R & Canter S (1984). Alcohol dependence and phobic state. II. A retrospective study. *Br J Psych* 144:58–63.

19. Dackis CA, Gold MS, Pottash ALC & Sweeney DR (1986). Evaluating depression in alcoholics. *Psych Res* 17:105–109.

20. Lewis C, Rice J & Helzer JE (1983). Diagnostic interactions: Alcoholism and antisocial personality. *J Nerv Men Dis* 171:105–113.

21. Lewis CE, Helzer J, Cloninger CR, Croughan J & Whitman BY (1982). Psychiatric diagnostic predisposition to alcoholism. *Compr Psych* 23:451–467.

22. Mayfield D (1968). Psychopharmacology of alcohol. II. Affective tolerance in alcohol intoxication. *J Nerv Ment Dis* 146:322–327.

23. Hesselbrock MN, Meyer RE & Keener JJ (1985). Psychopathology of hospitalized alcoholics. *Arch Gen Psych* 42:1050–1055.

24. Mullaney JA & Trippett CJ (1979). Alcohol dependence and phobias. Clinical description and relevance. *Br J Psych* 135:565–573.

25. Mayfield DG (1979). Alcohol and affect: Experimental studies. In Goodwin DW & Erickson CK (eds.), Alcoholism and Affective Disorders, pp. 99–107. New York: SP Medical and Scientific Books.

26. Dackis CA, Bailey J, Pottash ALC, Stuckey RF, Extein IL & Gold MS (1984). Specificity of the DST and TRH test for major depression in alcoholics. *AM J Psych* 141:5.

27. Fowler RE, Liskow BI & Tanna VL (1980). Alcoholism, depression, and life events. *J Affect Disord* 2:171–185.

28. Schuckit MA (1989). Drug and Alcohol Abuse, 3rd ed. New York: Plenum.

29. Jaffe JH (1989). Drug addiction and drug abuse. In Gilman AG, Goodman LS, Rall TW & Murad F (eds.), The Pharmacological Basis of Therapeutics, 6th ed, pp. 523–540. New York: Macmillan.

30. Weissman M & Myers T (1980). Clinical depression in alcoholism. *Am J Psych* 137:372–373.

31. Weiss RN & Mirin D (1989). The dual diagnosis alcoholic: Evaluation and treatment. *Psych Ann* 19:261–265.

32. Stefanis CN & Kokkevi A (1986). Depression and drug use. *Psychopathol* 19:124–131.

33. Miller NS & Mirin SM (1989). Multiple drug use in alcoholics: Practical and theoretical implications. *Psych Ann* 19:248–255.

34. Miller NS, Gold MS, Belkin BM & Klahr AL (1989). Family history and diagnosis of alcohol dependence in cocaine dependence. *Psych Res* 29:113–121.

35. Kofoed L, et al: (1986). Outpatient treatment of patients with substance abuse and coexisting psychiatric disorders. *Am J Psych* 143:867–872.

36. Alterman AI, Erler FR & Murphey E (1981). Alcohol abuse in the psychiatric hospital population. *Addict Behav* 6:69–73.

37. Alterman AI, Erdlen DI & Laporte DJ (1982). Effects of illicit drug use in an inpatient population. *Addict Behav* 7:231–241.

38. Schwartz SR & Goldfinger SM (1981). The new chronic patient: Clinical characteristics of an emerging subgroup. *Hosp Commun Psych* 32:470–474.

39. Alterman AI (1985). Substance abuse in psychiatric patients. In Alterman AI (ed.): Substance Abuse and Psychopathology. New York: Plenum.

40. Safer D (1987). Substance abuse by young adult chronic patients. *Hosp Commun Psych* 38:511–514.

41. Drake RE, Osher FC & Wallach MA (1989). Alcohol use and abuse in schizophrenia: A prospective community study. *J Nerv Ment Dis* 177:408–414.

42. Ananth J, Vandewater S, Kamal M, Brodsky A, Gamal R & Miller M (1989). Missed diagnosis of substance abuse in psychiatric patients. *Hosp Commun Psych* 40:279–299.

43. Minkoff K (1989). An integrated treatment model for dual diagnosis of psychoses and addiction. *Hosp Commun Psych* 40:1031–1036.

44. Peyser HS (1989). Alcohol and drug abuse: Underrecognized and untreated. *Hosp Commun Psych* 40:221.

45. Lehman AF, Myers P & Corty E (1989). Assessment and classification of

patients with psychiatric and substance abuse syndromes. *Hosp Commun Psych* 40:1019–1024.

46. Tamerin JS, Mendelson JH (1969). The psychodynamics of chronic inebriation. Observations of alcoholics during the process of drinking in an experimental group setting. *Am J Psych* 125:886.

47. McNamee HB, Mello NK & Mendelson JH (968). Experimental analysis of drinking patterns of alcoholics: Concurrent psychiatric observations. *Am J Psych* 124:1063.

48. Nathan PE, Titler NA & Lowenstein LM (1970). Behavioral analysis of chronic alcoholism. *Arch Gen Psych* 22:419.

49. Tamkin AS, Carson WF, Nixon DH & Hyer LA (1987). A comparison among some measures of depression in male alcoholics. *J Stud Alc* 48:176–178.

50. Tunving K (1985). Psychiatric effects of cannabis use. *Acta Psych Scan* 72:209–217.

51. Schuckit MA (1983). Alcoholic patients with secondary depression. *Am J Psych* 140:711–714.

52. Schuckit MA (1985). The clinical implications of primary diagnostic groups among alcoholics. *Arch Gen Psych* 42:1043–1049.

53. Weissmann M, Rottinger M & Kleber H (1977). Symptoms and patterns in primary and secondary depression. *Am J Psych* 34:854–862.

54. Hesselbrock MN, Hesselbrock VM, Tennen H, Meyer RE & Wormman KL (1983). Methodological considerations in the assessment of depression in alcoholics. *J Consult Clin Psychol* 53:399–405.

55. Petty F & Nasrallah H (1981). Secondary depression in alcoholism: Implications for future research. *Compr Psych* 22:587–595.

56. Rounsaville BJ, Kosten TR, Weissman MM & Kleber HD (1986). Prognostic significance of psychopathology in treated opiate addicts. *Arch Gen Psych* 43:739–745.

57. Khantzian EJ & Teece C (1983). DSM-III psychiatric disorders of narcotic addicts. *Arch Gen Psych* 40:649–655.

58. Gawin FH & Kleber HD (1986). Abstinence symptomatology and psychiatric diagnosis in cocaine abusers: Clinical observations. *Arch Gen Psych* 43:107–113.

59. Ludenia K, Donham GW, Holzer PD, Sands MM (1984). Anxiety in an alcoholic population: A normative study. *J Clin Psychol* 40:356–358.

60. Schuckit MA & Montero MG (1988). Alcoholism, anxiety, depression. *Br J Addict* 83:1373–1380.

61. Winokur G & Holemon E (1963). Clinical and sexual aspects. *Acta Psych Scan* 39:384–412.

62. Woodruff RA, Guze SB & Clayton PJ (1972). Anxiety neurosis: Clinical and psychiatric outpatients. *Compr Psych* 13:165–170.

63. Stavynski A, Lamontagne Y & Lavallee Y-J (1986). Clinical phobias and

avoidant personality disorder among alcoholics admitted to an alcoholism rehabilitation setting. *Can J Psych* 31:714–719.

64. Sheehan DV, Carr DB, Fishman SM, Walsh MM & Peltier-Saxe D (1985). Lactate infusion in anxiety research: Its evolution and practice. *J Clin Psych* 46:158–165.

65. Goodwin DW & Guze SB (1980). Psychiatric Diagnosis. New York: Oxford University Press.

66. Sherer MA (1988). Intravenous cocaine: Psychiatric effects, biological mechanisms. *Biol Psych* 24:865–885.

67. Siegal RK (1984). Cocaine smoking disorders: Diagnosis and treatment. *Psych Ann* 14:728–732.

68. Roelofs S & Dikkenberg GM (1987). Hyperventilation and anxiety: Alcohol withdrawal symptoms decreasing with prolonged abstinence. *Alcohol* 4: 215.

69. Brown SA, Irwin M & Schuckt MA: Changes in anxiety among abstinent male alcoholics. *J Stud Alc,* in press.

70. Mayfield D & Allen D (1967). Alcohol and affect: A psychopharmacological study. *Am J Psych* 123:1347–1351.

71. Mayfield DG & Coleman LL (1968). Alcohol use and affective disorder. *Dis Nerv Syst* 29:467–474.

72. Pauleikhoff B (1953). Uber die Seltenheit von Alkholabusus bei zyklothym. *Depressiven, Nervenarzt* 24:445–448.

73. Campanella G & Fossi G (1967). Considerazioni sui rapporti fra alcoolismo e manifestazioni depressive. *Rass Stud Psich* 52:614–632.

74. Pitts FN, Winokur G (1966) Affective disorder VII: Alcoholism and affective disorder. *J Psych Res* 4:37–50.

75. National Household Survey on Drug Abuse (1985). National Institute on Drug Abuse. U.S. Washington, DC, Government Printing Office.

76. Aigner TG & Balster RL (1978). Choice behavior in rhesus monkeys: Cocaine versus food. *Science* 201:534–535.

77. Bozarth MA & Wise RA (1985). Toxicity associated with long-term intravenous heroin and cocaine self-administration in the rat. *JAMA* 254:81–83.

78. Miller NS, Dackis CA & Gold MS (1987). The relationship of addiction, tolerance and dependence to alcohol and drugs: A neurochemical approach. *J Subst Abuse Treat* 4:197–207.

79. Dorus W & Senay EC (1980). Depression demographic dimensions and drug abuse: *Am J Psych* 137:699–704.

80. Cummings CP, Prokop CK & Cosgrove R (1985). Dysphoria: The cause or the result of addiction? *Psych Hosp* 16(13):131–134.

81. Pettinati HM, Sugerman AA & Maurer HS (1982). Four year MMPI changes in abstinent and drinking alcoholics. *Alc Clin Exp Res* 6:487–494.

82. Vaillant GE (1984). The course of alcoholism and lessons of treatment. In

Grinspoon L (ed.): Psychiatry Update. Washington, DC: American Psychiatric Press.

83. Brown SA 7 Schuckit MA (1988). Changes in depression among abstinent alcoholics *J Stud Alc* 49:412–416.

84. Woodruff RA, Guze SB, Clayton PJ & Carr D (1973). Alcoholism and depression. *Arch Gen Psych* 28:97–100.

5

Epidemiology of Psychiatric and Addictive Disorders: Methodology and Perspective

OVERVIEW

There are several factors that influence the outcome and interpretation of epidemiologic studies. These factors include:

1. The population being sampled
2. Diagnostic factors
3. Longitudinal factors
4. Treatment factors
5. Study design
6. The study research design
7. The biases and expectations of the examiner
8. The length of the study
9. Treatment intervention.

Prevalence rates vary widely regarding the comorbidity of psychiatric and substance-use disorders. Much of the striking discrepancy of epidemiologic data is attributable to who did the study, where was the study conducted, and what was studied.[1]

The term "comorbidity" itself implies the presence of two distinct disorders—psychiatric illness and addiction. Deciding whether these illnesses merely coincide, are associated syndromes, primary disorders, or secondary to another disorder remain debated yet crucial issues. Epidemiologic findings on comorbidity result from the influence that each of the above nine factors has on epidemiologically derived knowledge about comorbidity.

After examination of the data in light of these factors, it can be concluded that 1) patients in psychiatric settings commonly have comorbid and independent addictive disorder and 2) patients in addition settings uncommonly have comorbid psychiatric illness despite common psychiatric symptoms.

METHODS

Assessing the prevalence of the comorbidity of psychiatric and addictive disease using epidemiologic methods results in artifactually high rates. Use of a clinical sample will yield falsely high rates, because alcohol and other drug use is associated with exacerbation of mental illness. Cross-sectional design will inflate rates of psychiatric comorbidity in addicts, who attribute alcohol or drug use to psychological symptoms until well into recovery.

Application of exclusionary criteria for independent diagnosis is subject to investigator bias, particularly about the unproven yet popular "self-medication" hypothesis. The psychiatric symptoms that are common in active addiction generally clear within weeks to months of treatment of addiction but do not respond to standard psychopharmacologic treatment for primary mental illness. When lengthy follow-up periods are employed, alcohol- and other drug-induced psychiatric syndromes typically resolve.

It can be concluded that although patients treated in psychiatric settings often have comorbid and independent addictive illness, patients treated in addiction settings uncommonly have comorbid psychiatric illness despite common psychiatric symptoms.

Population Factors

Subjects are derived from either clinical or nonclinical samples. Clinical samples may be divided into inpatient or outpatient, public or private, and addiction or psychiatry treatment settings. There have been adequate numbers of studies done in each to provide an analysis of the influence of the sampled population on epidemiologic data.

Clinical populations yield higher comorbidity rates than the general population. To the extent that individuals with multiple disorders are more disabled or distressed, such individuals tend to seek treatment; thus comorbid patients will be over-represented in clinical samples. In clinical settings, the rate for a particular disorder reflects the treatment provided at the site. For example, a general psychiatric setting will contain higher rates of chronically mentally ill patients because of orientation of the clinicians. Prevalence rates for comorbidity are higher for inpatient compared with outpatient treatment settings, greater for public compared with private settings, and for reimbursement-driven diagnoses where one disorder is reimbursed but not another.

Combining these variables, the overall prevalence rate in clinical psychiatric populations for addiction is 50%. In other words, a psychiatric patient has a one in two likelihood of having an addictive disorder. The prevalence rates for addictive disorders vary widely when further broken down into specific psychiatric diagnosis, as indicated in Table 5.1, column 2.[2-5]

On the other hand, studies reveal that the prevalence rates for psychiatric disorders in clinical populations derived from addiction treatment

TABLE 5.1. Ratios of Comorbidity Prevalence Rates Compared By Setting

Diagnosis: Comorbidity Addiction	Prevalence Rate: Psychiatry Setting[a]	Prevalence Rate: Addiction Setting[b]	Ratio Psychiatry Setting To Addiction Setting
Depressive disorder	30	5	7.5
Bipolar disorder	50	0.8	62.5
Schizophrenia	50	1.1	27.3
Antisocial personality disorder	80	0.6	133.3
Anxiety disorder	30	3	15
Phobic disorder	23	6	38.8

[a]Percent of patients diagnosed with comorbid addictive disorder.
[b]Percent of patients diagnosed with comorbid psychiatric disorder.

facilities are considerably lower and typically the same as those found in the general populations derived from addiction treatment facilities are considerably lower and typically the same as those found in the general population. This has been relatively well documented in addiction populations, as seen in the second column of Table 5.1.[6,7]

The last column in Table 5.1 further indicates the ratios that these dramatically different rates yield when diagnosis is compared for comorbidity in both settings. As a way of looking at these striking differences, the ratios of the prevalence rates for psychiatric settings to addiction settings have been calculated. While at first surprising, these ratios provide insight into the reason why psychiatric disorders are found so commonly among addictive disorders in some reports. For example, using the ratio for comorbidity for Bipolar Affective Disorder to illustrate how different epidemiologic truth will appear depending on site, one sees that a psychiatric clinician would conclude that Bipolar Affective Disorder is commonly associated with addiction. However, clinicians working in an addiction setting would conclude that addiction is rarely associated with Bipolar Affective Disorder.

Public community mental health population samples have markedly more chronically mentally ill patients than the private treatment sector. Public psychiatric samples yield the following prevalence rates for comorbid addictive diagnoses: 30% for schizophrenia, 50% for schizo-affective disorders, 30% for affective disorders, and 35% for personality disorders. The rates in outpatient private psychiatric settings are not as well documented but appear to contain lower rates for comorbidity among the chronically mentally ill. Again, to the extent that comorbidity causes greater disability, this may reflect downward socioeconomic drift to public treatment settings.[8-12]

High rates of addictive comorbidity are recognized in the young adult chronic patient, in whom alcohol and drug addiction is inversely correlated with age. Initial data derived from psychiatric inpatients suggested that as a group, schizophrenic patients preferred psychotomimetics and stimulants but not depressants. This fueled speculation that the alcohol/drug used by the young adult chronic patient is selected to self-medicate psychiatric symptoms. However, community-based studies indicate that the young adult chronic patients, like their nonmentally ill peers, are far more likely to use alcohol and marijuana than stimulants.

Moreover, nearly 70% of schizophrenic patients acknowledge using drugs or alcohol for the same reason their age peers report: "to get high."

Emergency room samples and community-based studies strongly support the finding that drug and alcohol use—even mild use—destabilizes the young chronic mentally ill patient and increases the likelihood of hospitalization. Comorbid young chronic mentally ill individuals have thus been overrepresented in the psychiatric treatment population, especially in recent years.[2-5,13-14]

Epidemiological Catchment Area Studies. Comorbidity rates are also quite discrepant between clinical and nonclinical samples. The most extensive population-based study of comorbidity is the Epidemiological Catchment Area Study (ECA). The ECA Study found that alcohol and drug disorders were the most common disorders among the psychiatric disorders. Alcoholism and drug addiction summed were almost equivalent to the other disorders combined (Fig. 5.1).

The ECA Study rates for the combined psychiatric and addictive disorders are similar to those in Table 5.2, column 2. For comparative purposes, the prevalence rates derived from clinical psychiatric settings seen

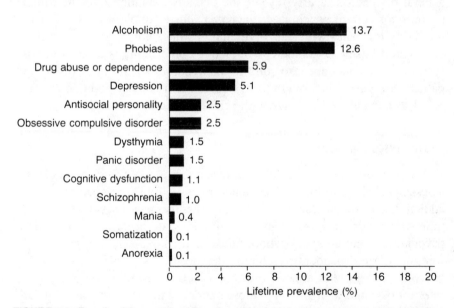

FIGURE 5.1. *Results of the combined five-site epidemiologic catchment area study, showing the lifetime prevalence of major psychiatric disorders as defined by criteria from DSM-III. (Reprinted with permission from* Journal of Studies on Alcohol, *Vol. 49, pp. 219–224, 1988. Copyright by Alcohol Research Documentation, Inc., Rutgers Center of Alcohol Studies, Piscataway, NJ 08855.)*

TABLE 5.2. Prevalence Rates for Comorbidity in the Psychiatric Setting Compared With the General Population (ECA Study)

Diagnosis: Comorbidity Addiction	Prevalence Rate: Clinical Setting[a]	Prevalence Rate: Nonclinical Male[a]	Prevalence Rate: Nonclinical Female[a]	Ratio: Clinical to Nonclinical[a]
Depressive disorders	30	8	23.4	3.8/1.3
Bipolar disorders	50	0.8	3.1	62.5/16.1
Schizophrenia	50	2.4	7.2	20.8/6.9
Antisocial personality disorders	80	14.6	10.1	5.5/7.9
Anxiety disorders	30	2.1	7.9	14.3/3.8
Phobic disorders	23	13.5	33.1	1.7/0.7

[a]Percent of patients diagnosed with addiction disorders.

in Table 5.1 are included in Table 5.2 column 2. A comparison of the ratios for prevalence rates of comorbidity in psychiatric settings compared to the general population clearly reveals the bias towards high rates in clinical settings for certain psychiatric diagnoses. For example, the ratio for comorbidity for males with schizophrenia illustrates how a psychiatric clinician would falsely conclude that addictive comorbidity is quite common. Instead, these data appear to confirm the hypothesis that dually diagnosed patients are very much overrepresented in the treatment population compared to nonaddicted patients with schizophrenia.[7,15]

Diagnostic Factors

The perspective of the clinician or researcher is a key determinant in the assessment of comorbidity prevalence rates. If one's perspective is that addiction is an independent disorder that directly causes psychiatric symptoms and syndromes, one uses exclusionary criteria that directly causes psychiatric symptoms and syndromes, one uses exclusionary criteria before making independent psychiatric diagnoses. As a result of excluding psychopathology that arises from the addictive disorder, the prevalence rates for psychiatric disorders in those patients with addictive disorders are generally in the range for those rates in the general population.

If one's perspective is that psychiatric disorders or symptoms directly cause addiction, one finds high prevalence rates for psychiatric disorders in addiction populations because exclusionary criteria (found in DSM-III-

R) are not applied. The "self-medication" hypothesis—that is, that alcohol and other drugs are used to self-medicate underlying and primary mental illness—remains a pervasive perspective that falsely elevates the prevalence rate of psychiatric diagnosis in addiction populations.

While self-medication of an underlying condition (most often a psychiatric rather than medical condition) is often cited in the literature as an explanation of alcohol and other drug use, the hypothesis cannot be validated when tested. In fact, several studies show that people addicted to alcohol and other drugs use their drugs of choice despite a worsening of drug-and alcohol-induced psychiatric symptoms.[20]

Longitudinal Factors

Follow-up provides perhaps the only valid way to establish the stability of comorbidity prevalence rates. If mental and addictive disorders are truly comorbid, either will persist after the other is in remission. By design, a postintoxication period is not employed in cross-sectional or retrospective studies, which therefore will elevate prevalence rates for psychiatric syndromes induced by drugs and alcohol.

The lack of a careful, prospective follow-up in clinical studies is also in part responsible for the artifactually high rates of psychiatric comorbidity found among those with an addictive diagnosis and vice-versa.[1,21]

The prevalence of psychiatric symptoms in the general population can be estimated to exceed that for psychiatric disorders by two- or threefold (Fig. 5.2). The prevalence of psychiatric symptoms in addictive disorders can be estimated to exceed that for psychiatric disorders by seven- to eightfold (Fig. 5.3).

It has been demonstrated that subjects who are psychiatrically symptom-free develop clearly definable psychiatric syndromes indistinguishable from those defined in DSM-III-R when exposed to alcohol and other drugs. Cocaine infusions in human volunteers produce paranoid delusions that closely follow the blood levels of cocaine. Other studies with alcohol demonstrate that severe depression develops with intoxication in otherwise symptom-free subjects. These affective changes have been correlated with blood alcohol levels, and correspond to known pharmacokinetics of alcohol.[1,16]

Moreover, when clinical populations are examined over time, psychiatric symptoms such as anxiety and depression correspond to periods of alcohol intoxication, diminish with periods of abstinence, and reappear

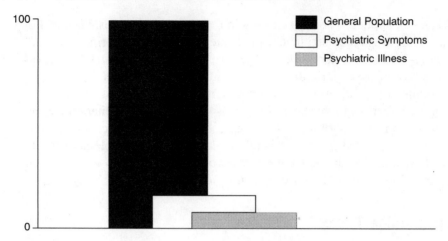

FIGURE 5.2. *The prevalence of psychiatric illness and symptoms in the general population.*[29]

with relapse. In general, similar results are found for the courses in other drug dependencies where the psychiatric syndromes follow the course of drug use, and are not etiological or independent in themselves.[21–22]

The question of the length of follow-up has been examined for many drugs, including alcohol, for the major psychiatric syndromes. For alcohol, 2–4 weeks may be needed for the pharmacological effects to recede,

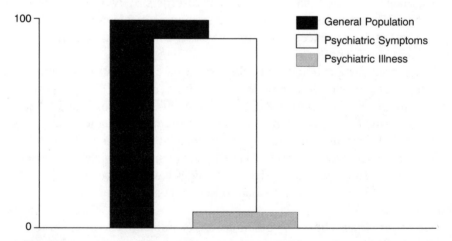

FIGURE 5.3. *The prevalence of psychiatric illness and symptoms in the chemically dependent population.*[29]

although a normal mood may appear within days. A similar course for resolution of cocaine-induced psychiatric symptoms has been documented. For longer-acting drugs such as benzodiazepines or methadone, the course may be protracted.[1,16,23]

Treatment Factors

A differential response to treatment interventions can distinguish the comorbidity of psychiatric disorders from addictive disorders. Studies performed on alcoholics employing pharmacological treatments for psychiatric illness do not show a favorable response in either the psychiatric symptoms or addictive course. Preliminary studies in drug addicts suggest that certain therapeutic pharmacological agents (desipramine for cocaine and clonidine and buprenophine for heroin) have a beneficial effect in promoting abstinence in acute and subacute withdrawal in cocaine and heroin addicts, similar to the use of benzodiazepines in alcoholics. However, these therapeutic agents do not have demonstrated efficacy in prophylaxis or relapse prevention for these addictive drugs, as would be predicted if "underlying" psychiatric disorders caused the drinking or drug use.[24] Treatment-outcome studies indicate that specific treatment of the alcohol and other drug addiction will result in the amelioration of the associated psychiatric syndromes and alter the course of the addictive disorder. Abstinence and specific treatment of the addictive disorder resulted in the resolution or diminution of affective, anxiety, psychotic, and personality disturbances in the vast majority of the patients.[25]

Some studies assume that treatment of the psychiatric symptoms will result in a lowered morbidity and mortality from the addictive disorder. This view holds that the addictive disorders are dependent on the psychiatric disorders, and etiologically linked to them. Beyond anecdotal reports, there is little systematic evidence to support this popular but unproven position. Our concern is that to insist on the priority of the psychiatric disorder in diagnosis and treatment will prevent the definitive treatment that will reduce the psychiatric morbidity and mortality caused by addictive disorders.[15]

It is clinically established that the successful treatment of true, independent psychiatric disorders is only possible once the addictive disorder is under control (i.e., abstinence from hallucinogens and depressants). Moreover, compliance with psychiatric treatments is usually poor in the setting of active addictive disorders. Studies show that those chronic psychiatric patients with untreated addictive disorders experience a greater number of relapses, greater severity of illness, poor medication use, heavier utilization of psychiatric services, and generally poorer outcome than those without an addictive disorder.[26-28]

Study Design

The basic design of data acquisition is also important in understanding comorbidity rates. Retrospective analysis yields higher rates for psychiatric comorbidity than a prospective analysis in which the stability of diagnoses can be tested over time. This is because 1) alcohol and other drugs can produce psychiatric syndromes, 2) patient self-reports tend to deemphasize alcohol and other drug use in the genesis of psychiatric symptoms, and 3) patients and clinicians alike tend to view psychiatric symptoms as either independent or the cause of alcohol and other drug use. In contrast, longitudinal studies reveal that psychiatric syndromes are more likely to be a result of alcohol and other drug use.[1,16]

The importance of prospective design is illustrated by the much lower prevalence rates for comorbidity in addicted patients when a period of withdrawal and abstinence is allowed before psychiatric diagnosis is made. The recommended period before establishing independent psychiatric comorbidity distinct from that arising secondary to the pharmacological effects and other addiction-induced changes is between 4 weeks to 2 years. However, the drop-off in diagnosable psychiatric illness over time depends on the diagnosis. Depressive and psychotic symptoms tend to resolve in days to weeks, whereas anxiety symptoms and personality changes diminish over months to years.

Depressive symptoms occur in 98% of alcoholics at some time. One-third will meet criteria for persistent depression that interferes with functioning for at least 2 weeks; for the vast majority, the depressive symptoms resolve with abstinence and alcoholism treatment. Administration of moderate doses (three to five drinks) of alcohol can produce depressive symptoms in normal subjects under experimental conditions. Similar alcohol doses given to healthy women may produce mood disruptions that can still be measured days after the conclusion of the experiment. These and other studies show that continuous, heavy drinking produces a "depressive syndrome" of alcohol intoxication. This "depressive syndrome" is associated with other drugs such as stimulants, cannabis, sedative-hypnotics, and opiates.[1,16]

The cross-sectional analysis typically done for addictive disorders in psychiatric populations without longitudinal follow-up results in unstable and inflated rates of psychiatric comorbidity that are in fact related to, rather than truly comorbid with, the addictive disorders. Even longitudinal studies will inflate rates of anxiety and personality disorders relative to psychotic and affective disorders if insufficient time is allowed. The most skilled clinician cannot reliably make accurate diagnoses that have predictive value using a point-prevalence method of analysis; large epidemiologic studies rarely employ such skilled clinicians. A cross-sectional epidemiologic study is best viewed as instructive of the high rate of psychiatric symptomatology and organic psychiatric disorders associated with addictive disorders without regard to etiology and therefore actual comorbidity.

Retrospective recall derived from addicted patients will also falsely inflate rates of psychiatric comorbidity. For example, abstinent alcoholics will retrospectively attribute drinking to anxiety and depression but be found to be free of these symptoms on examination. When these same alcoholics are given alcohol under experimental conditions, anxiety and depression develop in proportion to the increase in the amount and duration of alcohol consumption. Upon detoxification, the psychiatric symptoms resolve.

The subjects do not recall the severe symptoms that developed during intoxication and will continue to explain drinking on the basis of anxiety and depression. The attribution of drinking and drug use to psychiatric symptoms as post hoc rationalizations extends to hallucinations and delusions in psychotic patients, and personality difficulties in patients with personality disorders.[17]

If data are gathered retrospectively shortly after a recent episode of alcohol or other drug use, the self-report will result in exaggerated rates of psychiatric disorders due to the addict's rationalization of the use. While it may be accurate to assume that an alcoholic or drug addict interviewed in an addiction-treatment setting will reliably acknowledge frequency and duration of use, the individual's interpretation of why she or he uses remains distorted until sober for a prolonged period of time, often until the addict understands his or her addictive use of alcohol and drugs through treatment or self-help involvement.[17–18]

Prospective analyses reveal that psychological stats and personality variables do not predict the onset of drinking or alcoholism. These studies do not find that psychiatric diagnoses or symptoms precede or lead to higher rates of addiction. When longitudinal follow-up occurs over time after onset through the abstinent, treated state, the psychiatric symptoms and personality abnormalities associated with addictive use and intoxication resolve in most of those affected, with the young chronically mentally ill as exceptions. However, it is worth noting that addictive comorbidity in the young chronically mentally ill patient affects symptoms most commonly associated with the addictive illness: hostility, noncompliance, and disruptive behaviors. Where studied, young chronically mentally ill patients with addictive comorbidity cannot be distinguished from their non-addicted mentally ill peers by primary psychiatric diagnosis or by symptoms such as hallucinations, delusions, or paranoia.[3,13,19]

REFERENCES

1. Miller NS, Mahler JC & Belkin BM, et al. (1991). Psychiatric diagnosis in alcohol & drug dependence. *Ann Clin Psych* 3:79–89.
2. Drake RE & Wallach MA (1989). Substance abuse among the chronic mentally ill. *Hosp Commun Psych* 40:1041–1046.
3. Pepper B, Kirshner MC & Ryglewicz H (1981). The young adult chronic patient: Overview of a population. *Hosp Commun* 32(7):463–474.
4. Drake RE, Osher EC & Wallach MA (1989). Alcohol use and abuse in schizophrenia: A prospective community study. *J Nerv Ment Dis* 177(7), 408–414.
5. Barbee JC, Clark PD & Crapanzano BS, et al (1989). Alcohol and substance abuse among schizophrenic patients presenting to an emergency psychiatric service. *J Nerv Ment Dis* 177(7):400–407.
6. Myers JK, Weissman MM & Tschler GL, et al (1984). Six-month prevalence of psychiatric disorders in three communities. *Arch Gen Psych* 41:959–967.
7. Robins LN, Helzer JE & Przybeck TR, et al (1988). Alcohol disorders in the community: A report from the epidemiologic catchment area. In Rose RM & Barrett J. (eds.) Alcoholism: Origins and outcomes. New York: Raven Press.
8. Caton CL, Gralnick A & Bender S, et al (1989). Young chronic patients and substance abuse. *Hosp Commun Psych* 40(10):1037–1040.
9. Alterman AI, Erdlen FR & Murphy E (1981). Alcohol abuse in the psychiatric hospital population. *Addict Behav* 6:69–73.
10. Lamb HR (1982). Young adult chronic patients: The new drifters. *Hosp Commun Psych* 33(6):465–468.
11. Schwartz SR & Goldfinger SM (1981). The new chronic patient: Clinical characteristics of an emergency subgroup. *Hosp Commun Psych* 470–474.

12. Sheets JL, Prevost JA & Reihman J (1982). Young adult chronic patients: Three hypothesized subgroups. *Hosp Commun Psych* 33(3):197–203.

13. Hekimian LJ & Gerson S (1968). Characteristics of drug abusers admitted to a psychiatric hospital. *JAMA*. 205:75–80.

14. Rosenheck R, Massari L & Astrachan B, et al (1990). Mentally ill chemical abusers discharged from VA inpatient treatment: 1976-88. *Psych Q* 61(4):237–249.

15. Regier DA, Farmer ME & Rae DS, et al (1991). Comorbidity of mental disorders with alcohol and other drug abuse: results from the epidemiological catchment area (ECA) study. *JAMA* 264(19):2511–2518.

16. Schuckit MA & Montero MG (1980). Alcoholism, anxiety, depression. *Br J Addict* 83:1373–1380.

17. Tamerin JS, Mendelson JH (1969). The psychodynamics of chronic inebriation. Observations of alcoholics during the process of drinking in an experimental group setting. *Am J Psych* 125:886.

18. Vaillant GE & Milofsky E (1982). The etiology of alcoholism. *Am Psychol* 37(5):494–503.

19. McCarrick AK, Manderscheid RW & Bertolucci DE (1985). Correlates of acting-out behaviors among young adult chronic patients. *Hosp Commun Psych* 36(8):848–853.

20. Khantzian EJ (1985). The self-medication hypothesis of addiction disorders: Focus on heroin and cocaine dependence. *Am J Psych* 142:1259–1264.

21. Schuckit MA (1973). Alcoholism and sociopathy-diagnostic confusion. *Q J Stud Alc* 34:157–164.

22. Brown SA, Irwin M & Schuckit MA (1991). Changes in anxiety among abstinent male alcoholics. *J Stud Alc* 52(1):55–61.

23. Schuckit MA, Irwin M & Brown SA (1990). The history of anxiety symptoms among 171 primary alcoholics. *J Stud Alc* 31(1):34–41.

24. Miller NS (1991). The pharmacology of alcohol and drugs of abuse and addiction. New York: Springer-Verlag.

25. Harrison PA, Hoffman NG & Streed SG (1991). Drug and alcohol addiction treatment outcome. In Miller NS (ed.). Comprehensive handbook of drug and alcohol addiction. New York: Marcel-Dekker.

26. Minkoff K (1989). An integrated treatment model for dual diagnosis of psychosis and addiction. *Hosp Commun Psych* 40(10):1031–1036.

27. Kosten TR & Kleber HD (1988). Differential diagnosis of psychiatric comorbidity in substance abusers. *J Subst Abuse Treat* 5:201–206.

28. Helzer JE & Pryzbeck TR (1988). The co-occurrence of alcoholism with other psychiatric disorders in the general population and its impact on treatment. *J Stud Alc* 49(3):219–224.

29. Miller NS, Fine J (1993). Current epidemiology of comorbidity of psychiatric and addictive disorders. *Psychiatric Clinics of North America* 16(1):1–10.

PART III

Etiology of Psychiatric and Addictive Disorders

6

Course and Prognosis
of the Disorders

FOCUS

Prospective Studies

It is critical to understand the course of addiction in order to institute proper treatment. Prospective studies are needed to understand that addiction is not a result of unhappy childhood, familial discord, and personality disorder. Prospective studies reduce the confounding selection bias that has resulted in hopelessness toward treating chronically relapsing addicts.

Prospective studies not only confirm diagnosis but substantiate a clear clinical picture. Decades of follow-up are required to understand that addiction is often a progressive disorder. In the case of multiple symptoms, prospective study can elucidate "cause and effect" relationships. In other words, prospective study clarifies treatment goals. (In a depressed alcoholic, should we treat the depression, the alcoholism, or both?) Finally, only a prospective design can demonstrate the recovery processes.[1] While this chapter pertains to studies of alcoholism, clinical experience and studies strongly suggest that other drug addictions follow a prognosis similar to that for alcoholism.

Etiology

Many believe that the addiction results from the insecurity of earliest childhood. Because addiction profoundly distorts the individual's own perspective of relevant childhood memories, the only study design suited to test this generalization is a prospective one. In a study of a reexamination of junior high school boys, few significant differences were observed in the childhoods of alcoholics and nonalcoholics.[2] There were no differences in IQ between alcoholics and nonalcoholics. Whereas many more adult alcoholics than nonalcoholics were diagnosed as mentally ill, as children, the alcoholics were not more emotionally disturbed, nor had they come more often from emotionally troubled families. In childhood, alcoholics and nonalcoholics showed no differences in their capacity for school work or part-time employment. But as adults, alcoholics were much less likely to have had stable employment than nonalcoholics. No differences had appeared between the groups' relationships with their mothers, in terms of either maternal affection or maternal supervision. The implication is that alcoholics may exaggerate childhood difficulties after the fact to rationalize difficulties caused by alcoholism.

While many alcoholics do come from chaotic families, the effect of broken homes upon adult alcoholism vanishes when one controls for parental alcoholism, a potent cause of chaotic home life. Of the 51 men who had *few* childhood environmental weaknesses but who did have an alcoholic parent, 27% became alcohol dependent as adults. On the other hand, of the 56 men with *many* environmental weaknesses but no alcoholic parent, only 5% became alcohol dependent.[2]

In another prospective study, children with nutritional disorders, glandular disorders, "strong inferiority feelings," phobias, and "more feminine feelings" were *not* more likely to develop alcoholism. Importantly, boys with "strong encouragement of dependency" from their mothers and evident oral tendencies (thumb sucking, playing with their mouths, early heavy smoking, and compulsive eating) were actually *less* likely to develop alcoholism in adulthood.[1,2] Contrary to widespread beliefs, alcoholics *before* the onset of their alcoholism were outwardly more self-confident, less disturbed by normal fears, more aggressive and active, and more inclined toward heterosexuality.

Depression, secondary to addiction, is so frequently associated with alcoholism that psychiatric texts have consistently suggested that depression is a major cause of alcoholism. However, prospective studies suggest that this, too, is an illusion. The MMPIs of 38 men in college were compared with their MMPIs many years later when they were admitted to an alcohol clinic.[3] Only those who developed alcoholism eventually developed MMPIs that showed an elevated depression scale. The composite

MMPI of the subjects, once alcoholic, revealed the pathological profile of a self-centered, immature, dependent, resentful, and irresponsible person who was unable to face reality, i.e., (D) and (Pd) scales. In another study, the same observations on the MMPI were made in reverse sequence. At time of admission for alcoholism treatment, alcoholics manifested pathological elevations on the MMPI depression scale. After four years of abstinence, their mean values on the MMPI depression scale had returned to normal.[3]

Onset and Progression

There is individual variation in the evolution of alcoholism. Variations occur in the rapidity of onset, the progression of symptoms, and the eventual severity of alcoholism. For example, in one study the progression of alcoholism was more rapid in subjects from the lower end of the socioeconomic spectrum. Also, alcoholism among people with sociopathic personalities was characterized with a far more rapid onset and was more extreme than among other alcoholics.[4] Genetic differences among alcoholics (greater genetic loading) may explain variations in time of onset and rapidity of course of alcoholism.[5]

INTERACTIONS

Treatment populations are biased in several ways. Individuals who frequent clinics—whether for heart disease, tuberculosis, alcoholism, or any other chronic illness—tend to be more dependent, more physically ill, and more psychologically vulnerable than those who do not frequent clinics. Clinical samples tend to exclude those who spontaneously recover and who have alternative social supports and fewer personality supports. Prospective follow-up of and entire cohort avoids these biases by beginning with a normal population sample and then following it until those at risk have developed the disease.[6,7]

Because of sampling bias, alcoholics usually appear to be persons with personality disorders. Three premorbid personality types have been repeatedly postulated to play an etiologic role in alcoholism: 1) the emotionally insecure, anxious, and dependent;[6,7] 2) the chronically depressed;[8] and 3) the sociopathic.[9] However, long-term studies suggest that such personality patterns are often the result and not the cause of the alcoholism.[9]

Because of the observed association of alcoholism with bipolar affective disorder, some investigators have suggested that alcoholism might be a variant of major depressive disorder.[8] However, in an impressive 30-year follow-up study of the life course of over 1,700 Scandinavian alcoholics, a researcher determined that the prevalence of psychotic depression (0.35%) was, if anything, less than the lifetime prevalence observed in the general population.[10]

These findings that suggest major depressive disorder and alcoholism are quite independent disorders have been confirmed from a variety of sources.[2,3,13,18] In other words, if alcoholism is often observed in affectively disordered patients, it is because such patients are particularly likely to elicit psychiatric attention rather than because alcoholism is caused by affective disorders.

In a prospective study of alcoholics with late onset,[11,12] "bleak childhoods and psychological instability" in college had predicted, and presumably played a causal role, in the young adults' development of personality disorder and "oral" traits (pessimism, passivity, self-doubt, and heightened dependency). However, those men who developed alcoholism did not come disproportionately from this subgroup of emotional instability.[13] Once they began to drink alcoholically, however, oral-dependent traits and personality disorder became very common.

A destructive myth is that it is futile to treat alcoholics, especially those who use public clinics and emergency rooms. This misconception, too, results from selection bias and from cross-sectional designs that tend to count relapses rather than remissions. In a study of a 78-month interval, roughly 5,000 clients received over 19,000 detoxifications. One-eighth of these 19,000 admissions encompassed the 2,500 easily forgotten clients who never returned. Another one-eighth, however, were visits from the 25 indelibly remembered clients who returned sixty times or more. Thus, the intractable 0.5% were admitted as often and became far more deeply etched in clinicians' consciousness than did the 50% who never came back and who must have included the best outcomes.[14]

PROGNOSES

One reason why our understanding of alcoholism is so confused is that investigators who scrutinize the behavior of alcoholics for short periods of time come to doubt that alcoholism is a stable or progressive disorder.

Indeed, some believe that there are as many alcoholisms as there are problem drinkers. Certainly, the elderly retired stockbroker who first comes to medical attention due to cirrhosis and polyneuritis manifests differently from the young motorcyclist who comes to police attention due to drunken episodes of belligerance and community complaints. They come to the attention of different people, but is their illness really different?

Viewed over the short term, however, all alcoholism appears extremely unstable and in no sense progressive. In conceptualizing the clinical course of alcoholism, methodological considerations are crucial. On the one hand, the course of a chronic relapsing disease may appear very unstable if many mild cases are included, data are gathered by questionnaires, deaths are excluded, periods of observation are short, syndromes are broken down into individual symptoms, and integrated individual case histories are excluded.

On the other hand, the course of a chronic disease may appear stable and progressive if only severe cases are included, data are gathered by skilled clinical interviewers, all deaths are reported, symptoms, however individually unstable, are treated as clusters, long periods of observation are used, and individual lives rather than statistical analyses are scrutinized.

TREATMENT

Another advantage of prospective study is that it can help us determine effective treatment goals. In a prospective study of a community sample, 21 former alcoholics who had achieved the most stable abstinence (mean duration of 10 years) did not significantly differ in psychosocial adjustment from men who had never been alcoholic.[14] In other words, their abstinence was associated with full recovery in stability of personality.

In contrast, the psychosocial adjustment of alcoholics who had only recently become abstinent (less than 3 years) did not seem very different from that of active alcoholics. The three groups did not differ, however, in terms of childhood predictors associated with midlife psychosocial adjustment. The implication from these and other data is that while abstinence is the treatment goal of choice for most severe alcoholics, recovery from alcoholism requires prolonged convalescence to see improved psychosocial adjustment.[4]

Long-term follow-up also answers the question, "Can alcoholics be taught to return to social drinking?" Recently, in a comparatively well-controlled study, researchers suggested that a major etiologic factor in alcoholism was a failure to self-monitor blood alcohol levels.[15] The Sobells'[15] effort to teach alcoholics to drink socially provided the illusion that increasing alcoholics' awareness of such internal cues would facilitate their return to asymptomatic drinking.

Their findings at 2 years were impressive and influential. However, careful examination of their 2-year data reveals that the reason that patients trained in controlled drinking had the fewest "problem days" was that they had even *more abstinent days* than the patients who received abstinence training. A 10-year reevaluation of the Sobells' patients by Pendery et al.[16] confirmed that the Sobells' original deduction was incorrect. The six patients who recovered did so by achieving stable abstinence, and 13 of the 14 remaining patients died or repeatedly relapsed to alcohol dependence. The Sobells' study served to confirm that alcoholism is often a progressive, fatal disease.

Over the short term, the progressive nature of addiction is often not apparent, and the effect of treatment is magnified. Addicted people tend to present themselves for medical attention at their clinical worst and at the time when their symptoms are most exacerbated. Thus, if follow-up has a brief or rigid time frame, most addicted patients will appear to improve regardless of the treatment offered.[17]

In a prospective 8-year study of clinic alcoholics, 100 alcoholics were studied in terms of premorbid variables known to affect prognosis.[18] These patients were then followed every 18 months for 8 years (1972–1980). The authors examined the relationship between AA attendance, premorbid variables, and outcome. At the end of the 8 years, of the 29 patients with stable remissions of 3 years or more, 15 patients had made 300 or more visits to AA. Only one of the 37 still active alcoholics had the same number of visits to AA. As expected, social stability on admission predicted stable abstinence 8 years later for the group as a whole, but social instability on admission predicted AA attendance of the subsequent 8 years. Thirty-two patients attended AA meetings 100 or more times (mean 600 visits) between 1972 and 1980. Of these individuals, the number with stable employment and living arrangements went from two in 1972 to 15 in 1980. In sum, the alcoholics who were socially stable on admission tended to become abstinent without AA; but for admitted socially unstable alcoholics, frequent AA attendance appears to be an important intervening variable for recovery.

Finally, how do we explain the fact that over time alcoholics enjoy a 50% recovery rate? What natural treatment variables are working to help alcoholics to recover?

In a follow-up of an entire cohort of 120 inner-city alcoholics from adolescence until the age of 47, 49 men had achieved a year or more of abstinence.[14] Only one-third of the 49 had sought professional help during the first year of their abstinence, but over half had found an "external superego" or some form of "natural behavior modification" that altered the consequences of the alcohol use.[14] The external superego could include disulfiram, probation, or a medical affliction that made heavy drinking aversive. Over half found a substitute dependency such as gambling, meditation, smoking, eating, or compulsive over-involvement in a job or hobby.[14]

CONCLUSIONS

There are many lessons to be learned from the prospective study of alcoholism. One is that long-term follow-up shatters our retrospective illusions. A second lesson to be learned is therapeutic humility. In addition to studying the effects of effective therapeutic interventions, we must study those who have recovered from alcoholism without our help. Still a third lesson is hope. While alcoholism is both a baffling and a patient disorder, unlike most chronic diseases alcoholism may enjoy a high rate of stable remission.[1]

REFERENCES

1. Vaillant GE (1984). The course of alcoholism and lessons for treatment. Chapter 19. *Psychiatry Update vol. III*, Grinspoon L(ed.). Washington, DC: APA Press.
2. Vaillant GE & Milofsky ES (1982a). The etiology of alcoholism: A prospective viewpoint. *Am Psychol* 37:494–503.
3. Kammeier ML, Hoffman H & Loper RG (1973). Personality characteristics of alcoholics as college freshman and at time of treatment. *Q J Stud Alc* 34:390–399.
4. Vaillant GE (1983). *Natural History of Alcoholism.* Cambridge, MA: Harvard University Press.
5. Goodwin DW (1979). Alcoholism and heredity. *Arch Gen Psych* 36:57–61.

6. Simmel E (1948). Alcoholism and addiction. *Psychoanal Q* 17:6–31.
7. Blane HT (1968). *The Personality of the Alcoholic: Guises of Dependency.* New York: Harper & Row.
8. Winokur G, Clayton PJ & Reich T (1969). *Manic-Depressive Illness.* St. Louis, MO: CV Mosby.
9. Robins LN (1966). *Deviant Children Grown Up: A Sociological and Psychiatric Study of Sociopathic Personality.* Baltimore: Williams & Wilkins.
10. Sundby P (1967). *Alcoholism and Mortality.* Oslo, Norway: Universitets Forlaget.
11. Morrison JR (1974). Bipolar affective disorder and alcoholism. *Am J Psych* 131:1130–1133.
12. Schlesser MAG, Winokur G & Sherman BM (1980). Hypothalamic-pituitary-adrenal axis activity in depressive illness. *Arch Gen Psych* 37:737–743.
13. Vaillant GE (1980). Natural history of male psychological health. VIII. Antecedents to alcoholism and "orality." *Am J Psych* 17:181–186.
14. Vaillant GE & Milofsky ES (1982b). Natural history of male alcoholism. II. Paths to recovery. *Arch Gen Psych* 39:127–133.
15. Sobell MB & Sobell LC (1976). Second-year treatment outcome of alcoholics treated by individualized behavior therapy: Results. *Behav Res Ther* 14:195–215.
16. Pendery ML, Maltzman IM & West LJ (1982). Controlled drinking by alcoholics? New findings and a reevaluation of a major affirmative study. *Science* 217:169–175.
17. Polich JM, Armor DJ & Braiker HB (1981). *The Course of Alcoholism.* New York: Wiley.
18. Vaillant GE, Gale L, Milofsky E (1982). Natural history of male alcoholism. II. Relationship between different diagnostic dimensions. *J Stud Alc* 43:216–232.

7

*Genetics of
the Disorders*

OVERVIEW

The complex issue of comorbidity can be examined by identifying which illnesses are inherited independently or together and what are the interactions between genetic and environmental factors that promote illness or protect against it. The studies of inheritance, as well as precise clinical description and laboratory measurements, can lead to more precise characterization of causal mechanisms in comorbidity.

Family, twin, and adoption studies can point to specific characteristics that may be further evaluated by genetic-linkage studies. Currently, there is a greater, richer literature on genetics relating to addiction to alcohol than other drugs.

Together, these studies suggest that there is a substantial genetic component to the development of alcoholism. Genetic studies of comorbidity show that anxiety symptoms in alcoholics appear to be a consequence of heavy drinking, rather than an independent disorder. Genetic evidence shows alcoholism to be independent of antisocial personality disorder, although some cases of alcoholism, particularly those characterized by early onset, may also be associated with even earlier onset of criminal or other antisocial behavior.

While depressive symptoms are common among people addicted to alcohol and other drugs, depression appears to be inherited separately from alcoholism. For many addicted people, a depressive syndrome is a complication of addiction rather than a second, independent illness. Such findings further underscore the need to separate the phenotype of drug dependence into more clinically distinct subgroups, based on coexistent disorders, laboratory findings, and family history.

DIAGNOSIS

Family Studies

Comorbidity is the occurrence of two (or more) independent diseases in the same individual, either at the same time or on a lifetime basis (lifetime comorbidity). Comorbidity within the family is the occurrence of a second illness within the proband's family at a rate above that expected in the population at large. When such familial associations are seen, individuals with the first, the second, and both illnesses may be compared in order to identify possible etiologic factors.

Familial prevalence does not establish a genetic basis for these illnesses. It simply means that the prevalence of the disorder among relatives of a proband with the disorder is higher than its prevalence in the general population. Once the familial occurrence of an illness is established, study of its inheritance can clarify its genetic relationship to comorbid conditions.

Often the first step is to demonstrate the familial occurrence of a disorder. Familial transmission has been demonstrated in other psychiatric disorders, including affective disorder,[1,2] schizophrenia,[3] antisocial personality disorder,[4] anxiety disorders,[5] Briquet's syndrome,[6] and attention deficit disorder,[7] among others.

Importantly, familial alcoholism is one of the most solidly based findings in psychiatry. Despite great diversity in populations selected, diagnostic practices, and research strategies employed, researchers have consistently concluded that the risk of alcoholism is elevated up to sevenfold among first-degree family members of alcoholics.[8,9] While women are less often affected than men (both in the general population and within alcoholic families), there is no sex difference in transmission; that is, relatives have the same degree of risk for alcoholism whether the proband is male or female.[10]

Adoption and Twin Studies

Family studies alone can only suggest the presence of heritable factors. Whether a disorder is biologically transmissible may be established on the basis of comparisons of genetic transmission between various classes of relatives. Adoption, twin, and high-risk studies are considered the primary methods of separating genetic and learned environmental determinants of risk for illness. In the case of alcoholism, evidence from twin, adoption, and high-risk studies strongly supports the conclusions that heritable, nonenvironmental factors have substantial influence on risk of illness.[9,11–13]

However, these studies also demonstrate, as with many other common complex diseases (such as juvenile-onset diabetes or hypertension), that alcohol dependence does not follow any easily identified pattern of inheritance. Thus, its appearance depends on an interaction between inborn, constitutional factors, and postnatal exposure and experiences.[14] Moreover, both adoption and twin studies indicate the existence of variations in alcohol dependence with distinct patterns of inheritance and degree of susceptibility to postnatal influences.[13,15,16]

Etiology

Establishing a biological marker specific for alcohol dependence would be a significant step forward. In particular, demonstration of linkage between the disease and a known chromosomal site could rapidly lead to precise identification and molecular characterization of a genetic factor. Elucidation of the function of the normal allele(s) and finding the disease-related allele(s) could contribute greatly to our understanding of the pathogenesis of alcohol dependence.

While a variety of markers have been proposed,[17,18] recent interest has focused on a possible association with the dopamine D2 receptor.[19] The A1 allele at the dopamine D2 receptor was found in 69% of alcoholics, versus 20% of nonalcoholic controls.[19] Other studies have not replicated these results.[20] Instead, the A1 allele was found in 38% of alcoholics versus 30% of nonalcoholics in one study and, in another, no linkage with the D2 dopamine receptor locus in two families was found. An association was found between the A1 allele and alcoholism (in 41% of alcoholics versus 12% of controls), with an even more striking difference in that the allele was found in 60% of the severe alcoholics in this sample.[20] However, this study, as others, was unable to demonstrate linkage to the D2 receptor site.

Finally, the specimens reported with an association between the A1 allele and the dopamine D2 receptor[19] were reexamined.[20] A progressive decrease in dopamine binding sites among alcoholics as compared to nonalcoholics was found. The lowest number of sites was found in the homozygous A1A1 subjects, suggesting that genotype at the D2 locus, through its expression of receptors, might influence susceptibility to some form of alcoholism.[20]

Research is being carried out on the inheritance of other forms of drug dependence but is less advanced.[23] While animal studies support the role of genetic factors in alcohol and other drug-seeking behavior,[24] demonstration of intergenerational transmission in humans has proven difficult for several reasons.

First, relative to alcohol dependence, other drug dependence remains relatively less common. In the ECA study, lifetime prevalence of opioid abuse and dependence, for example, was found to be 0.7%, compared to 11–16% for alcohol abuse and dependence.[25,26] Moreover, legal sanctions against drug use and social disapproval tend to make data gathering and recruitment of subjects more difficult.[27]

Another difficulty is that, on a lifetime basis, though drug users may have specific drug preferences, they tend not to restrict use to one drug or class of drug, thus complicating studies of transmission. As a result, researchers have at times assumed a single underlying spectrum of vulnerability to alcohol and all illicit drugs or grouped illicit drugs together without respect to pharmacologic properties.[14]

Finally, changes in the availability of illicit drugs would be expected to alter observed patterns of inheritance. Even if genetic factors played a major role in conveying susceptibility to dependence on a given drug (such as cocaine or heroin), without exposure the trait would not be revealed.

Nonetheless, evidence exists to suggest a familial liability to drug abuse and dependence. Using a family history protocol to study 305 probands admitted for drug abuse or dependence, 97 with alcohol abuse/dependence only, 27 with drug abuse/dependence, and 177 with alcohol plus other drug abuse/dependence was found.[28] Probands with drug abuse/dependence (amphetamine and cannabis abuse/dependence being the most common) more frequently reported having a family history of drug dependency than probands with alcohol dependence (18.5% vs. 3%) and also more often reported first-degree relatives with both alcohol and other drug use (26% as compared to 14%).

Diagnoses in a large family study of opiate addicts were associated with high rates of antisocial personality (ASP), major depression, alcoholism, and drug abuse among first-degree relatives.[29] Their study was large enough to allow subdivision of opiate addicts into groups without other Research Diagnostic Criteria (RDC) diagnoses, opiate addiction plus major depression, or opiate addiction plus ASP. They had difficulty in demonstrating specific intergenerational transmission of opiate use, since only 1% of the parents had used opiates, but their data nonetheless showed familial aggregation of drug abuse, with rates ranging from 17.5–22.8% of first-degree relatives, versus 3.3% among relatives of normal controls, corresponding to a 13.7-fold increase in adjusted odds of drug use given a family history of opiate addiction.[29]

Another large family study evaluated 350 inpatients admitted for drug abuse, slightly over half of whom were opiate users, another one-third were cocaine users, and the remainder primarily used sedative–hypnotics.[30] Among first-degree relatives overall, 9.5% had a drug-abuse diagnosis. But the rate of drug dependence among relatives differed substantially based on the proband's drug of choice, from 16% of male relatives of cocaine users to 2% of male relatives of sedative–hypnotic users. In contrast, rates of alcoholism among family members were comparable across groups, again suggesting specific aggregation of drug dependence within families.[30]

Thus, despite significant obstacles to such investigations, evidence from three large family studies suggests the familial association of drug dependence. However, there have been few studies that have explicitly tried to separate genetic and environmental factors. The only reported study of twins[13] found that concordance for drug abuse/dependence (by DSM-III criteria) was significantly higher in monozygotic than dizygotic male, but not female, twins. However, the MZ/DZ ratio of concordance for abuse and dependence was similar across sex (1.45 for males versus 1.37 for females), suggesting that the negative finding in females was due to lack of statistical power.

A study of 443 adoptees by Cadoret et al. also suggested the heritability of drug dependence but found that it was related to a biological background of alcohol problems and ASP. Adoptees with drug dependence but not ASP tended to have a biological background of ASP, which predicted ASP in the adoptee, which was in turn highly correlated with drug dependence.[31]

INTERACTIONS

Interaction of Genetics and Addiction

In sum, it seems clear that alcoholism and other drug dependence aggregate in families. There is strong evidence for the existence of genetic liability for alcoholism and weaker, though still considerable, support for the role of genetic factors in other drug dependence

Depression. Depression does not confer an increased risk for alcoholism. Perhaps the best-studied situation is the familial cooccurrence of alcoholism and depression. Studies have concluded that, although these disorders often occur together both in the individual and in their families, the disorders are transmitted separately. Subjects with depression but not alcoholism have an excess of depression, but not alcoholism, in their relatives; those with alcoholism and depression tend to transmit both.[32,33]

Similarly, based on adoption data, no significant excess of depression among parents of drug abusers as compared to controls (2.5% vs. 4.8%) was found, nor was an excess of treated drug abuse seen in parents of adoptees with affective disorder versus controls (6.3% vs. 3.9%).[34]

Anxiety. Contrary to popular belief, anxiety disorders, do not appear to convey a risk for alcoholism.[36] It is likely that most anxiety symptoms in alcoholics are directly related to heavy drinking, rather than reflecting an independent disorder.[35]

Personality Disorders. ASP conveys the highest risk of any disorder for dependence on alcohol or other drugs, and family studies of alcohol and drug dependence have consistently found elevated rates of ASP in relatives.[10,29] The association between ASP and problematic alcohol use is so close, in fact, that ASP has often been considered to be a part of the syndrome or a complication of alcoholism rather than necessarily being a distinct entity.[39-41] However, in the larger view, while most persons ASP suffer from alcoholism (drug addiction), most alcoholics/drug addicts do not have ASP disorders.[41] No appreciable difference in rates of ASP among relatives of probands with opiate addiction, regardless of any secondary diagnosis the proband had, including ASP, was found.

Adoption studies have found evidence of specificity of inheritance of alcoholism and ASP and genetic independence of the two disorders.[42,43]

Since both ASP and alcoholism are heterogeneous phenotypes,[44,45] this conflict may result from using definitions that are too broad: in order to clarify the familial association (or independence) of these disorders, more homogeneous subgroups of both disorders need to be defined.

On the basis of a large adoption study and subsequent work, it has suggested that at least two more homogeneous subforms of alcoholism exist.[46,47] Analysis of records on 862 men and 913 women born in Stockholm between 1930 and 1949, of known paternity and adopted by non-relatives at an early age, revealed two patterns of alcohol abuse. Type 1 alcoholism is characterized by later onset of alcohol-related difficulties, benders, guilt over drinking, and alcoholic liver disease, but not criminality. Prolonged hospitalization of natural parents prior to adoption and low socioeconomic status in the adoptive parents appeared to be risk indicators for severity; without such exacerbating factors, course of illness tended to be mild. Daughters of biological fathers with Type 1 background tended to have an increase in alcohol abuse, but not criminality, somatoform disorders, or other psychiatric disorders.[46,47]

Characteristics of Type 2 alcoholism include early onset of alcohol problems, fighting while intoxicated, drunk driving, and inability to abstain from alcohol. Such alcoholics' biological fathers tended to have a background of both treatment for alcoholism and of significant criminality; mothers had no excess of either. Regardless of postnatal environment, their adopted-away sons had a ninefold increase in risk of alcohol abuse, yielding an estimate of the heritability of liability to this form of alcohol abuse of 90% in men. Unlike the daughters of Type 1 men, daughters of Type 2 fathers showed no increase in either alcohol dependence or criminality, but did have a significant increase in somatoform disorders.[46,47]

REFERENCES

1. Dinwiddie SH (1993). Genetic and family studies in psychiatric illness and alcohol and drug dependence. *J Addict Dis* 12(13):17–28.
2. Rice JP, Reich T, Andreasen NC, Endicott J, Van Eerdewegh M, Fishman R, Hirschfeld RMA & Klerman GL (1987). The familial transmission of bipolar illness. *Arch Gen Psych* 44(5):441–447.
3. Rice JP, McGuffin P. Genetic etiology of schizophrenia and affective disorders. In: Cooper AM, Guze SB, Judd L, Klerman GL, Michels R, Cavenar JO, Solnit AJ (eds.), *Psych* Philadelphia, Lippincott, 1(62), 1–24.

4. Cloninger CR, Reich T & Guze SB (1975). The multifactorial model of disease transmission: II. Sex differences in the familial transmission of sociopathy (antisocial personality). *Br J Psych* 127:11–22.

5. Weissman MM (1988). The epidemiology of anxiety disorders: Rates, risks and familial patterns. *J Psych Res* 22(Suppl 1):99–114.

6. Cloninger CR, Reich T & Guze SB (1975). The multifactorial model of disease transmission: III. Familial relationship between sociopathy and hysteria (Briquet's syndrome). *Br J Psych* 127:23–32.

7. Biederman J, Munir K, Knee D, Habelow W, Armentano M, Autor S, Hoge SK & Waternaux C (1986). A family study of patients with attention deficit disorder and normal controls. *J Psych Res* 20(4):263–274.

8. Cotton NS (1979). The familial incidence of alcoholism. *J Stud Alc* 40(1):89–116.

9. Merikangas KR (1990). The genetic epidemiology of alcoholism. *Psychol Med* 20:11–22.

10. Guze SB, Cloninger CR, Martin R & Clayton PJ (1986). Alcoholism as a medical disorder. *Compr Psych* 27(6):501–510.

11. Goodwin DW, Schulsinger F, Lermansen L, Guze SB & Winokur G (1973). Alcohol problems in adoptees raised apart from alcoholic biological parents. *Arch Gen Psych* 28(2):238–243.

12. Cadoret RJ, Cain CA & Grove WM (1980). Development of alcoholism in adoptees raised apart from alcoholic biologic relatives. *Arch Gen Psych* 37(5):561–563.

13. Pickens RW, Svikis DS, McGue M, Lykken DT, Heston LL & Clayton PJ (1991). Heteogeneity in the inheritance of alcoholism. *Arch Gen Psych* 48(1):19–28.

14. Dinwiddie SH & Cloninger CR (1991). Family and adoption studies in alcoholism and drug addiction. *Psychiatric Ann* 21(4):206–214.

15. Cloninger CR, Bohman M & Sigvardsson S (1981). Inheritance of alcohol abuse. Cross-fostering analysis of adopted men. *Arch Gen Psych* 38(8):861–868.

16. Bohman M, Sigvardsson S & Cloninger CR (1981). Maternal inheritance of alcohol abuse. Cross-fostering analysis of adopted women. *Arch Gen Psych* 38(9):965–969.

17. Hill SY, Goodwin DW, Cadoret R, Osterland CK & Doner SM (1975). Association and linkage between alcoholism and eleven serological markers. *J Stud Alc* 36(7):981–92.

18. Hill SY, Aston C & Rabin B (1988). Suggestive evidence of genetic linkage between alcoholism and the MNS blood group. *Alc Clin Exp Res* 12(6):811–814.

19. Blum K, Noble EP, Sheridan PJ, Montgomery A, Ritchie T, Jagadeeswaran P, Nogami H, Briggs AH & Cohn JB (1990). Allelic association of human dopamine D2 receptor gene in alcoholism. *JAMA* 1990; 263(15):2055–2060.

20. Bolos AM, Dean M, Lucas-Derse S, Ramsburg M, Brown GL & Goldman D (1990). Population and pedigree studies reveal a lack of association between the dopamine D2 receptor gene and alcoholism. *JAMA* 264(24):3156–3160.

21. Parsian A, Todd RD, Devor EJ, O'Malley KL, Suarez BK, Reich T & Cloninger CR (1991). Alcoholism and alleles of the human D2 dopamine receptor locus. *Arch Gen Psych* 48)77):655–663.

22. Noble EP, Blum K, Ritchie T, Montgomery A & Sheridan PJ (1991). Allelic association of the D2 dopamine receptor gene with receptor-binding characteristics in alcoholism. *Arch Gen Psychiatry* 48(7):648–54.

23. Pickens RW & Svikis DS (1991). Genetic influences in human substance abuse. *J Addict Dis* 10(1–2):205–213.

24. Crabbe JC & McSwigan JD, Belknap JK (1985). The role of genetics in substance abuse. In: Galizio M & Maisto SA (eds.), *Determinants of Substance Abuse*, pp. 13--64. New York: Plenum.

25. Anthony JC & Helzer JE (1990). Syndromes of drug abuse-dependence. In: Robins LE, Regier DA, (eds.), *Psychiatric Disorders in America*, pp. 116–154. New York: Free Press.

26. Robins LN, Helzer JE & Weissman MM, et al. (1984). Lifetime prevalence of specific psychiatric disorders in three sites. *Arch Gen Psych* 41(10):949–956.

27. Kozel NJ & Adams EH (1989). Epidemiology of drug abuse: An overview. *Science* 234:970–974.

28. Meller WH, Rinehart R, Cadoret RJ & Troughton E (1988). Specific familial transmission in substance abuse. *Int J Addict* 23(10):1029–1039.

29. Rounsaville BJ, Kosten TR, Weissman MM, Prusoff B, Pauls D, Anton SF & Merikangas K (1991). Psychiatric disorders in relatives of probands with opiate addiction. *Arch Gen Psych* 48(1):33–42.

30. Mirin SM, Weiss RD, Griffin ML & Michael JL (1991). Psychopathology in drug abusers and their families. *Compr Psych* 32(1):36–51.

31. Cadoret RJ, Troughton E, O'Gorman TW & Heywood E (1986). An adoption study of genetic and environmental factors in drug abuse. *Arch Gen Psych* 43(12), 1131–1136.

32. Cloninger CR, Reich T & Wetzel R (1979). Alcoholism and affective disorders: Familial associations and genetic models. In: Godwin DW & Erickson C, (eds.), *Alcoholism and the Affective Disorders*, pp: 57–86. Spectrum.

33. Merikangas KR, Leckman JF, Prusoff BA, Pauls DL & Weissman MM (1985). Familial transmission of depression of depression in alcoholism. *Arch Gen Psych* 42(4):367–372.

34. von Knorring A-L, Cloninger CR, Bohman M & Sigvardsson S (1983). An adoption study of depressive disorders and substance abuse. *Arch Gen Psych* 40(9):943–950.

35. Noyes R, Crowe RR & Harris EL, et al. (1986). Relationship between panic disorder and agoraphobia: A family study. *Arch Gen Psych* 43:227–232.

36. Munjack KJ & Moss HB (1981). Affective disorder and alcoholism in families of agoraphobics. *Arch Gen Psych* 38:869–871.
37. Kushner MG, Sher KJ & Beitman BD (1990). The relation between alcohol problems and the anxiety disorders. *Am J Psych* 174(6):685–695.
38. Schuckit MA, Irwin M & Brown SA (1990). The history of anxiety symptoms among 171 primary alcoholics. *J Stud Alc* 51(1):34–41.
39. Schuckit MA (1973). Alcoholism and sociopathy—diagnostic confusion. *Q J Stud Alc* 34:157–164.
40. Cleckley H (1982). *The Mask of Sanity.* St. Louis: Mosby.
41. Hesselbrock VM, Hesselbrock MN & Stabeneau JR (1985). Alcoholism in men patients subtyped by family history and antisocial personality. *J Stud Alc* 46(1):59–64.
42. Caboret RJ, O'Gorman TW, Troughton E & Heywood E (1985). Alcoholism and antisocial personality. *Arch Gen Psych* 42(2):161–167.
43. Cadoret RJ, Troughton E & O'Gorman TW (1987). Genetic and environmental factors in alcohol abuse and antisocial personality. *J Stud Alc* 48(1):1–8.
44. Cloninger CR & Reich T (1983). Genetic heterogeneity in alcoholism and sociopathy. In: Kety SS, Rowland LP, Sidman RL, Matthysse SW (eds.) *Genetics of Neurological and Psychiatric Disorders* pp. 145–165. New York, Raven Press.
45. Whitters A, Troughton E, Cadoret RJ & Widmer RB (1984). Evidence for clinical heterogeneity in antisocial alcoholics. *Compr Psych* 25(2):158–164.
46. Cloninger CR, Bohman M, Sigvardsson S & von Knorring A-L (1985). Psychopathology in adopted-out children of alcoholics. The Stockholm adoption study. In: Galanger M, (ed.), *Recent Development in Alcoholism* 3:37–51.
47. Cloninger CR (1987). Neurogenetic adaptive mechanisms in alcoholism. *Science* 236:410–416.

8

Addictive Disease as a Psychiatric Disorder

DEFINITION: WHAT IS A DISEASE?

According to *Webster's Ninth New Collegiate Dictionary,*[4] disease is "an impairment of the normal state of the living animal or plant body that affects the performance of the vital functions"; sickness is listed as a synonym. An obsolete definition is "trouble."[1] This is a relatively inclusive definition that would allow many conditions to qualify as a disease. *Dorland's Illustrated Medical Dictionary, Twenty-Seventh Edition*[2] contains a definition of disease as "any deviation from or interruption of the normal structure or function of any part, organ, or system (or combination) of the body that is manifested by a characteristic set of symptoms and signs, and whose etiology, pathology, and prognosis may be known or unknown." Most dictionaries define disease as an illness or a sickness. Alcoholism and drug addiction fit exactly into this definition because an addiction to alcohol and drugs is a definite morbid process that produces characteristic and identifiable signs and symptoms affecting many organ systems in the body.[3]

When studies have been performed on the nature of alcoholism and whether or not it is a disease, some interesting results have been obtained. In 1979, a study revealed that 85% of general practitioners agree that alcoholism is a disease—the same percentage that regarded coronary artery disease, hypertension, and epilepsy as a disease. A 1988 Gallop poll found that when the public was asked if alcoholism were a disease, 78% agreed strongly, 10% agreed somewhat, 6% disagreed somewhat, 5% disagreed strongly, and 1% had no opinion. But the poll indicated that the exact meaning of "disease" remains unclear in the public mind. Asked which of a number of options described their feelings about alcoholism, 60% said it is a disease or illness, 31% a mental or psychological problem, 23% a lack of willpower, 16% a moral weakness, and 6% were unsure. (The total is greater than 100% due to multiple responses.)

HISTORY: DISEASE CONCEPT OF ADDICTION

The concept of disease dates back to 5th century B.C. Greece when Hippocrates, the father of medicine, set down explanations of diseases he had observed. He postulated that diseases were caused by an imbalance in the elements of earth, air, fire, and water and other ingredients of nature. Psychiatric disorders were caused by being possessed by evil spirits that overtook the body and mind. Medicine was rather slow in shaking these conceptualizations of disease. Even as late as the 19th century, certain medical diseases such as syphilis, and most psychiatric disorders, including schizophrenia, manic-depressive illness, and alcoholism, were considered defects of character and moral degeneracies.[5]

In the early 19th century, mental illness began acquiring legitimacy as a disease. Physicians in the United States first recognized alcoholism as a disease through the writings of Benjamin Rush, who was among the founders of the American Psychiatric Association. Rush identified alcoholism as a disease in which alcohol serves as the causal agent, loss of control over drinking behavior as the characteristic symptom, and total abstinence as the only effective cure. Curiously, the field of alcoholism has not yet surpassed this simple but brilliant clinical observation made by a discerning psychiatrist.[17]

The disease concept of alcoholism was legitimized in the mid-twentieth century when an official body of physicians for the first time acknowledged that alcoholism was a disease.[6] The American Medical Association published an official declaration in a journal article entitled "Hospitalization of Patients with Alcoholism," in which The Council on Mental Health, its Committee on Alcoholism, and the profession in general recognized the syndrome of alcoholism as an illness which justifiably should have the attention of physicians.[3,6] Although this statement constitutes the formal acceptance of the disease concept of alcoholism by the American medical profession as a whole, it does not mean that it was accepted by physicians unanimously or even by a majority.[8]

Certain physicians were particularly important in shaping and supporting the disease concept of alcoholism. While working with alcoholics in Towns Hospital in New York City, Dr. William Silkworth arrived at a simple formula to explain his clinical observations of alcoholism. He ascertained that alcoholism is a physical allergy to alcohol, which exists in only those who are destined to become alcoholics, and not in those who are temperate drinkers.[8]

Dr. Harry Tiebout, a psychiatrist, worked closely with members of Alcoholics Anonymous to advance some formalization of the disease concept espoused by the recovered alcoholics. He published articles in leading medical journals about psychodynamic concepts that could be used to describe the intrapsychic phenomena in the disease of alcoholism. He emphasized the importance of the psychological defense mechanisms of denial, rationalization, and minimization in the propagation of alcoholism.[9]

The popularization of the disease concept of alcoholism originates with the nonphysician E.M. Jellinek who wrote a lengthy, scholarly book entitled, *The Disease Concept of Alcoholism.*[3] In the book, he analyzed data and opinion from a variety of sources and arrived at the conclusion that a majority of the evidence indicates that alcoholism is a disease. He basically viewed alcoholism as an addiction similar to other drug addictions. He also pointed out that the term *alcohol addiction* would not gain favor because of the stigma attached to the term addiction.[3]

The growth of Alcoholics Anonymous and the development of effective treatment of addiction has contributed greatly to credibility of the disease concept. However, a parallel accumulation of scientific evidence has provided the long-awaited documentation of the disease concept of alcoholism. Genetic studies of alcoholism have clearly established that alcoholism has similar characteristics to other diseases since it may be transmitted genetically. Genetic messages are encoded in the genes, which are composed of biochemical components called deoxyribonucleic acid (DNA). The gene for addiction has not been identified as yet.[10]

ETIOLOGY

The Disease Model of Addiction to Alcohol and Other Drugs

There is an enormous overlap between addiction to alcohol and addiction to other drugs. Polydrug addiction is the norm, not the exception, and, except for specific pharmacologic issues and timelines, the processes of progression, treatment, recovery, and relapse are nearly identical for addiction to alcohol and other drugs. For these and other reasons, it is almost useless to discuss addiction to alcohol as a disease without also including addiction to other drugs as a disease. Although there are differences, particularly in the consequences between the use of alcohol and drugs, the essential characteristics of the diseases are identical. Therefore, the consideration of alcoholism as a disease must include addiction to other drugs as a disease.[11]

Addiction is defined by behaviors of addiction, which are 1) preoccupation with the acquisition of alcohol or other drugs, 2) their compulsive use in spite of adverse consequences, and 3) a pattern of relapse to alcohol and other drugs in spite of adverse consequences.[11] Loss of control characterizes all those behaviors. The addictive use of alcohol and other drugs inevitably leads to the development of adverse consequences because of the persistent loss of control. This loss of control, once established, exists for a lifetime. In other words, the alcoholic and drug addict will not be able to use alcohol or drugs without experiencing a consistent loss of control at some point following a resumption of use after a period of abstinence.[11-13]

Loss of Control. The primary foundation of alcoholism as a disease rests on the acceptance of the loss of control over alcohol by the alcoholic.[3,13] The loss of control is the cardinal manifestation of the disease,[13] the essential feature that leads to a multitude of adverse consequences. The loss of control is manifested in many aspects of the addicted person's life, including disturbances in interpersonal relationships, and adverse medical, psychiatric, and spiritual consequences.[13]

The key point that is difficult for dissenters from the disease concept to accept is that the addicted person has lost this control over the use of alcohol or other drugs because of a disease of the body, mind, and spirit. The dissenters contend that the addicted person has chosen to drink volitionally, although often to relieve some intolerable condition. The fallacy in the "free will" concept of addiction is clear but difficult to refute if the "loss of control" explanation of addiction is not accepted.[13]

Studies have been performed to examine the addicted person's loss of control over alcohol and other drug use. Several studies have demonstrated that alcoholics cannot use alcohol normally or nonaddictively over their lifetime once the diagnosis of alcoholism is made.[12] One longitudinal study confirmed that less than 1% of alcoholics drank normally. However, other studies present findings that alcoholics can be taught to drink normally over time.[12] Some studies bring alcoholics into the laboratory and ask questions and observe the drinking behaviors of the alcoholics. The findings are that alcoholics do show a loss of control with the use of alcohol.[14]

Denial. Methodological biases exist when studying addicted people in the cross-sectional state as well as over time, particularly in the active state of drinking or alcoholism. The central problem is the denial that is part of the disease of addiction. This denial may lead to difficulties in establishing the criteria for the diagnosis as well as identifying the adverse consequences. Any underestimation of the denial will lead to problems in confirming the loss of control in addicted people. Corroborative history from outside sources who know the addicted person is often necessary to penetrate or circumvent the denial. Not all studies take these precautions in their methods.[13]

In the first step in Alcoholics Anonymous the alcoholic must accept his or her loss of control over alcohol. It is implied, if not explicitly stated, that this loss of control extends over a lifetime. "We admitted we were powerless over alcohol—that our lives had become unmanageable."[8] The word "powerless" is equivalent to the loss of control, and the word "unmanageable" represents the adverse consequences of the powerlessness. In order for the alcoholic to begin recovery from the alcoholism, responsibility for the loss of control must be assumed. A common reason for relapse to alcoholic drinking is an inability or unwillingness to accept this fundamental aspect of the disease. Relapse because of the lack of acceptance of the loss of control may occur after a brief or prolonged period of abstinence.

The alcoholic can comprehend the first step, and recognize the loss of control over alcohol, if it is attributed to a disease.[8] Because "willpower" over the loss of control of alcohol use is ultimately ineffective, insistence on correcting a weak character or treating an underlying psychiatric or emotional disorder will not prevent relapse to alcohol or other drug use. The addicted person is already filled with self-condemnation, and a further exaggeration of the guilt by making the addict at "fault" for his or her abnormal drinking or drug use will impede their accepting responsibility for the addiction and its consequences.[15]

Adaptive versus Disease Model for Addiction

Origins of the Adaptive Model. In contrast to the disease model is the popular "adaptive model," which reflects an ancient conception of addiction and has evolved into modern psychosocial theories. These psychosocial theories originate from notions of causality in religion, morality, and late nineteenth- and early twentieth-century psychology. The religious concept of free will and willpower in disease has continued throughout centuries. People became ill because of a lack of moral character and "true grit." Many of the psychosocial theories remain cemented in moral causality.[15]

The disease model evolved for not only addiction to alcohol and other drugs, but for other medical, surgical, and psychiatric conditions. The principle reasons for the adoption and application of the disease model is that it fits the observations and provide a pragmatic approach that works for diagnosis and treatment.[13]

The adaptive model may be intuitively appealing, but does not withstand scientific validation. Intuition can support the assumption that the earth is flat and at the center of the universe, or that the earth is round and is part of a solar system around which it revolves. Through careful observation and testing, scientific validation serves to demonstrate the fallacies of the intuitive mind. The disease model is as deterministic, probablistic, and mechanical as science itself. The scientific model has been an effective way for medicine to advance. To revert back to the adaptive model with emotional suppositions and religious intonation is to impede medical progress and, unfortunately, remain with a model that does not work.[13,15]

According to the disease model, the interaction between alcohol and other drugs and the brain is responsible for the initiation of the disease. The disease model states that a genetic vulnerability is expressed as a predisposition to develop an addiction when exposed to alcohol and other drugs. Alcohol and drugs are thought to affect neurotransmitters in key areas of the brain to sustain addictive behavior.[16] The drive states such as hunger, thirst, sex, and others are associated with a reward system in the limbic system in a primitive portion of the brain. An effect of alcohol and other drugs is to stimulate both the drive states and the reward center, and may produce a link between all of them through memory in the hippocampus of the limbic system.[18]

In this way addiction to alcohol and other drugs is a "biochemical disease," just as are manic-depressive illness and schizophrenia. The biochemical theories for these psychiatric disorders are no further advanced than those for alcoholism and drug addiction. The current biochemical explanations of bipolar disease and schizophrenia are based on hypotheses about neurotransmitter affects in the brain. These neurochemical explanations have much promise but have yet to be definitively proven. There are several biochemical theories of addiction to alcohol and other drugs involving the same neurotransmitter systems, such as dopamine, serotonin, gamma-aminobutyric acid (GABA), and others, which are thought to be operative in the expression of the other psychiatric disorders.[16]

Tenets of the Adaptive Model. The adaptive model states the reverse; i.e., that economic, family, individual, and social problems, stresses, evils, and depravities lead to addictive use. This model holds that prior to the onset of addiction, the addicted person has failed to achieve maturity in economic independence, self-reliance, and responsibility toward others. Because of these failures, the individual seeks and chooses to use alcohol and drugs to further self-destruction. The important ingredients to the equation in the adaptive model are that the addiction results from environmental problems prompting a lack of maturity.[15]

Genetics of Alcoholism

Research confirming the heritability of alcoholism has helped to support Jellinek's disease model.[3] Many scientific studies have clearly documented that alcoholism has a genetic component to it, as do many other medical and psychiatric disorders. Plutarch noted in biblical times that the "drunkard begot drunkards."[10]

The genetic studies have used four major methods for studying alcoholism as a primary disease. The first method was utilized by Jellinek himself,[3] who termed *familial alcoholism* as a diagnostic category. Jellinek and many others found that alcoholism ran in families, such that an alcoholic had a much greater chance of having a family member who is alcoholic than a nonalcoholic. In fact, the studies on families of alcoholics have found that over 50% of the alcoholics have a family history positive for alcoholism. Furthermore, if an alcoholic had at least one family member who was alcoholic, they were likely to have additional family members who were alcoholics.[10]

Adoption studies performed abroad and in the United States have shown dramatically that biological background plays a determining role in the development of alcoholism. Twin studies are also revealing in confirming a genetic predisposition to alcoholism. Identical twins are more likely to be concordant for alcoholism than fraternal twins according to many studies performed in the United States and abroad.[10]

High-risk studies have shown that those who are at risk to develop alcoholism share characteristics with alcoholics and have characteristics that differ from those of nonalcoholics. A high-risk individual is not yet an alcoholic but has a blood relative who is. The importance of high-risk studies is that there may be markers that we can identify that are specific for alcoholism and that are present before its onset.[10]

Heavy Drinking

Epidemiological Catchment Area Study. Heavy drinking does occur in the absence of alcoholism, and as such may not be considered a disease.[17] Heavy drinking does not include addictive drinking, in that loss of control over alcohol is not present. What distinguishes heavy drinking from alcoholism is that the heavy drinker can, and often will, quit or abstain when the consequences from the drinking are serious enough to warrant it. The ability to control drinking to ward off adverse consequences is the hallmark of the heavy drinker, whereas the alcoholic continues to drink in spite of the adverse consequences.[17]

According to a large national study in which 20,000 people were interviewed in five cities, the Epidemiological Catchment Area Study (ECA) found that heavy drinking and alcoholism both occurred in about 15% of the population.[18]

Heavy Drinking as a Counter to Alcoholism as a Disease. Some opponents to the disease concept of alcoholism offer heavy drinking as an explanation of alcoholism. Fingarette argued in a book entitled *Heavy Drinking: The Myth of Alcoholism as a Disease*[17] that alcoholism is not a disease, and in fact does not exist. He concludes that alcoholics do not

experience a loss of control over alcohol use, and presents several studies to support his contention. He ignores many studies that do show loss of control in alcoholics, as well as the self-report of thousands to millions of alcoholics in recovery who attest to their powerlessness over the use of alcohol.

Curiously, Fingarette's definition of heavy drinking would qualify for many clinicians' definition of alcoholism. He affirms that heavy drinking becomes a central activity with consequences affecting the drinker's life. This definition of heavy drinking is essentially one of addictive drinking in which a preoccupation with and compulsive use of alcohol is characteristic. He stops short of calling heavy drinking alcoholism.[17]

Importantly, Fingarette asserts that alcoholics are not helpless; that they can take control of their lives. "In the last analysis, alcoholics must want to change and choose to change." He concludes that alcoholism is not a disease; the assumption of personal responsibility, however, is a sign of health, while needless submission to spurious medical authority is a pathology. Proponents of the disease concept would not disagree with Fingarette on any of those points. The cornerstone of recovery according to the disease concept of alcoholism is personal responsibility. The alcoholic must assume responsibility for his or her alcoholism (drug addiction) before recovery can begin and certainly be maintained. This is true of many diseases, particularly chronic ones that are not curable.

The Self-Medication Hypothesis

Psychoanalysis. Psychodynamic theory has provided a useful conceptualization and terminology for the description of some of the intradynamic processes involved in alcoholism (drug addiction). The terms *conscious* and *unconscious* and *defense mechanisms* are particularly helpful in describing the character of the addictive process and the intrapsychic consequences of the addictive mode. Conscious and unconscious denial, minimization, rationalization, and other psychodynamic processes are psychological mechanisms by which alcoholism is perpetuated and sustained intrapsychically.[19]

Psychoanalytic theory has reflected a popular view of alcoholism that has existed for centuries. This historical view is that alcoholism is caused by some disorder or disease other than alcoholism; i.e., alcoholism is not a primary disease. In other words, alcoholism may exist, but is not a disease as such; rather it is secondary to or a manifestation of an underlying, causative disorder. The psychoanalytic model has attempted to explain alcoholic drinking by a number of psychodynamic theories.[20]

The ego is the mediator between the powerful forces of the impulsive id and the punitive superego, which, according to psychoanalytic thinking, operate in the unconscious mind. Whenever there is a conflict between these primitive drives, guilt may result, and the ego is in a dissonant state. The disharmony in the ego, through its failed attempts to mediate conflict, motivates the ego to seek relief in escape; one mode of potential tension relief is through drinking.[19,20]

This explanation may be valid for alcohol and drug "use," but it does not account for addictive use, nor is it indicative of a disease. Psychoanalytic theory only provides a rationale for the use of alcohol and drugs; it does not explain why alcoholics continue to use alcohol and drugs long after the adverse consequences outweigh the benefits. The conflicts created by addictive drinking often exceed those that may have motivated the drinking in the first lace. The original distress to the ego is lost in the overwhelming disruption from diseased drinking.[19,20]

According to psychodynamic principles, once the conflicts are resolved through psychotherapy, which may be extensive and prolonged, the alcoholic will no longer need to drink to self-medicate the underlying distress to the ego. The major drawback to this approach is that it often fails to work unless the drinking behavior is terminated. The alcoholic is either unable or unwilling to abstain from alcohol by solving underlying conflicts. According to the disease model, the drinking must cease and other behaviors conducive to continued abstention must be instituted before the conflicts can be assessed and resolved by the alcoholic.[19,20]

Biological Psychiatry. The self-medication hypothesis is often used in biological psychiatry.[20] This hypothesis suggests that addiction to alcohol and other drugs is due to individual attempts to treat some other illness, including anxiety, depression, or personality disorders. The emphasis is on the need to self-medicate with alcohol and drugs the distress that originates from the underlying psychiatric disease.

A common example is the diagnoses of anxiety and depression and the use of alcohol and drugs. The theory is that because depression produces psychological pain, the sufferer of depression will use alcohol and drugs to obtain relief, as in the psychoanalytic model. Once again, this is a model that is based on the popular and old conception of motivated use of alcohol and other drugs. It not only fails to justify addictive or diseased use, but it also does not fit the clinical picture of what actually happens in alcoholics and those who are depressed.[21,22]

Studies have clearly shown that alcohol and other drug use produces depression, but do not show that depression leads to alcohol and drug use. In one study, three groups were given alcohol and their mood and affect were measured.[23] The three groups were depressed alcoholics, depressed nonalcoholics, and nondepressed nonalcoholics (normals). Surprisingly, the depressed alcoholics showed the least benefit in euphoria and improved affect from the drinking of alcohol. The depressed nonalcoholics received the greatest benefits, followed by the normals. These observations confirm that alcoholics do not drink to feel better; indeed makes them feel worse.[24] It appears that alcoholics drink in spite of the depression and not because of it.[23]

Furthermore, an analysis of the drinking behavior of nonalcoholic people with bipolar disorder yielded similar results. Patients with manic–depressive disorder showed that they reduced their drinking during their depressive episodes and increased their drinking during their manic episodes. The reason for increased drinking during mania is that many behaviors of excess are greater with the hyperactivity and poor judgment of the manic. The reason for reduced drinking during depression may be related to the overall effects of alcohol, which are to depress the mind and mood. Alcohol is categorized as a depressant by its pharmacological actions on the brain.[23]

Although it has often been assumed that addictive use is a manifestation of an underlying anxiety disorder, no studies have demonstrated that anxiety leads to addictive drinking and drug use. However, studies have clearly shown that alcohol and drugs produce anxiety in either the intoxicated state or during withdrawal. For instance, chronic alcohol intake produces repetitive withdrawal states during which anxiety is produced as a function of the discharging sympathetic nervous system. Similarly, cocaine induces the sympathetic nervous system to produce rather severe states of anxiety, including panic disorders, as with alcohol.[14]

The biological models of addiction are important to consider because they stress an underlying biochemical mechanisms for behavior, mental state, and psychiatric disorders. Because alcoholism represents in part a physical "allergy" to alcohol, the basis is some change in the brain chemistry that is responsible for the expression of the disease of alcoholism when alcohol interacts with the brain cells. Further studies on the neurochemical origins of psychiatric disease will help our understanding of the origins of alcoholism and drug addiction because both disorders are rooted in abnormalities in brain function.

Legal Perspectives

An early case that reached the Supreme Court of the United States resulted in the ruling:

> that the drinking of intoxicating liquor might develop from a harmless indulgence into a baneful disease of chronic disease alcoholism. It is common knowledge and the warning is evident that indulgence in intoxicating liquors, unless restrained, . . . leads to excessive indulgence and one need not be warned that if continued, the craving for alcoholic liquor may lead to habitual drunkenness and the unfortunate self-imposed consequences.[24]

In this decision, the court acknowledges not only that alcoholism is a disease, but that this is common knowledge. It also believes that the individual is responsible for the taking the risks of drinking alcohol in the first place in face of a multitude of evidence that the consumption of alcohol can lead to chronic alcoholism. The self-imposed consequences originate from the decision to drink and not the disease of alcoholism according to the this interpretation.[24]

A Pennsylvania court decided that:

> A caveat must be entered. We do not hold that chronic alcoholism is as a matter of law a self-inflicted injury. Our decision is that the evidence which trial judge found credible justifies the conclusion that the disability suffered by this insured was self-inflicted.[24]

A Maryland court ruled that:

> There is no evidence on the record legally sufficient for the jury to find that the chronic alcoholism of the insured is the result of his conscious purpose or design. . . . On the contrary the testimony tends to show that he had vainly exercised his will to restrain and control his desire. The result of his disease is a weakness of will and of character which caused him to yield to liquors. The drinking in the first stages was voluntary but there was not testimony that the drinker was then aware of the latent danger in his habit; and so while his consumption of liquor was a voluntary act, yet his ignor-

ance of its insidious effect does not make the act a voluntary exposure of himself to the unexpected danger of the disease of chronic alcoholism. The result of the indulgence of an appetite does not necessarily determine that the result was self-inflicted because if the actor does not apprehend or is ignorant of the danger of his act, he may not be held to have voluntarily inflicted upon himself the consequences.[24]

This decision covers the aspect of the insidious nature of alcoholism, and because of denial the alcoholic is often not aware of severity of the drinking as well as the consequences from the drinking. Inherent, but not explicitly stated, is the loss of control over the alcohol use and the subsequent adverse consequences of the alcoholism.[24]

The United States Supreme Court recently ruled that two alcoholics were not entitled to benefits from the Veterans Administration because they suffered from chronic alcoholism. The court was clear that it decided not to rule on whether or not alcoholism is a disease. It restricted its decision as to whether or not the alcoholics were guilty of willful misconduct. The court did not deny that the source of the willful misconduct was the disease of alcoholism. The court was careful to avoid a legal debate over a condition that rests on scientific and medical evidence.[24]

Finally, the courts on many levels—municipal, county, state, and federal—regularly take into consideration the disease of alcoholism in rendering its decisions regarding the individual and the consequences of alcoholism. The courts do not excuse the alcoholic of the consequences of the alcoholism, which would only enable the alcoholic to continue drinking. What the courts do is provide the alcoholic with a choice: Face the full punishment for the offense related to the alcoholism or accept a plan for retribution.

The legal system allows for remorse and restitution for many crimes, and frequently adjusts the sentence accordingly. It is a consistent practice for the judge to allow the alcoholic to accept responsibility for the treatment of his or her disease, express regret for the consequences, and demonstrate restitution by voluntarily choosing to undergo a formal treatment program for the alcoholism. In this way, alcoholism has no special legal status, and the alcoholic is held accountable for his or her alcoholism. Most importantly, it provides society with a corrective approach to a widespread disease. Thousands of alcoholics have initiated recovery with this particular legal intervention.

TREATMENT

Comparisons with Other Diseases

The treatment of addictive disease illustrates the paradoxical nature of many aspects of a disease with a strong physical component that also has so many behavioral and mental effects. It is interesting that the treatment of addiction resembles treatments for other well-accepted "medical" diseases.

Physicians are more uncertain about the diagnosis of coronary artery disease as a disease because the "root" etiologies are attributable to lifestyles under the individual's control and not to an invasion of some external forces that render the individual a victim. The diagnosis of coronary artery disease has become increasingly complex. Many different factors, which are subject to error, are integrated into a diagnosis of coronary artery disease, including personal reports from the patient and electrocardiographic findings.[25]

Interestingly, effective treatment of early coronary artery disease depends much more on changing lifestyles than receiving medical treatments. Coronary artery disease has been associated with certain diets high in fats, obesity, type A, or hard-driving, stress-oriented personalities, smoking, and high blood pressure. All of these conditions are believed to be under the control of the individual, and for this reason alone, coronary artery disease may be becoming less of a "disease" in the sense that is readily accepted by the public[25]

It may be that any condition that involves some volition on the part of the individual to initiate or maintain will never fully qualify as a disease. A paradox is that in order to recover from alcoholism, an individual must exercise some commitment of will toward abstinence from alcohol consumption, according to the disease concept. However, the term *disease* explicitly means that the individual has lost the capacity to consistently control how much and how often he or she drinks and the ability to accurately predict the consequences of the drinking. From where does the control arise to offset the autonomous state of addiction?

Alcoholism is also like essential hypertension in that neither has a known specific etiology but both conditions cause physical disease. Hypertension is heavily affected by social factors and may even have chronic alcohol consumption such as in alcoholism as a cause. Alcohol withdrawal is characterized by a discharging of the sympathetic nervous system, which results in an elevation of blood pressure and pulse rate. The physical and psychological adverse complications from hypertension are as diverse as those caused by alcoholism.[25]

The preferred treatment of hypertension is frequently a change in diet, loss of weight, reduction in stress, and changes in those aspects of lifestyle that come under the power of the will. The treatment of alcoholism requires changes in lifestyle and attitudes that are in some ways similar to the treatment of hypertension. Furthermore, the adverse consequences of alcoholism accrue in both conditions if left untreated; generally, the greater the number, the longer the course of the diseases.

Victim State in the Treatment of Alcoholism

The individual who has a disease is a victim in that he or she has no control over its onset and progression. This motion may have originated in ancient times, when the gods intervened in the helpless victim's life to produce some unfortunate change. The gods may have been angry and decided to punish someone because of a reason unrelated to that person, or the individual was responsible for a wrong but not one warranting the severity of the punishment. At any rate, the gods produced a victim, and the victim was not responsible for the malady possessing him.

Having cancer or a genetic disease is an example of a victim state. A cancer victim is someone who has developed a malignancy, which is an uncontrolled growth of a tissue in the body. The tissue growth overtakes the normal functions of the organs, and eventually the ability of the body to sustain life is lost. We do not ordinarily hold the individual responsible for the cancer. Yet how else will the individual seek and accept any treatment that is available? The individual who continues to deny he or she either has or can have cancer will not seek early diagnosis and treatment. Are not these choices decisions over which the individual has control and the freedom to exercise that control? How many victims of cancer see themselves as invincible and unrealistically avoid believing they may develop cancer, thereby avoiding the responsibility of seeking treatment?

Studies have shown that individuals may have more control over the onset and development of cancer than we had previously thought. For many types of cancer, prevention is becoming a reality. Lung cancer may be caused by cigarette smoking, cervical cancer may be a result of certain sexual practices and whether or not one has been pregnant, stomach cancer may be associated with particular types of diets, and breast cancer may be associated with taking birth control pills.

In order for the addicted person to recover, he or she must resolve the conflicts between the twisted conscience and the distorted perceptions of reality.[26] The source of the conflicts is the uncontrolled drinking that must cease (and abstinence maintained) before any meaningful resolution can take place. Addiction is a three-part disease. First, there is the physical allergy or predisposition to use alcohol or other drugs in an uncontrolled pattern. Second, it is a mental illness—the obsession that the addicted person either has or will have control of the consumption at some time, either in the present or future, despite repeated evidence to the contrary. And third, it is a spiritual disease that results from the compulsive use of alcohol or other drugs, in which the person uses and lives in conflict with himself or herself and others.

Those who judge the addicted person through their own experiences with alcohol (and possibly, other drugs) prevent addiction from being accepted as a disease. By definition, normal drinkers control the amount they drink and have no consistent pattern of adverse effects from their drinking. Unfortunately, because of this introspective position, they apply their experience with alcohol to the alcoholic, who cannot control his or her drinking. The two realities do not match, and alcoholism is considered a lack of willpower over alcohol that the normal drinker appears to possess. In actuality, because predisposition to alcoholism may be genetic, the ability to drink consistently with control may be under genetic control and not under the will of the individual as much as previously believed.

The obstacle that may be under genetic control and not under the will of the individual as much as previously believed.

The obstacle that may produce the greatest difficulty is the religious dogma that using alcohol and other drugs (or at least excessive use) is a sin or morally wrong. This is a view that is responsible for moral judgments that condemn alcoholics and addicts, and only serve to prevent diagnosis and treatment. How many people would come forth to complain about a health problem if it were judged to be a moral problem?

Pharmacological Treatment

A major factor determining whether a clinical state is accepted as a disease is the use of pharmacological agents. The use of medications is consistent with the passive, victim state so important to the disease concept. A drug requires limited volitional action on the part of the victim to treat the disease other than taking the medications and tolerating any side effects.

There are no known medications that specifically and directly treat the addiction to alcohol or other drugs. The lack of pharmacological agents makes it less appealing to the scientifically oriented physician who seeks a drug solution to these diseases. However, addiction to alcohol and other drugs is similar to other diseases such as hypertension, coronary artery disease, and cancer for which there are no pharmacological agents to treat their root causes.

REFERENCES

1. *Webster's Ninth New Collegiate Dictionary* (1986). Springfield, Massachusetts: Merriam-Webster.
2. *Dorland's Illustrated Medical Dictionary* (1988). 27th ed., Philadelphia: Saunders.
3. Jellinek EM (1960). *The Disease Concept of Alcoholism.* New Haven College and University Press. In association with Hillhouse Press, New Brunswick, New Jersey.
4. Gallup Poll conducted March 8–12, 1988 Princeton, NJ
5. Meyer RE (1988). Overview of the concept of alcoholism, *Alcoholism: Origins and Outcome,* Rose RM & Barrett J (eds.), New York: Raven Press.
6. Gordis E (1989). Guest editorial: The disease concept of alcoholism. *Psychiatr. Hosp.,* 20(4):151–152.
7. Rush B (1870). *An Inquiry into the Effects of Spirituous Liquors in the Human Body.* Boston: Thomas & Andrews.
8. Alcoholics Anonymous. New York, Alcoholics Anonymous World Services.
9. *The Doctor's Opinion* (1976). New York: Alcoholics Anonymous World Services.
10. Goodwin DW (1985). Alcoholism and genetics. *Arch Gen Psych,* 42:171–174.
11. Miller NS & Gold MS (1989). Suggestions for changes in DSM-III-R criteria for substance use disorders. *Am J Drug Alc Abuse,* 15(2):223–230.
12. Helzer JE, Robins LN & Taylor JR, et al. (1985). The extent of long-term moderate drinking among alcoholics discharged from medical and psychiatric treatment facilities. *N Engl J Med,* 312(26):27.
13. Milam JR & Ketchum K (1981). *Under the Influence.* Seattle, WA: Madrona Publishers.

14. Miller NS, Dackis CA, & Gold MS (1987). The relationship of addiction, tolerance and dependence: A neurochemical approach. *J Subst Abuse Treat,* 4:197–207.

15. Alexander BK (1987). The disease and adaptive model of addiction: A framework evaluation. *J Drug Issues*

16. Tabakoff B, & Hoffman PL (1980). Alcohol and neurotransmitters, *Alcohol Tolerance and Dependence* Rigter H & Crabbe JE (eds.), New York: Elsevier.

17. Fingarette H (1988). *Heavy Drinking: The Myth of Alcoholism as a Disease.* Los Angeles: University of California Press.

18. Robins LN, Helzer JE, Przybeck TR, & Regier DA (1988). Alcohol disorders in the community: A report from the epidemiological catchment area, *Alcoholism: Origins and Outcome* pp. 15–28. Rose RM & Barrett J (eds.), New York: Raven Press.

19. Brenner C (1974). *An Elementary Textbook of Psychoanalysis.* New York: Doubleday.

20. Khantzian EJ (1985). The self medication hypothesis of addictive disorders: Focus on heroin and cocaine dependence. *Am J Psych* 142(11):1259–1264.

21. Schuckit MA (1983). The history of psychiatric disorders. *Hosp Commun Psych.* 34(11):1022–1027.

22. Guze SB, Cloninger CR, Martin R & Clayton PJ (1988). Alcoholism as a medical disorder, *Alcoholism: Origins and Outcome,* pp. 83–94. Rose RM and Barrett J (eds.), New York: Raven Press.

23. Mayfield D (1979). Alcohol and affect: Experimental studies, *Alcoholism and Affective Disorders* Goodwin DW & Erickson CK (eds.). New York: SP Medical and Scientific Books.

24. Seessel TV (1988). Beyond the Supreme Court ruling on Alcoholism as willful misconduct: It is up to Congress to act. *JAMA,* 259(2):248.

25. Vaillant GE (1983). *The Natural History of Alcoholism: Causes, Patterns and Paths to Recovery.* Cambridge: Harvard University Press.

26. Tiebout HM (1953). Surrender versus compliance in therapy. *Q J Stud Alc* 14:58–68.

9

Developmental Factors

Before the more definitive cross-fostering studies[1] were available, few investigators believed that the association between parent and child alcoholism might be more hereditary than environmental. According to Vaillant,[2] when we are on land and view fish under water, we tend to trust our eyes and not the student of parallax who tells us that the location of the fish is an illusion. Similarly, the parallax of retrospective vision distorts what our "eyes" tell us about the etiology of addiction.

COURSE

Vaillant[3] states, "In spite of a great diversity of personality structures among alcoholics there appears in a large proportion of them a low tolerance for tension coupled with an inability to cope with psychological stresses." In the most recent edition of the *Comprehensive Textbook of Psychiatry*, Selzer[4] writes: "Alcoholic populations do display significantly more depression, paranoid thinking trends, aggressive feelings and acts, and significantly lower self-esteem, responsibility, and self-control than nonalcoholic populations. Despite occasional disclaimers, active alcoholics do not resemble a randomly chosen population." Other retrospective clinical studies of alcoholism have equated the antecedents of alcoholism with those of the oral dependent personality.[5]

Because addiction to alcohol and other drugs profoundly distorts the individual's personality, his or her social stability, and recollection of relevant childhood variables, retrospective impressions are suspect.[6] In recent years, six prospective studies[2,7–11] have demonstrated many fallacies in our retrospective conception of the alcoholic's personality.

It was observed that, contrary to popular beliefs, alcoholics were, if anything, premorbidly outward, more self-confident, aggressive, and heterosexual than their peers.[7,12] Alcoholism thus appears to be the cause rather than the result of passive–dependent traits,[2] elevations on the D and Pd scales of the Minnesota Multiphasic Personality Inventory,[9] passivity, low self-esteem, and introversion.[10] Alcoholism also can cause, rather be the result, of an unhappy childhood, broken families, and personality disorders.

Premorbid antisocial behavior has been identified as an important predictor of alcoholism,[13,14] but these two important prospective studies were derived from samples that premorbidly exhibited a disproportionate amount of antisocial behavior. The independent contribution of five major psychosocial variables to the development of addiction were examined: 1) ethnic background, 2) alcoholic heredity, 3) antisocial behavior prior to the development of alcoholism, 4) boyhood emotional adjustment, and 5) presence or absence of familial instability.

ETIOLOGY

In an important study by Vaillant, four childhood and family variables—childhood environmental strengths,[15] boyhood competence,[16] childhood emotional problems, and IQ—significantly predicted independent ratings of adult mental health made 33 years later. These variables predicted sociopathy less well, and they were only marginally correlated with adult alcoholism. Other variables—delinquent parents, multiproblem families (childhood environmental weaknesses), poor infant health, and premorbid antisocial personality—correlated most powerfully with sociopathy, less so with alcoholism, and only marginally with subsequent mental health. Finally, the variables that seemed significantly associated with adult alcoholism but not with sociopathy or poor mental health were alcoholism in parents, alcoholism in ancestors, hereditary background, and cultural background. The association between alcoholism and premorbid etiological variables was not really affected by whether alcoholism was defined according to the medical model of the DSM-III or the social deviance model of Cahalan.

Alcoholics with alcoholic relatives were three times more likely than those with no alcoholic relatives to develop alcohol dependence. This relationship remained significant but not as dramatic if parents and siblings (who could exert environmental effects, genetic effects, or both) were excluded from the comparison and the more conservative alcoholism in ancestors scale was substituted.

Alcoholism, especially in young men, may be a cause as well as a symptom of antisocial behavior. Those with serious premorbid behavior problems were four times as likely to develop alcohol dependence, but since there were only 16 men with severe behavior problems in Vaillant's study, premorbidly antisocial behavior cannot be invoked as a major etiological factor for most alcoholics.

Ethnicity and Culture

Parental ethnicity is highly correlated with the men's subsequent use of alcohol. Those of Irish extraction were seven times more likely to manifest alcohol dependence than the 130 men of Italian, Syrian, Jewish, Greek, or Portuguese extraction.[2]

The relationship between alcohol use and culture is extremely complex,[17-20] but the relationship can be reduced to a single common denominator—cultural characteristics of alcohol dependence.[2] The non-Moslem Mediterranean countries have no sanctions against children learning to drink, but have strong sanctions against drunkenness in adults. Conversely, the Irish and North American cultures forbid drinking in adolescence and have long considered total prohibition of alcohol, but do give approval to drunkenness in male adults. For purposes of statistical depiction, other Northern European countries are assigned an intermediate position. Although the French teach children responsible drinking, they also condone drunkenness and alcohol use independent of meals.[3]

The interaction between parental culture and familial alcoholism is interesting. Among men of Irish extraction, the presence of alcoholic relatives only slightly increases the risk of alcohol dependence in the subjects: many Irish subjects with alcoholic relatives became lifelong teetotalers. Among other ethnic groups (both among the Southern Europeans, in whom alcoholism is rare, and among the Northern Europeans and Native Americans, in whom it is common), alcohol dependence occurs five times as often in men with several alcoholic relatives as it does in men with no alcoholic relatives. Psychological stress and vulnerability are not irrelevant in alcoholism, but prospective and multifactorial study designs show diminished importance of these factors.

For the most part, the premorbid variables that most clearly predict alcoholism do not predict mental health, and vice versa. In an exhaustive review of the prospective literature on childhood-to-adult studies, if IQ is excluded, correlations of .2 to .4 are the highest observed between ratings of childhood and adult behavior.[22] We are taught that "the child is father of the man." Based on prospective studies, the relationship is a limited one.[23]

Prospective Studies of Predictors

Alcoholic heredity, school behavior problems, and not being brought up in a Mediterranean culture each make an important contribution to the explained variance in subsequent alcohol problems.[2] In addition to these three variables, boyhood competence makes a small additional independent contribution to alcohol abuse. If the number of alcoholic relatives is controlled for, multiproblem families are not associated with an increased number of alcohol-related problems, but they are associated with an increased number of antisocial problems. Similarly, childhood environmental strength is significantly correlated with both alcoholism and sociopathy, but the environmental variable explains less than 1% of additional variance.

Having many alcoholic relatives is associated with an increased risk of alcoholism, but family studies cannot distinguish the effect of genes (having a blood relative with alcoholism) from that of environment (being raised by an alcoholic parent or surrogate parent). However, review of all available cross-fostering studies that have distinguished heredity from environment[23-25] suggests that alcoholic biological relatives (even if physically absent) apparently contribute far more to the observed increased risk for alcoholism in children than alcoholics in the environment. These observations would help explain why the association of disorganized families with subsequent alcoholism disappears if familial alcoholism is controlled.

Premorbid antisocial behavior contributes significant independent variance to the likelihood of adult alcoholism. Certainly, antisocial inner-city youths are at greater risk for developing all types of drug abuse,[10,26-28] and the rate of alcohol abuse that was observed among delinquents in one study was higher than the rate observed among the controls.[28] Findings from a longitudinal study of college men indicate that middle-class adolescents who become alcoholics also exhibit greater impulsivity than their peers.[2,12]

Importantly, the relationship between alcoholism and antisocial personality is a two-way street. Antisocial symptoms are often a result rather than a cause of alcoholism. The three variables that account for the greatest independent variance in adult sociopathy are school behavior problems, boyhood competence, and poor infant health. The ethnic and familial factors that are important in alcoholism are unimportant in sociopathy.

It remains to be proven that demographic variables,[30] occupation,[31] social peer groups,[32] availability of legal services,[33] societal instability,[21] affective illness,[34] attribution and expectancy effects,[35] and other, as yet unidentified, factors contribute significant independent variance to the development of alcohol dependence.

Available prospective studies suggest that if one controls for antisocial childhood, cultural attitudes toward alcohol and alcoholism, alcoholic heredity, and most especially for the *effects* of alcohol abuse and alcoholism, then many of the childhood and adult personality variables to which adult alcoholism has traditionally been attributed will appear as "carts before the horses."

Vaillant's (2) findings suggest that even when they employed prospective design, previous investigators may have sometimes erroneously interpreted their data to support the retrospective illusion that alcoholism *must* be a symptom of personality disorder.[8,10,14,36] For example, in concluding that dominant father, "immigrant" Catholicism, and low social class protected against the development of alcoholism, the McCords failed to note that, in Cambridge and Somerville in 1940, such individuals were predominantly first- and second-generation Italians. Italian-American drinking practices, rather than other characteristics, may have protected their children from later alcohol dependence. Similarly, although alcoholic fathers and alcoholic mothers in the McCords'[10] study parented a disproportionate number of alcoholic subjects, the McCords wrote that "evidence for an hereditary explanation of the disorder was unlikely."

REFERENCES

1. Goodwin DW (1979). Alcoholism and heredity. *Arch Gen Psych* 36:57–61.
2. Vaillant GE (1980). Natural history of male psychological health: VIII. Antecedents of alcoholism and "orality." *Am J Psych* 137:181–186.

3. Vaillant GE (1984). The course of alcoholism and lessons for treatment. In Grinspoon L (ed.), *Psychiatry Update,* vol. III, pp. 311–319. Washington DC: American Psychiatric Press.

4. Selzer ML (1980). Alcoholism and alcoholic psychoses. In Kaplan HL, Freedman AM & Sadock BJ (eds.), *Comprehensive Textbook of Psychiatry.* Baltimore: Williams & Wilkins.

5. Blane HT (1968). *The Personality of the Alcoholic: Guises of Dependency.* New York: Harper & Row.

6. Vaillant GE & Milofsky ES (1982). The etiology of alcoholism: A prospective viewpoint. *Am Psychol* 37(5):494–503.

7. Jones MC (1968). Personality correlates and antecedents of drinking patterns in adult males. *J Consult Clin Psychol* 32:2–12.

8. Jones MC (1971). Personality antecedents and correlates of drinking patterns in women. *J Consult Clin Psychol* 36:61–69.

9. Kammier ML, Hoffmann H & Loper RG (1973). Personality characteristics of alcoholics as college freshmen and at time of treatment. *Q J Stud Alc* 34:390–399.

10. McCord W & McCord J (1960). *Origins of Alcoholism.* Stanford: Stanford University Press.

11. Robins LN, Bates WN & O'Neal P (1962). Adult drinking patterns of former problem children. In DJ Pittman & CR Snyder (eds.), *Society, Culture and Drinking Patterns.* New York: Wiley.

12. Loper RG, Kammier ML & Hoffmann H (1973). MMPI characteristics of college freshman males who later became alcoholics. *J Abnorm Psychol* 82:159–162.

13. Powers E & Witmer H (1959). *An Experiment in the Prevention of Delinquency.* New York: Columbia University Press.

14. Robins LN (1966). *Deviant Children Grown Up: A Sociological and Psychiatric Study of Sociopathic Personality.* Baltimore: Williams & Wilkins.

15. Vaillant GE (1974). Natural history of male psychological health: II. Some antecedents of healthy adult adjustment. *Arch Gen Psych* 31:15–22.

16. Vaillant GE, Vaillant CO (1981). Natural history of male psychological health: X. Work as a predictor of positive mental health. *Am J Psych* 138:1433–1440.

17. Greely A & McReady WC (1980). *Ethnic drinking subcultures.* New York: Praeger.

18. Heath DB (1975) A critical review of ethnographic studies of alcohol use. In Gibbons RJ (eds.), *Research Advances in Alcohol and Drug Problems (vols. 2).* New York: Wiley.

19. Marlatt GA & Rohsenow DJ (1980). Cognitive processes in alcoholic use: Expectancy and the balanced placebo design. In Marlow NK (ed.), *Advances in Substance Abuse: Behavioral and Biological Research.* Greenwich, CT: Jai Press.

20. Stivers R (1976). *A Hair of the Dog.* University Park, PA: Pennsylvania State University Press.

21. Pittman DJ & Snyder CR (1962). *Society, Culture and Drinking Patterns.* New York: Wiley.

22. Kohlberg L, LaCrosse J & Ricks D (1972). The predictability of adult mental health from childhood behavior. In Wolman BB (ed.), *Manual of Childhood Psychopathology.* New York: McGraw-Hill.

23. Bohman M (1978). Some genetic aspects of alcoholism and criminality. *Arch Gen Psych* 35:269–276.

24. Goodwin DW, Schulsinger F, Moller N, Hermansen L, Winokur G & Guze SB (1974). Drinking problems in adopted and non-adopted sons of alcoholics. *Arch Gen Psych* 31:164–169.

25. Schuckit MA, Goodwin DW & Winokur G (1972). A half-sibling study of alcoholism. *Am J Psych* 128:1132–1136.

26. Chein I (1964). *The Road to H.* New York: Basic Books.

27. Robins LN (1966). *Deviant Children Grown Up: A Sociological and Psychiatric Study of Sociopathic Personality.* Baltimore: Williams & Wilkins.

28. Robins LN (1974). *The Vietnam Drug User Returns* (Special Action Office Monograph, Series A, No. 2). Washington, DC: Government Printing Office.

29. Glueck S & Glueck E (1950). *Unraveling Juvenile Delinquency.* New York: The Commonwealth Fund.

30. Cahalan D (1970). *Problem Drinkers: A National Survey.* San Francisco: Jossey-Bass.

31. Plant ML (1979). *Drinking Careers.* London: Tavistock.

32. Jessor R & Jessor SL (1975). Adolescent development and the onset of drinking. *Q J Stud Alc* 36:27–51.

33. Terris MA (1967). Epidemiology of cirrhosis of the liver: National mortality data. *Am J Pub Health* 57:2076–2088.

34. Winokur G, Clayton DJ & Reich T (1969). *Manic Depressive Illness.* St. Louis: Mosby.

35. Marlatt GA & Rohsenow DJ (1980). Cognitive processes in alcoholic use: Expectancy and the balanced placebo design. In Marlow NK (eds.), *Advances in Substance Abuse: Behavioral and Biological Research.* Greenwich, CT: JAI Press.

36. Lisansky-Gomberg ES (1968). Etiology of alcoholism. *J Consul Clin Psychol* 32:18–20.

PART IV

Laboratory Diagnosis

10

Clinical Indications
for Testing

OVERVIEW

The principle indications for drug testing in current practice are:[24-34]

- Evaluation of a new patient, especially when the clinical picture suggests drug use.
- Evaluation of all adolescents, especially those with behavioral problems.
- Evaluation of all high-risk patients (e.g., those with significant exposure and access to drugs).
- Evaluation of all new patients with acute and chronic syndromes, especially when the presentation is atypical or there is a failure to respond to treatment.
- Evaluation of an unexpected or unexplained mental state or performance change.
- Monitoring response to inpatient and outpatient treatment for drug and alcohol addiction and other psychiatric illness.
- Employment monitoring when as agreement to test exists between employers and employees.
- Methadone maintenance.

Table 10.1 describes common settings in which drug testing is used. The need for drug testing is underscored by statistics that indicate that

TABLE 10.1: Examples of Situations for Drug Testing

- Clinical Settings: primary care, emergency departments, intensive care units.

    Clinical problems that suggest testing: apparent intoxication; apparent overdose; apparent withdrawal; acute psychotic symptoms such as delusions, paranoia, and hallucinations; altered mental status; seizures; cardiac arrhythmias; chest pain; serious and unexplained trauma, injury, and burns.

- Addiction Medicine Settings: medically-managed inpatient treatment, intensive outpatient treatment, outpatient treatment, and aftercare–continuing care.

    Testing during intake to confirm drug use; testing to monitor decrease in long-lasting drugs during acute and subacute withdrawal; testing to confirm ongoing sobriety.

- Workplace Settings.

    Preemployment screenings.
    Probable cause, such as injury or abnormal behavior at work.
    Random testing of employees.

drug use, particularly illicit use, is widespread. In a large-scale drug screening of U.S. government employees, one in six members of the federal work force were found to use illicit drugs regularly, and 44% of all new employees screened had used drugs such as marijuana and cocaine within the previous year. In another large-scale drug screening, one-third of applicants to the New York Transit Authority had positive tests for drugs in their urine during preemployment evaluation. A spot check of U.S. Navy personnel in San Diego, California, and Portsmouth, New Hampshire, in 1983 revealed that 47% were smoking marijuana. This figure is now down to 2% after widespread adoption of drug-screening programs.[1]

In most instances, the five major drugs of interest in drug testing are marijuana, cocaine, amphetamines, opiates, and phencyclidine (PCP), although screening for other drugs may be indicated. Polydrug use, abuse, and addiction are the rule. For example, as many as 80% of alcoholics under the age of 30 use another drug in addition to alcohol, most commonly marijuana, followed by cocaine and PCP. A little known fact is that 98% of all cocaine addicts have used marijuana, and from 50–75% of opiate users have used or are using marijuana, benzodiazepines, and cocaine. Furthermore, 90% of Americans have at least tried alcohol, and from 10–20% or more have a problem with alcohol. Twenty-five million people have at least tried cocaine, 5–6 million use it regularly, and 12–13 million use it once a year.[2,3] The need for drug screening extends beyond illicit drugs to legal prescription medications, as 81 million prescriptions were filled in 1985 for benzodiazepines. According to the 1985 Drug Abuse Warning Network (DAWN) reports, benzodiazepines were "mentioned" in 18,492 emergency room (ER) visits, morphine and heroin in 14,696 ER visits, and cocaine in 13,501 visits.[4] These ER visits were for a variety of reasons pertaining to medical and psychiatric problems directly or indirectly related to the drug use.

In the national household study done by the National Institute for Drug Abuse (NIDA) in 1985, the lifetime prevalence of use by individuals 18–25 years old was 60% for marijuana, 11.5% for hallucinogens, 17.3% for stimulants, 11.0% for sedatives, 12.2% for tranquilizers, 11.4% for analgesics, and 1.2% for heroin.[4] This prevalence rate indicates that nearly half the U.S. population has used marijuana and substantial numbers have used other drugs. From these statistics alone, it is evident that drug use is no longer the province of the less fortunate or "the other guy." Convenient cliches and stereotypes cannot be used to explain drug use, as drugs are used by many individuals in all walks of life.[5] It is a pervasive practice with adverse consequences affecting almost everyone.

When to Test for Drugs

Drug and alcohol use can induce virtually any psychiatric symptom or syndrome as well as many medical symptoms and syndromes that are indistinguishable from the idiopathic form (see Table 10.2). The severity of the alcohol- and drug-induced psychopathology may range from mild anxiety and sadness to frank mania and delirium, and there are many variations between these two extremes. Because the symptoms and syndromes caused by drugs and alcohol are frequently indistinguishable from those with other etiologies, it is important to identify drugs and alcohol in the history or confirm their presence by drug testing.

Some of the major psychiatric syndromes induced by drugs and alcohol are mania, depression, anxiety disorders, personality disorders, schizophrenia, eating disorders, and delirium and dementia (organic mental disorders). Some of the major medical syndromes are gastrointestinal, cardiovascular, endocrinological, traumatic, rheumatological, and dermatological in origin. These conditions may be induced either during the period of drug intoxication and/or withdrawal, depending on the particular drug action.[6-13]

TABLE 10.2: Common Psychiatric and Medical Problems Associated with Psychoactive Substance Use

Sedative–hypnotic intoxication	Depression, paradoxical intoxication, amnestic disorder, blackouts
Sedative–hypnotic withdrawal	anxiety, panic, phobias, insomnia, delirium, hallucinosis, tremor
Cocaine intoxication	mania, personality disturbances, hypertension, cardiac arrhythmias, anorexia, and self-inflicted excoriating lesions of the skin
Cocaine withdrawal	severe depression with suicidal thinking, agitation, hyperphagia, and hypersomnia
PCP intoxication	mania, personality disturbances with violent outbursts, hypertension, cardiac arrhythmias, and vivid visual and auditory hallucinations
PCP withdrawal	impulsivity, poor judgment, and depression with suicidal thoughts
Heroin use	associated with endocarditis, arthritis, acquired immune deficiency syndrome (AIDS), and other consequences of intravenous drug use
Organic solvents	organic brain syndromes, such as delirium and dementia, cardiac arrhythmias, and hepatocellular damage
Marijuana	anxiety, depression, poor concentration and memory loss, hallucinations, paranoid ideation and delusions, poor motivation, and a general deterioration in personality

Cocaine, for instance, causes mania, personality disturbances, hypertension, cardiac arrhythmias, anorexia, and self-inflicted excoriating lesions of the skin during intoxication. During withdrawal, it induces severe depression with suicidal thinking, hyperphagia, and hypersomnia. PCP intoxication produces mania, personality disturbances with violent outbursts, hypertension, cardiac arrhythmias, and vivid visual and auditory hallucinations, whereas the withdrawal is characterized by impulsivity, poor judgment, and depression with suicidal thoughts. Heroin use may be associated with endocarditis, arthritis, acquired immune deficiency syndrome (AIDS), and other consequences of intravenous drug use. The practice of inhalation of organic solvents, such as glues, aerosols, and gasoline, produces organic brain syndromes, such as delirium and dementia, cardiac arrhythmias, and hepatocellular damage,[3,14–17] all of which may or may not be reversible. Marijuana has many effects on brain and behavior that typically include anxiety, depression, poor concentration and memory loss, hallucinations, paranoid ideation and delusions, poor motivation, and a general deterioration in personality.

The diagnosis of an alcohol or other drug problem is greatly enhanced by drug testing, especially when the clinical picture suggests the presence of abuse, addiction, tolerance, physical dependence, or abuse. Furthermore, it is critical that the physician clearly understand the terms, definitions, and concepts as described in Chapter 2 in order to adequately diagnose and describe drug problems as well as to use drug testing effectively and efficiently.[18]

As mentioned earlier, addiction is characterized by the preoccupation with the acquisition of drugs, compulsive use in spite or adverse consequences, recurrent use, and inability to control or reduce the use effectively, resulting in a pattern of recurrent use or relapse after abstinence. The behaviors of addiction are universal; they transcend norms or standards of use and are not dependent on the characteristics of a particular drug.[19]

The development of tolerance is the need to increase the dose of a drug to maintain the same effect, or the loss of an effect at a constant dose of a drug. Pharmacological dependence occurs when stopping the drug results in predictable signs and symptoms, depending on the particular drug. Characteristically, the signs and symptoms or withdrawal are suppressed by the drug[19] when it is given in sufficient doses at an appropriate time during withdrawal.

Contrary to popular notions, tolerance and physical dependence are not specific for addiction. While addiction is frequently accompanied by tolerance and physical dependence, these may and frequently do occur without the development of addiction. For instance, opiate analgesics are used in the treatment of acute pain, with subsequent rapid development of tolerance and the onset of a predictable withdrawal syndrome on cessation of use, but frequently without preoccupation, compulsive use, and relapse to opiate use. Predictably, tolerance and physical dependence are necessary adaptations and responses of the brain to regular use of a drug. Because dependent use is frequently repetitive, pharmacological tolerance and dependence readily occur in addiction.[20] Also, the detection of tolerance may be impeded by denial of use (common in addiction) and by subtle, insidious onset of tolerance, as is true of alcohol addiction.

To successfully diagnose drug addiction, it is important to recognize and circumvent these obstacles to the clinical diagnosis. Some of the reasons for the inadequate diagnosis of substance use disorders include:

- Denial, rationalization, and minimization by people with substance use disorders.
- Denial, rationalization, and minimization by institutions and others, such as businesses, employers, coworkers, and physicians.
- Substance use problems and other types of impairment in physicians and other health care professionals.
- A lack of knowledge, experience, and expertise regarding the diagnosis of abuse, addiction, physical tolerance, and dependence.
- A lack of awareness that effective treatments for addiction to alcohol and other drugs exist, are available, and are effective.
- Rapidly diminishing reimbursement for substance-use disorders.

Drug testing can aid in reducing these obstacles by providing documentation and confirmation of drug use and addiction,[21-23] despite impediments to identification.

REFERENCES

1. Pottash ALC, Gold MS & Extein I (1982). The use of the clinical laboratory. In Sederer LI, (ed.), *Inpatient Psychiatry: Diagnosis and Treatment.* Baltimore: Williams & Wilkins.
2. DeMillo L, Gold MS & Martin D (1986). Evaluation of substance abuse. In Gold MS & Pottash ALC, (eds.), *Diagnostic and Laboratory Testing in Psychiatry,* New York: Plenum.
3. Gold MS & Estroff TW (1985). The comprehensive evaluation of cocaine and opiate abusers. In Hall RCW & Beresford TP, (eds), *Handbook of Psychiatric Diagnostic Procedures,* New York: Spectrum.
4. NIDA (1985). *National Household Survey on Drug Abuse.* National Institute on Drug Abuse. Washington, DC: U.S. Govt. Printing Office.
5. Wolfe SM (1987). Drug-induced tranquility. *Health Lett* 6–8.
6. Verebey K, Gold MS & Mule SJ (1986). Laboratory testing in the diagnosis of marijuana intoxication and withdrawal. *Psych Ann* 16:235–241.
7. Estroff TW & Gold MS (1984). Medication and toxin-induced psychiatric disorder. In Extein I & Gold MS, (eds.), *Medical Mimics of Psychiatric Disorders,* Washington DC: American Psychiatric Press.
8. Estroff TW & Gold MS (1986). Medical and psychiatric complications of cocaine abuse and possible points of pharmacologic intervention. *Adv Alc Subst Abuse* 5:61–76.
9. Estroff TW & Gold MS (1984). Psychiatric misdiagnosis. In Gold MS, Lydiard RB, Carman JS, (eds.), *Advances in Psychopharmacology: Predict-*

ing and Improving Treatment Response, pp. 34–66. Boca Raton, FL: CRC Press.

10. Weissman MM, Pottenger M & Kleber H, et al. (1977). Symptom patterns in primary and secondary depression: A comparison of primary depressives with depressed opiate addicts, alcoholics and schizophrenics. *Arch Gen Psych* 34:854–862.

11. Thacore VR & Shukla SRP (1976). Cannabis psychosis and paranoid schizophrenia. *Arch Gen Psych* 33:383–386.

12. Beamish P & Kiloh LG (1960). Psychoses due to amphetamine consumption. *J Ment Sci* 106:337–343.

13. Extein I, Dackis CA & Gold MS, et al. (1986). Depression in drug addicts and alcoholics. In Extein I & Gold MS, (eds.), *Medical Mimics of Psychiatric Disorders,* pp. 133–162. Washington, DC: American Psychiatric Press.

14. Gold MS & Washton AM (1984). *Adverse Effects on Health and Functions of Cocaine Abuse; Data from 800 Cocaine Callers: Trends, Patterns and Issues in Drug Abuse.* Natl Inst Drug Abuse Res Monogr Ser 1, (2), Rockville, MD: National Institute for Drug Abuse.

15. Gold MS, Dackis CA & Pottash ALC, et al. (1986). Cocaine update: From bench to bedside. In Stimmel B, (ed.), *Advances in Alcohol & Substance Abuse,* vol. 6, pp. 1–5. New York: Haworth Press.

16. Estroff TW & Gold MS (1987). Chronic medical complications of drug abuse. *Psych Med* 3:267–286.

17. Yago KB, Pitts FN & Burgoyne RW, et al. (1981). The urban epidemic of phencyclidine (PCP use: Clinical and laboratory evidence from a public psychiatric hospital emergency service. *J Clin Psych* 42:193–196.

18. Miller NS & Gold MS (1987). The medical diagnosis and treatment of alcohol dependence. *Med Times* 115:109–126.

19. Jaffe JH (1985). Drug addiction and drug abuse. In Gilman AG, Goodman LS, Rall TW & Murad F, (eds.), *The pharmacological Basis of Therapeutics,* 7th ed., pp. 532–581. New York: Macmillan.

20. Miller NS, Dackis CA & Gold MS (1987). The relationship of addiction, tolerance, dependence: A neurochemical approach. *J Subst Abuse Treat* 4:197–207.

21. Gold MS, Pottash ALC & Estroff TW, et al. (1984). Laboratory evaluation in treatment planning. In Karusu TB, (ed.), *The Psychiatric Therapies, Part I: The Somatic Therapies,* Washington DC: APA Commission on Psychiatric Therapies.

22. Verebey K, Martin D & Gold MS (1986). Drug abuse: Interpretation of laboratory tests. In Gold MS, Pottash ALC, (eds.), *Diagnostic and Laboratory Testing in Psychiatry,* pp. 155–169. New York: Plenum.

23. Gold MS, Pottash AC & Estroff I (1984). The psychiatric laboratory. In Bernstein JG (ed.), *Clinical Psychopharmacology,* pp. 29–58. London: John Wright.

24. Estroff TW & Gold MS (1984). Medication and toxin-induced psychiatric disorder. In Extein I & Gold MS (eds.), *Medical Mimics of Psychiatric Disorders,* Washington DC: American Psychiatric Press.

25. Estroff TW & Gold MS (1986). Medical and psychiatric complications of cocaine abuse and possible points of pharmacologic intervention. *Adv Alc Subst Abuse* 5:61–76.

26. Estroff TW & Gold MS (1984). Psychiatric misdiagnosis. In Gold MS, Lydiard RB, Carman JS (eds.), *Advances in Psychopharmacology: Predicting and Improving Treatment Response,* pp. 34–66. Boca Raton, RL: CRC Press.

27. Weissman MM, Pottenger M & Kleber H, et al. (1977). Symptom patterns in primary and secondary depression: A comparison of primary depressives with depressed opiate addicts, alcoholics and schizophrenics. *Arch Gen Psych* 34:854–862.

28. Thacore VR & Shukla SRP (1976). Cannabis psychosis and paranoid schizophrenia. *Arch Gen Psych* 33:383–386.

29. Beamish P & Kiloh LG (1960). Psychoses due to amphetamine consumption. *J Ment Sci* 106:337–343.

30. Extein I, Dackis CA & Gold MS, et al. (1986). Depression in drug addicts and alcoholics. In Extein I & Gold MS, (eds.), *Medical Mimics of Psychiatric Disorders,* pp. 133–162. Washington, DC: American Psychiatric Press.

31. Gold MS & Washton AM (1984). *Adverse Effects on Health and Functions of Cocaine Abuse: Data from 800 Cocaine Callers: Trends, Patterns and Issues in Drug Abuse.* Natl Inst Drug Abuse Res Monogr Ser 1, (2) Rockville, MD: National Institute for Drug Abuse.

32. Gold MS, Dackis CA & Pottash ALC, et al. (1986). Cocaine update: From bench to bedside. In Stimmel B, (ed.), *Advances in Alcohol & Substance Abuse,* vol. 6, p. 125. New York: Haworth Press.

33. Estroff TW & Gold MS (1987). Chronic medical complications of drug abuse. *Psych Med* 3:267–286.

34. Yago KB, Pitts FN & Burgoyne RW, et al. (1981). The urban epidemic of phencyclidine (PCP use: Clinical and laboratory evidence from a public psychiatric hospital emergency service. *J Clin Psych* 42:193–196.

11

Methodology and Guidelines for Testing

DEFINITIONS

Sensitivity and Specificity

The sensitivity and specificity of a drug test determine greatly the utility of the test. *Sensitivity* is the ability to detect the presence of the drug at low levels, while *specificity* is the degree of accuracy in detecting only the drug desired. It is important to note that the methods used for drug testing vary greatly in their sensitivity and specificity.[1-5]

Unfortunately, many physicians who use and interpret drug tests are unaware that some of the most commonly used laboratory tests tend to be low in both sensitivity and specificity. Thin-layer chromatography (TLC) has both low sensitivity and specificity; enzyme immunoassay (EIA) has high sensitivity but less specificity. Moreover, some tests yield only qualitative information, detecting the presence of the drug without reliably measuring its quantity. Quantitative tests, in contrast, give information on the amount of the drug that is present in body fluids, which is important in differentiating low levels of drugs that persist for prolonged periods from higher levels from recent use.[2,6,8,11] For instance, a steadily declining urine level of cannabinoid metabolites followed by an abrupt significant rise in the metabolites indicates recent use of marijuana.

Source of Specimen

The target of the methodology in drug testing is measuring either the parent drug, its metabolite, or both. Although urine and blood may both be assayed, it is important to know that urine contains 1000 times more drug than blood, and therefore is the preferred specimen in most instances. However, examination of blood is useful in identifying recent use, as detection in the blood indicates that the drug has been ingested close in time to sampling so that biotransformation and elimination have not yet occurred. For example, cocaine is detectable in blood for only a number of hours, but by certain methods it can be detected for days in the metabolite form.[9,12]

The drug screens for various laboratories vary in the number and types of drugs that are assayed and the methodologies of tests employed. Usually, a clinician must specify the drugs of interest or at least be aware of the type of tests performed by the laboratory. Otherwise, only those drug tests deemed routine by the laboratory will be done[2,8,11] and only according to their selected methodologies.[9,12]

Elimination Time

Elimination time is an important factor in clinical interpretation of results of drug testing. For any given test, it is important to know how long a result is likely to be positive in relation to the time of last use of the drug. Some drugs have a relatively long elimination time, especially if the metabolite is also identifiable; that is, marijuana itself is detectable for days while its metabolites, Δ-9-THC (tetrahydrocannabinol) and 11-nor-THC-9-carboxylic acid (THCA), are detectable for weeks by certain methods. Even short-acting periods after the parent drug has been cleared; that is, cocaine is 98% eliminated from the blood in 5 hours, while its metabolite, benzoylecgonine (BE), is detectable for 2–4 days. It is critical that the test for a drug be ordered sufficiently close in time to the drug ingestion so as to be able to detect it by any method.[2,8] A commonly used drug, alcohol, is metabolized rapidly, so that blood and urine are positive for only hours after last use. Alcohol's metabolites, for example, acetic acid, are too common to the body and efficiently utilized in endogenous biochemical pathways to be reliably measured.

Cutoff Levels

The cutoff value reflects the level of the sensitivity of the drug test. It determines whether a test is reported as positive or negative by the laboratory, and depends on the capability of the methodology as well as the needs of the clinician. The cutoff value is ordinarily selected by the laboratory but can be specified by the physician, according to the clinical indications for drug testing. Frequently the level is set high to avoid false-positives (a false-positive result is a positive result obtained when the drug is not actually present) and litigation. This is sometimes overly defensive, however, as valid and reliable results are obtainable if a lower or more sensitive cutoff value is used.[6,12] It is important to emphasize that the physician can order whatever cutoff value is needed or desired, but the value may need to be specified by the laboratory. For instance, a cutoff value for cannabinoids of 100 ng/ml will miss many detected in the sample.[6,12]

Contrary to popular belief, false-negative results are far more common that false-positive results in clinical practice. A study done by the Centers for Disease Control (CDC) found that 75% of the participating labs reported false-negatives on a urine specimen containing 4000 ng/ml of the cocaine metabolite BE, a value far above concentrations that are evident clinically in usual states of use at the time of detection by most laboratories and by usual methods. Another survey by the CDC confirmed that high rate of false-negative results by finding that 91% of the labs had unacceptable false-negative rates for cocaine and BE.[6,12]

Also, most clinicians are now aware that marijuana, PCP, LSD, and other commonly used or abused illicit drugs are not identified at all in most TLC systems, which are still used by many laboratories. False-positive results are very unusual but should be confirmed routinely by laboratories with a more sensitive and specific test such as gas chromatography/mass spectrometry (GC/MS).[14,15]

The confusion arising from the use of drug testing may be partly due to such variables. These variables in drug testing are frequently not sufficiently appreciated by most clinicians, who rely on laboratory testing in clinical practice in addition to the myriad of clinical variables. Further, detectability of a drug depends on the type of drug, size of the dose, frequency of use, the route of administration, and individual variation in drug metabolism. In turn, these variables are dependent on the time of the last dose, the sample collection method, and the sensitivity and specificity of the analytical method used for drug testing.[11,12]

METHODS

The analytical methods available for drug testing are of two basic types: chromatographic and competitive binding/immunoreactive. Chromatographic techniques include:

- Thin-layer chromatography (TLC)
- Gas–liquid chromatography (GLC)
- High-pressure liquid chromatography (HPLC)
- Combined gas chromatography/mass spectrometry (GC/MS).[9,11]

Competitive binding/immunoreactive techniques include:

- Radioimmunoassay (RIA)
- Enzyme immunoassay (EIA).[2,8,22]

Thin-Layer Chromatography

TLC is reserved mainly for detecting toxic ranges of only a few selected drugs in drug screening. Although it is relatively fast and inexpensive, an experienced technician is required to process and interpret the TLC plates. Further, TLC is a qualitative test—it yields only a positive or negative result, without a quantitative measurement of the amount of drug present. Its main drawbacks, however, are its low sensitivity and low specificity. The minimum amount of drug or metabolite necessary to yield a positive result is 1000 to 2000 ng/ml, which is very large in comparison to other methods.[12]

TLC relies on a reproducible migration pattern by the drug on a thin layer of adsorbent (e.g., a silica-coated glass plate). Characterization of a particular drug is achieved by color reactions produced by spraying the plate with color-complexing reagents. The method was originally designed to detect very-high-dose, resent drug use or toxic blood levels from a number of drugs used simultaneously. It is a reasonable test in an emergency room, where the drugs taken are unknown and there is a need for quick determination of toxic levels.[2,8]

TLC should be ordered with extreme caution and interpreted with suspicion, as lower levels of drugs are not detected by this method, nor are TLC screens generally admissible as forensic evidence. Negative results for cocaine and other drugs are meaningless by the TLC method, and positive results should be confirmed by a second, more specific method because of the low specificity and sensitivity of TLC.[2,8]

Gas–Liquid Chromatography

GLC is an analytical method that separates molecules by use of a glass or metal tube that is packed with material of a particular polarity. The sample of drug is vaporized at the injection site and carried through the column by a steady flow of gas. The column terminates at a detector that permits recording and quantification. The time needed to pass through a column is the retention time, and each drug has a particular retention time for a given column.[2,8,12]

High-Pressure Liquid Chromatography

HPLC is similar to GLC but uses a liquid rather than a gas to propel the sample through the column. Some drug classes are better chromatographed on HPLC (i.e., tricyclic antidepressants and benzodiazepines), while other drugs are better detected with GLC, so that the two methods are complementary in a given laboratory. It is important to know that GLC and HPLC are significantly more specific and sensitive than TLC. However, these methods require extraction, derivation, column separation, and detection, all of which increase the time for testing.[2,8]

Gas Chromatography/Mass Spectrometry

GC/MS is the ultimate laboratory method of detection. It analyzes a given drug according to a fragmentation pattern that is specific for that particular drug. The fragmentation pattern is produced by the breaking of weaker bonds of the drug molecules under stress. A perfect match with a fragmentation pattern in a computer library is considered an absolute confirmation of the drug, and is referred to as "fingerprinting" of the molecules.[2,8]

The range of sensitivity of the method is less than 50 ng/ml, or 100–1000 times more sensitive and far more specific than the TLC system.

Common drugs of abuse and addiction are readily identified in small amounts (i.e., marijuana, cocaine, heroin). The expenses of the technique make GC/MS impractical for screening but vital for confirmation of drug presence and identity.[2,8]

Radioimmunoassay and Enzyme Immunoassay

RIA and EIA are immunological methods that employ antibodies against the specific drugs or competing drug molecules or enzymes, which are labeled with a radioactive tracer. Because the antibody sites are limited, the number of radioactively tagged molecules displaced is used to calculate the amount of unlabeled drug in the mixture.[2,8,12]

The principal drawback of the immunological method is the cross-reactivity of parent drugs and metabolites with the antibodies, which in reality is low. Although the cross-reactivity may produce a false-positive reaction, the result can be and should be confirmed by the more specific method, GC/MS. Because the sensitivity is high and the specificity still reasonably high, the EIA and RIA are commonly employed as screening techniques.[2,8,12]

The Enzyme Multiplied Immunoassay Technique (EMIT, trademark of SYVA Co.) is the test most widely used for marijuana. In general, the EIA system is very popular because it does not require timely extraction and centrifugation procedures. It lends itself to automation and is considerably less expensive than most other methods.

GC/MS, GLC, HPLC, and some RIA methodologies may be applied to all bodily fluids, including serum. Because blood levels are better indicators of recent use, it is sometimes important to obtain a blood level in evaluating a clinical state of intoxication. In contrast, RIA, EIA, and TLC are not ordinarily designed to detect drug levels in the blood, but are used in analyzing urine.[2,8,14]

DIAGNOSIS

It cannot be overemphasized that it is essential that all urine specimens be collected under direct supervision, including witnessing micturition. An unsupervised urine sample is always suspect, as urine samples can be substituted, contaminated, and adulterated easily, even by novices. Testing supposedly recently voided urine for basal body temperature may obviate the need for supervision in the future, but for now, testing should be supervised.[2,8]

A first-void urine (i.e., the first urination in the morning) has the highest concentration of drug and the highest specific gravity, and will therefore afford the greatest likelihood for detection of dilution. The drugs of interest and the type of methodology for drug testing need to be specified, and the cutoff value for the sensitivity selected or at least known. Urine and blood samples, when indicated, should be ordered for the following conditions: (i) for diagnosis, particularly for a differential diagnosis in atypical cases; and (ii) to monitor treatment progress on an inpatient or outpatient basis.[2,8,12]

For example, urine screens may be done several times a week. Drug testing during treatment acts as a deterrent to drug use and helps to identify reasons for those who relapse.[16–18]

The "office" testing procedure with the fastest turnaround and adequate accuracy is the EIA. Many offices, clinics, and even employers have the equipment and personnel to rapidly test urine samples. "Dipstick" testing offers no advantages and many disadvantages (false-positives and false-negatives). A test that is delivered to a good lab in the early evening should be reported to the physician the next morning by EIA or RIA even if GC/MS confirmation is pending. Labs are certified by CDC or National Pathology organizations (CAP), or more recently, for drug testing, by the National Institute on Drug Abuse (NIDA). We recommend knowing the laboratory to which you send your patient (or patient samples)—its certification, quality assurance programs, and proficiency testing. We also recommend a visit to the lab if at all possible.[6]

An illustrative example of how clinical testing can be useful is seen in the treatment of cocaine addiction. Cocaine is a commonly used drug, and its use is often denied by the users. Relapse to cocaine is high even in treatment programs, and the physician can use drug testing rather than self-reports to monitor response to treatment. For example, cocaine and its metabolite BE are detectable by TLC in the urine for only about 12–20 hours after cocaine is last used, by EIA to 48 hours, by RIA to 3–4 days, and by GC/MS to 7–8 days. It is important to know the clinical history of last use in relation to the time of collection, as well as whether the collection of the sample was supervised. This information is used in conjunction with cutoff value in order to interpret the results of the drug testing.[2,8,13]

Urine Drug Screening Parameters

Table 11.1 provides a summary of the National Institute on Drug Abuse federal employee drug-screening levels, confirmation levels, and the duration after last use that the drug can be expected to appear in the urine at these concentrations.

TREATMENT

The treatment of the drug- or alcohol-using patient requires a certain level of mutual trust. Drug testing simplifies the physician–patient relationship by taking detective-like drug-use interrogation out of the therapy. Urine is routinely taken, and consequences of positives follow. Urine testing should be expected as a part of treatment and, ideally, as a condition of treatment.[2,8]

The approach to the addicted patient requires skill and knowledge of the nature and prognosis of addictive illnesses. Of primary importance is that addiction be regarded as an independent illness. The causes of addictive illness are not known but the best available evidence reveals a biological

TABLE 11.1 Cutoff Limits and Duration for Urine Screening

Drug	NIDA Cutoff in ng/ml	Confirmation	Number of Days in Urine
Cocaine	300	150	<3
Amphetamines	1000	500	<2
Opiates	300	300	<2
Chronic marijuana use	100	15	<30
Single use of marijuana	100	15	<.7
Alcohol	—	—	<1
Barbiturates	—	—	<2
Phenobarbital	—	—	<7
Methadone	—	—	<4
Methaqualone	—	—	<7
PCP	25	25	<7

Compiled from: Council on Scientific Affairs (1987). Scientific issues in drug testing. *JAMA* 257:3110–3114; Osterloth JD, Becker CE (1990). Chemical dependency and drug abuse in the workplace. *Western J Med* May:506–513; Schwartz RH (1988). Urine testing in the detection of drugs of abuse. *Arch Int Med* 148:2407–2412.

basis for addictive use of drugs and alcohol. A caveat is that an alcoholic or drug addict is more likely to accept recommendations and suggestions if they are told they have an illness rather than a moral problem.[18]

An important perspective to use is that underlying conditions do not cause addictive use of drugs and alcohol, and probably do not cause significant use either. What generally happens is that the addict rationalizes the drug or alcohol use by arguing that the use is caused by depression, anxiety, or other reasons. However, studies show that these are frequently consequences of alcohol and drug use and not causes.[10]

The cardinal manifestations of drug and alcohol addiction are defense mechanisms—denial, minimization, rationalization, and projection. The addict mysteriously, and partly unconsciously, denies drug use despite direct evidence such as a positive drug screen or breathalyzer or a collateral source that confirms use. The addict frequently projects responsibility for problems onto someone or something else, i.e., "a series of misunderstandings and bad breaks."[10,18]

These defense mechanisms are best confronted with evidence of the consequences of the addictive use of drugs and alcohol. The denial can be penetrated with concrete examples. It is best to avoid judgmental attitudes and accusations that tend only to increase the denial and defensiveness. In addition, the addict is more likely to accept the confrontation if it is coupled with an explanation and offering of treatment for the addiction. In fact, confrontation without the hope of treatment should be avoided. Effective addiction treatment is available and should be made available to the addicted patients.[10,18]

In conclusion, laboratory testing can aid a clinician in making a differential diagnosis and eliminating drugs from active consideration as a cause of psychiatric symptoms. Testing of blood is useful in forensic and diagnostic questions when the clinician needs to know what drug or drugs the person was influenced by at the time (and hours before), relative to the mental status exam (change in behavior, accident, etc.).[2,12]

It is also useful in treatment planning and monitoring response to treatment in both inpatient and outpatient settings. In occupational settings, drug testing can be used as an early indication that a problem exists and also as a successful prevention tool. It is important that the physician have an understanding of available test methodologies, including their advantages and limitations, to use drug testing effectively in clinical practice.[2,11]

REFERENCES

1. Pottash ALC, Gold MS & Extein I (1982). The use of the clinical laboratory. In Sederer LI (ed.), *Inpatient Psychiatry: Diagnosis and Treatment,* Baltimore: Williams & Wilkins.

2. Gold MS & Dackis CA (1986). Role of the laboratory in the evaluation of suspected drug abuse. *J Clin Psych* 47 (Suppl):17–23.

3. Miller NS & Gold MS (1987). The medical diagnosis and treatment of alcohol dependence. *Med Times* 115:109–126.

4. DeMillo L, Gold MS & Martin D (1986). Evaluation of substance abuse. In Gold MS & Pottash ALC (eds.), *Diagnostic and Laboratory Testing in Psychiatry,* New York: Plenum.

5. Gold MS & Estroff TW (1985). The comprehensive evaluation of cocaine and opiate abusers. In Hall RCW & Beresford TP (eds.), *Handbook of Psychiatric Diagnostic Procedures,* New York: Spectrum.

6. NIDA (1985). *National Household Survey on Drug Abuse.* National Institute on Drug Abuse. Washington, DC: U.S. Govt. Printing Office.

7. Wolfe SM (1987). Drug-induced tranquility. *Health Lett* 6–8.

8. Verebey K, Gold MS & Mule SJ (1986). Laboratory testing in the diagnosis of marijuana intoxication and withdrawal. *Psych Ann* 16:235–241.

9. Jaffe JH (1985). Drug addiction and drug abuse. In Gilman AG, Goodman LS, Rall TW & Murad F (eds.), *The Pharmacological Basis of Therapeutics,* 7th ed., pp. 532–581. New York: Macmillan.

10. Miller NS, Dackis CA & Gold MS (1987). The relationship of addiction, tolerance, dependence: A neurochemical approach. *J Subst Abuse Treat* 4:197–207.

11. Gold MS, Pottash ALC & Estroff TW, et al. (1984). Laboratory evaluation in treatment planning. In Karusu TB (ed.), *The Psychiatric Therapies, Part I: The Somatic Therapies,* Washington, DC: APA Commission on Psychiatric Therapies.

12. Verebey K, Martin D & Gold MS (1986). Drug abuse: Interpretation of laboratory tests. In Gold MS & Pottash ALC (eds.), *Diagnostic and Laboratory Testing in Psychiatry,* pp. 155–167. New York: Plenum.

13. Gold MS, Pottash AC & Estroff I (1984). The psychiatric laboratory. In Bernstein JG (ed.), *Clinical Psychopharmacology,* pp. 29–58. London: John Wright.

14. CDC (1974). *Toxicology and Drug Abuse Survey III: Proficiency Testing.* Atlanta, GA: Centers for Disease Control.

15. Hansen JH, Caudill SP & Boone DJ (1985). Crisis in drug testing—Results of CDC blind study. *JAMA* 25:2382–2387.

16. Washton AM, Gold MS & Pottash AC (1985). Cocaine abuse treatment

outcome. In APA 138th Annual Meeting, *Abstracts of New Research,* Washington, DC: American Psychiatric Association.

17. Washton AM, Gold MS & Pottash AC (1987). Naltrexone in addicted physicians and business executives. *Natl Inst Drug Abuse Res Monogr Ser* 55:185–190.

18. Miller NS (1987). A primer of the treatment process for alcoholism and drug addiction. *Psych Lett* 5:30–37.

PART V

Clinical Characteristics

12

An Overview of Populations in Addiction Psychiatry

DEFINITION

People who are addicted to a psychoactive drug often are addicted to one or more other drugs, especially alcohol. The concurrent and simultaneous addiction to drugs and alcohol can be described as multiple drug addiction. Concurrent drug use is use of two or more drugs within the same period, i.e., one month; and simultaneous drug use is use of two or more drugs at the same time, i.e., cocaine and alcohol together. Whereas addicted people often have a primary *"drug of choice,"* they often have one or more *"secondary drugs of choice."*

Some people choose a secondary drug of choice that is pharmacologically similar to their primary drug of choice, i.e., from similar classes, such as sedatives. In such cases, the secondary drug of choice can be substituted for the primary drug, or can enhance the effects of the primary drug. For example, many people who have alcohol as their primary drug of choice will use benzodiazepines or marijuana as their secondary drug of choice.

Some people choose a secondary drug of choice that is pharmacologically dissimilar to their primary drug. In such cases, the secondary drug of choice may be used to decrease or minimize the unwanted effects of the primary drug. For example, many stimulant addicts will use alcohol to dampen the anxiety, agitation, and overstimulation that accompanies stimulant use.

It is important for physicians to understand that multiple drug addiction is the norm, not the exception, and that alcohol is frequently in the clinical picture.

Among people with multiple drug addiction, the interplay of drugs will determine the clinical presentation of the acute and chronic intoxication syndromes. The clinical features are a result of the combined effects of multiple drugs during intoxication, withdrawal, and prolonged abstinence syndromes, as well as toxic and psychosocial consequences. The challenge to the physician to diagnose multiple drug addiction and to determine detoxification schedules has increased dramatically in recent years. The resultant mixture of signs and symptoms may complicate the clinical picture sufficiently to make the diagnosis of any one drug intoxication impossible. Furthermore, other psychiatric syndromes that may be induced by alcohol, and particularly by other drugs, make diagnosis and treatment more complex.

Considerable overlap occurs among drug effects. The intoxicated state of one drug may mimic the withdrawal state of another. A stimulant picture is produced during intoxication and a depressant state during withdrawal by depressants. Psychotic symptoms are produced during intoxication by some drugs and during withdrawal by others (e.g., cocaine produces hallucinations and delusions during intoxication, and alcohol produces them during withdrawal). Moreover, because all the drugs involved in a multiple drug addiction produce psychiatric symptoms and syndromes, the clinical state of the multiply addicted individual frequently includes more severe psychopathological consequences.[1,2]

Addicts use combinations of drugs for a variety of reasons. The high (euphoria) from a stimulant is better maintained with a depressant (e.g., alcohol is often used with cocaine for this reason). A drug may be used to "treat" unwanted side effects of another drug (e.g., the undesirable effects of a cocaine high can be counteracted by opiates, alcohol, or other sedative–hypnotics). Moreover, depressants such as alcohol or benzodiazepines are used to "come down" or to "sedate" a cocaine-induced anxiety. As discussed earlier, one drug may be used as a substitute for another drug (e.g., over-the-counter stimulants, anticholinergics, and antihistamines may be used in lieu of cocaine or opiates when the latter are not available). A withdrawal effect of one drug may be alleviated by the intoxicating effect of another drug (e.g., a cocaine-induced depression may be temporarily relieved by alcohol, benzodiazepines, or marijuana).

ETIOLOGY

Medical and Psychiatric Sequelae of Addiction

Medical syndromes as sequelae of chronic alcoholism are not particularly common in the overall population of alcoholics, but still are present in a substantial minority. These include alcoholic liver disease, cardiomyopathy, oropharyngeal cancers, gastrointestinal ulcerations, and others. Accidents and trauma are also leading causes of morbidity and mortality in alcoholics, particularly among adolescents. Alcoholics represent from 25–50% of the total suicides in the United States and Europe. Although acute overdose from alcohol is rare, associated drug overdoses with alcohol use are common. The leading drugs that alcoholics tend to use in overdoses are benzodiazepines, tricyclic antidepressants, barbiturates, and other psychotropic medications. However, use of other drugs of addiction in overdoses may be higher than investigators have recorded, because of the difficulty in obtaining evidence for other drug use in clinical situations.[3]

The medical complications of multiple drug addictions are numerous, but not nearly as common as the psychiatric complications, with the exception of intravenous drug use, which is associated with substantial morbidity and mortality. Accidental, suicidal, and homicidal deaths remain common, especially among the young, for whom multiple drug use is significantly more predominant.

Persons addicted to intravenous drugs are at high risk of developing acquired immune deficiency syndrome (AIDS). Approximately 30% of AIDS cases in the United States are among intravenous drug addicts or are attributable to intravenous drug use. The intravenous drug addicts who themselves have AIDS readily transmit the virus to other drug dependents by sharing syringes and needles, having sexual contact, and engaging in other activities that involve an exchange of blood. In some cities, like New York, as many as 55–60% of intravenous drug dependents are seropositive for human immunodeficiency virus (HIV). Intravenous drug dependents represent about 1% of the population, or 2.5 million individuals.[4]

Other relatively common sequelae from intravenous drug use are viral and toxic hepatitis, endocarditis, lethal overdoses, pulmonary infections, allergic reactions, meningoencephalitis, brain abscesses, accidents, and trauma.[5]

Because of the use of denial and rationalization, alcoholics and drug dependents tend to minimize the nature and amount of their drug use. The sources of denial are diverse; they include organicity, the psychopathology of addiction, and the psychodynamics of conflict. The major mechanism by which the illogical state of addiction is allowed to continue, in spite of sometimes overwhelming adverse consequences from alcohol and drug use, is generated by forces often unrecognized by the dependent. Multiple drug dependence appears to reinforce this denial more strongly and makes it more difficult for the dependent to abstain from drug use because of substitution of one drug or alcohol for another. Importantly, the loss of control over one drug extends to another drug: the use of one psychoactive drug will disinhibit the individual and tend to lead to use of another.[6,7]

DIAGNOSIS

The findings of an important study have supported a common addiction syndrome for alcohol and other drugs, particularly opiates and cocaine.[8] The practice of multiple drug use by today's addict has many practical implications for diagnosis. The identification of only alcohol addiction in a patient is often tenuous and misleading. Because denial is a part of the addiction process, and because drugs are illegal and socially unacceptable, underreporting and underestimation of multiple drug use are to be expected in a clinical interview, especially if only the dependent person is interviewed. Corroborative sources increase the likelihood of obtaining a more accurate history; however, because of similar denial, these sources still may not reveal the total pattern and amount of alcohol and drug use. These corroborative sources may include family members, employer, and legal agencies, and may be supported by urine and blood testing for alcohol and drugs.

Although the contemporary alcoholic usually becomes addicted on alcohol first, most alcoholics under the age of 30 are addicted on at least one other drug and more often multiple drugs. Studies also show that a majority of drug addicts who become dependent on a drug first develop alcohol addiction later. Moreover, for many drug addicts, alcohol is the first drug used addictively. Finally, even in cases where alcohol is not the drug of choice for the drug addicted, it continues to be used addictively as an adjunct with a drug or in substitution of a drug.[9-12]

It is a frequent clinical observation that the multiple-drug-addicted individual has greater behavioral and mental disturbance than the person who is addicted to only one drug or alcohol. Frequently, multiple drug addiction begins in adolescence, when the personality is developing and the individual has not yet achieved a stable, integrated identity of self. However, the effects of alcohol and other drug addiction on an immature personality and personality development have not been well studied. The salient clinical observation is that the personality is adversely affected by acute and chronic use of alcohol and other drugs; the questions of how long these changes last and to what degree they change with recovery have not been addressed in studies.

Specifically, the pharmacological interactions with the brain critically affect the mind and behavior. Alcohol, marijuana, cocaine, opiates, sedative–hypnotics, and other drugs produce signs and symptoms of intoxication and withdrawal that include disturbances in mood, thinking, and vegetative states. These psychoactive effects on the brain and behavior are often chronic and cumulative in multiply addicted individuals. The degree of mental and cognitive disorganization is sometimes especially marked in this population because of the chronic dependence on multiple drugs.[5,13,14]

Obtaining answers to questions regarding the essentials of diagnosis is difficult with these reticent and impaired patients, even in obvious cases. The criteria for addiction, which include a preoccupation with, compulsive use of, and relapse to alcohol and other drugs, are denied by many addicted people who are actively using alcohol or other drugs. Obtaining answers to questions regarding the development of tolerance and physical dependence on alcohol and drugs is equally difficult. Persistent pursuit of such a patient in subsequent interviews, and a knowledge of the diagnostic characteristics of alcohol and other drug use, abuse, and addiction (particularly in the multiple drug addict), will often yield rewarding results.[15]

INTERACTIONS

Addictive and Psychiatric Disorders

Both acute and chronic alcohol and drug intoxication and withdrawal produce syndromes that must be differentiated from bipolar, depressive, anxiety, psychotic, personality, and other psychiatric disorders.[1,13,16] Alcohol-induced depression must be differentiated from major depression due to other causes, as defined in DSM-III-R. Alcohol hallucinosis with auditory and sometimes visual hallucinations needs to be differentiated from schizophrenia. The anxiety produced by repeated stimulation of the sympathetic nervous system in alcohol intoxication and withdrawal must be distinguished from the anxiety disorders of generalized anxiety, panic attacks, and phobias. Phobias such as agoraphobia, which are quite common in alcoholics, often resolve with abstinence from alcohol.[13]

Cocaine and other stimulant intoxication produce effects that must be distinguished from mania; euphoria, hyperactivity, and distorted self-image (the triad in mania) are principal pharmacological effects of cocaine intoxication. The withdrawal from cocaine, particularly in chronic use, is characterized by severe depression, with attendant signs and symptoms that resemble major depression. The chronic effects of cocaine are to induce paranoid delusions and hallucinations, both visual and auditory, which must be distinguished from schizophrenia. Furthermore, the anxiety generated by the pharmacological effects of chronic cocaine use is in the form of generalized anxiety, panic attacks, and intense agoraphobia.[1,17]

Marijuana, PCP, and other hallucinogens are drugs that product intense distortions of mood, affect, thinking, and perceptions. The resulting development of depression, manic behavior, delusions, and hallucinations must be differentiated from affective and psychiatric disorders. Other hallucinogens, such as LSD, methamphetamine, and psilocybin, share properties with marijuana.[18]

All these drugs have adverse effects on personality when used chronically in a dependent mode. Deterioration in personality and interference with development of the personality are produced by all the drugs when taken individually, including alcohol. The multiply addicted individual is more severely affected and experiences a more pronounced effect on the personality, which is manifested by a disturbance in interpersonal relationships.[12,15,19]

Flexibility of Diagnoses

Of foremost importance is maintaining a differential diagnosis with continuous review; the clinician should not be compelled to make a single, final, and irreversible diagnosis. Furthermore, it is essential to keep in mind that alcohol and drug addiction are independent disorders that produce these symptoms and syndromes. The treatment of multiple drug addiction with detoxification and abstinence will frequently be sufficient to establish the definitive diagnosis within days to weeks. However, occasionally the effects of alcohol and drugs will persist for protracted periods, so that a prolonged period of observation may be necessary before these effects can be ruled out. The mood disturbances and anxiety produced by alcohol, cocaine, and marijuana may endure for weeks and months, although they may lessen with the passing of time. The delusions and hallucinations will sometimes continue in all the drug states for prolonged periods. Finally, the deterioration in personality may take years to reverse, although a substantial start is initiated with abstinence and a commitment to a treatment program.[5,13]

Laboratory testing for drugs of addiction can be useful in differentiating psychiatric from drug-induced syndromes and identifying use of specific drugs. The accuracy depends on the sensitivity and specificity of the test employed, the recency of onset, the dose of the drug, and the method of specimen collection and cutoff value. A positive test is almost certain evidence of use of a particular drug, wherein a negative result is not confirmatory, although it suggests a lack of recent use. The rate of false-positives is low, and the rate of false-negatives is high.[20] As with any laboratory test in medicine, the results should be interpreted in the context of the clinical setting. It is imperative not to treat a particular result without a corresponding clinical syndrome that is relevant.

Prevalence

The findings of the ECA study for prevalence rates for comorbid psychiatric diagnoses indicate that psychiatric disorders are common among patients with addiction to alcohol and other drugs.[21] One-third of the total population in ECA sample met lifetime criteria for one of the DSM-III psychiatric diagnoses, and one-third of those with one diagnosis had a second diagnosis. The lifetime prevalence rates for psychiatric disorders were higher among those with alcoholism than those without alcoholism in the general population.

Among those with the diagnosis of alcoholism, almost half (47%) had a second psychiatric diagnosis. The cooccurrence of psychiatric disorders with alcoholism was more common in women than in men: 64% of female alcoholics had a second diagnosis, compared to 44% of men. In men, antisocial personality disorder was second to drug addiction as the most common psychiatric disorder among alcoholics, with a substantial relative risk for the presence of antisocial personality if alcoholism was diagnosed.

Phobias were particularly common among male alcoholics, followed by depression, schizophrenia, panic, and mania.

In alcoholic women, phobias and depression, followed by antisocial personality, panic, schizophrenia, and mania, were the psychiatric disorders cited in descending prevalence. Interestingly, the *relative risk* of a psychiatric diagnosis for women with alcoholism in relation to the general population was greatest for antisocial personality and least for depression and phobias, owing to the high rates of these latter disorders among nonalcoholic women in the general population. Furthermore, the prevalence of *relative risk* for psychiatric disorders was the same for women alcoholics as for men alcoholics, suggesting a common contribution from the alcoholism.[21]

Other studies indicate further that those patients with multiple drug addiction and psychiatric disorders have an overall poorer prognosis. These "dual-diagnosis" patients tend to be younger, are more often male, and have poorer medication compliance. In addition, they are nearly twice as likely to be rehospitalized at a 1-year follow-up. Multiple drug addiction appears to add to the problems of disruptive, disinhibited, and noncompliant behaviors in chronic mental illness.[22]

REFERENCES

1. Gold MS & Verebey K (1984). The psychopharmacology of cocaine. *Psych Ann* 14(10):714–712.
2. Jaffe JH (1985). Drug addiction and drug use. In Goodman LS & Gilman AG (eds.), *The Pharmacological Basis of Therapeutics* 6th ed, pp. 532–581. New York: Macmillan.
3. Ritchie JM (1985). The alipathic alcohols. In Gilman AG, Goodman LS, Rall TW & Murad F (eds.), *The Pharmacological Basis of Therapeutics* 7th ed, pp. 372–386. New York: Macmillan.
4. Des Jarlais DC & Friedman SR (1988). HIV and intravenous drug use. *AIDS* 2 suppl. 1:S65–S69.
5. Hoffman FG (1983). *A Handbook of Drug and Alcohol Abuse* 2nd ed. New York: Oxford University Press.
6. Miller NS & Mirin SM (1989). Multiple drug use in alcoholics in practical and theoretical implications. *Psych Ann* 19(5):248–255.
7. Milam JR & Ketchum K (1981). *Under the Influence.* Seattle, WA: Madrona.
8. Kosten TR, Rounsaville BJ, Babor TF, Spitzer RL & Williams JBW (1987).

Substance use disorders in DSM-III-R: Evidence for the dependence syndrome across different psychoactive substance. *Br J Psych* 151:834–843.

9. Galizio M & Maish SA (1985). *Determinants of Substance Abuse.* New York: Plenum.

10. Freed EX (1973). Drug abuse by alcoholics: A review. *Intern J Addict* 8:451–473.

11. Miller NS, Gold MS, Belkin B & Klahr AL (1990). The diagnosis of alcohol and cannabis dependence in cocaine dependents and alcohol dependence in their families. *Br J Addict* 84:1491–1498.

12. Miller NS & Mirin SM (1989). Multiple drug use in alcoholics in practical and theoretical implications. *Psych Ann* 19(5):248–255.

13. Schuckit MA (1983). Alcoholism and other psychiatric disorders. *Hosp Commun Psych* 34(11):1022–1027.

14. Miller NS, Dackis CA & Gold MS (1987). The relationship of addiction, tolerance and dependence: A neurochemical approach. *J Subst Abuse Treat* 4:197–207.

15. Miller NS & Gold MS (1989). Suggestions for changes in DMS-III-R criteria for substance use disorders. *Am J Drug Alc Abuse* 15(2):223–230.

16. Post RM (1975). Cocaine psychosis: A continuum model. *Am J Psych* 132:225–231.

17. Gawan FH & Kleber HD (1986). Abstinence symptomatology and psychiatric diagnosis in cocaine abusers: Clinical observations. *Arch Gen Psych* 43:107–113.

18. Redda KK, Walker CA & Barnett C (1989). *Cocaine, Marijuana, Designer Drugs: Chemistry, Pharmacology, and Behavior.* Boca Raton, FL: CRC Press.

19. Poldrugo F & Forti B (1988). Personality disorders and alcoholism treatment outcome. *Drug and Alc Depend* 21:171–176.

20. Verebey K & Turner CE (1991). Laboratory testing. In Frances RJ & Miller SI (eds.), *Clinical Textbook of Addictive Disorders* pp. 221–236. New York: Guilford Press.

21. Helzer JE & Pryzbeck TR (1988). The co-occurrence of alcoholism with other psychiatric disorders in the general population and its impact on treatment. *J Stud Alc* 49(3):219–224.

13

A Systematic Approach to Differential Diagnosis and Treatment

OVERVIEW

Psychiatric disturbance is frequently associated with psychoactive drug and alcohol use and addiction.[1,2] Differential diagnosis is important for the effective pharmacological and therapeutic treatment of the comorbid diagnosed patient.[3-5] Alcoholics Anonymous refers to the "insanity of alcoholism," and the term "dope fiend" evokes images of derangement and perversity. Many of the more dramatic attempts at prevention, both historically and recently, have relied on inferred risks of alcohol and drug use in provoking mental disturbance.

However, the actual relationship between abuse, addiction, and psychiatric dysfunction, can be articulated and understood. Clinical observation and currently existing data can provide the basis for practical methodology for evaluation and treatment.

A pragmatic model for diagnosis and treatment of psychiatric syndromes/disorders in association with drug and alcohol disorders can be based on clinically observable conditions consistent with the existing research knowledge. Causality and comorbidity of both disorder categories can be determined. A model can be developed that divides common clinical presentations into a few discrete syndromes. A standardized methodology, when applied to these syndromes, can provide guidelines for the evaluation, intervention, and diagnosis of psychiatric and addictive disorders.[6]

METHODS

Estimates of Prevalence

Psychiatric symptoms from alcohol and drug disorders occur more commonly than independent, coexisting psychiatric disorders. Psychosis can be used as a model to illustrate this fundamental point in differential diagnosis.

If organic mental syndromes and psychoactive substance use disorders are excluded, psychotic symptoms generally can be attributable to schizophrenia, delusional disorders, mood disorders, and psychotic disorders not elsewhere classified. The overall prevalence of these major psychiatric disorders can be assumed to be approximately 5%.[2,7] The actual one-month prevalence rates for the following psychiatric disorders are: "schizophrenic/schizophreniform disorders" 0.7% and "affective disorders" 2.9%, for a total of 3.6%. Adding "delusional disorders" and "psychotic disorders not elsewhere classified" brings the total to 4.6% (near 5%).[2,7]

For the purpose of this analysis, a rate of psychiatric illness of twice that for the general population will be assumed for the alcohol and drug addicted population (assuming a higher rate, i.e., three times normal, would not significantly change the outcome).

These assumed prevalences lead to the following conclusions. Approximately one out of 20 individuals in a general population (nonaddicted) being evaluated for active psychotic illness will be found to have such illness. In a group of 20 currently addicted individuals, two individuals (10/100) would suffer from such a psychotic illness. Conversely, 19 out of 20 individuals in the general population would be free of active psychotic illness, while 18 out of 20 chemically dependent individuals would be free of psychotic illness.

As noted previously, a more extreme assumption (i.e., a three-times normal prevalence of psychotic illness in the addicted) would result in 17 out of 20 individuals being free of psychotic illness. From the perspective of clinical service, it is important whether one, two, or three people out of twenty (5, 10, or 15%) will require treatment for major psychotic illness. However, from the perspective of diagnosis and epidemiology, psychotic illness is *not* found in most (70–95%) of the general population or the addicted population.

Individuals with current addictions (with intermittent and prolonged periods of intoxication and withdrawal), frequently manifest psychotic symptoms. Hallucinations, paranoid delusion, disturbance in the form of thought, and profound alterations in mood are common occurrences in the course of addictive illness. While independent psychotic illness is likely to be modestly, or even moderately increased in the addicted population, psychotic symptoms are dramatically increased. Therefore, psychotic symptoms have *less diagnostic validity for mental illness in the addiction population* than they do in the general population.

The evaluating clinician is thus faced with a significant diagnostic dilemma when evaluating an alcohol and/or drug addicted individual with psychotic symptoms. While having to maintain a higher than usual index of diagnostic suspicion for psychotic disorder, the majority of symptoms observed will not be indicative of independent psychiatric illness. The same paradigm can be used for other psychiatric disorders.

Comorbid Addiction and Psychiatric Symptoms

The clinician confronted by psychotic symptoms in a (presumably) addicted individual must be aware of the following:

- One cannot assume the existence of a preexisting psychiatric illness.
- One cannot rely on current symptomatology to assume the presence of, or to specify, a psychiatric diagnosis.
- One must entertain a relatively high index of suspicion of psychotic illness.
- One must provide acute treatment of psychotic symptoms.
- One must treat (or refer for treatment) the addictive illness and/or psychiatric disorder.

After initial stabilization, the clinician will be expected to plan the long-term treatment and to arrive at a diagnosis.

Guidelines for Diagnosis

An examination of the preceding discussion leads to certain conclusions that provide the basis for a rational method of approach.

Conclusion I. Due to the absence of a demonstrable psychiatric or "underlying" etiology of addiction and the poor diagnostic validity of nonspecific symptoms, a definitive psychiatric diagnosis is not possible during acute episodes in addicted people.

Conclusion II. The existence of addiction does not reduce the dangerousness of psychotic symptoms.

These conclusions dictate a simple and direct strategy. First treat the
presenting symptoms as clinically required; then observe the patient when
free of psychoactive drugs to evaluate the origin of the symptoms. A
psychiatric diagnosis independent of addiction is made only if symptoms
recur or persist after significant abstinence.

While simple and rational conceptually, the practical application of this
methodology is complicated by the fact that psychotic symptoms secondary to abuse and addiction may persist for prolonged periods of time
and that many, if not most, addicted patients, are not likely to become
drug-free easily, rapidly, or for long periods. However, while the goals of
the diagnostic plan (becoming free of psychoactive drug use and its attendant psychological disruption) may be achieved only in relative terms
and for a portion of patients, the diagnostic plan still represents the appropriate management of this patient population. Simply stated, addicted
individuals, with or without intercurrent psychiatric illness, do not get
better unless they achieve or approach abstinence. Addicted patients with
psychotic symptoms who continue to use alcohol or other drugs are unlikely to benefit from psychiatric medications, social intervention, or counseling (whether or not they also have psychotic illnesses).

Psychiatric medication, especially certain antidepressants, can be dangerous in combination with psychoactive drugs (e.g., chlorpromazine and
alcohol, MAOIs and cocaine). However, even when not pharmacologically
toxic, the coadministration of drugs of abuse and psychiatric medications
constitutes a losing battle. Psychoactive drugs are apt to be taken with
greater regularity and in larger doses than prescribed medication. Similarly, social service interventions can almost always be undermined by
addiction. Food stamps, tokens, checks, and housing will be bartered or
wasted by the active addicts. Living arrangements are destabilized and
counseling forgotten by the active user.

Overall Treatment Plan

The following treatment plan is therefore suggested:

1. Treat life-threatening complications.
   a) Treat overdose and withdrawal.
   b) Hospitalize psychiatrically for suicidality or dangerousness (on a
      locked ward with appropriately trained staff).

2. Support abstinence.

   a) Refer to treatment programs.

   b) Refer to AA/NA/CA and Double Trouble Groups.

   c) Provide ongoing personal support.

3. Use indicated psychiatric medications if symptoms persist and impair function and recovery.

4. Do not use cross-tolerant sedatives except for detoxification or acute sedation.

5. Discontinue medications and observe patient for recurrence of psychiatric symptoms.

6. Make psychiatric diagnosis based on reappearance or persistence or symptoms in absence of active alcohol/drug use.

7. Provide appropriate psychiatric medications and management based on clinical course over time.

Psychiatric Syndromes

The treatment of psychiatric disturbance in addicted individuals can be conceived as the treatment of the following syndromes:

- Intoxications
- Cognitive impairment due to organic mental syndromes
- Depressive type syndrome
- Paranoid type syndrome

Intoxications are acute mental syndromes. They can be characterized by fluctuations in level of consciousness, activity, and awareness of environment. They are transient and should be treated with support, observation, restraint, and medical intervention when necessary (i.e., talking down, sleeping off, sedating). Within a few hours, intoxication symptoms will usually clear and the patient may manifest one of the other syndromes noted (i.e., protracted benzodiazepine withdrawal).

Cognitive impairment such as chronic memory and disorientation difficulties requires neurological evaluation to determine etiology and prognosis (apart from persistent effects of alcohol and drugs) and should be so referred.

The remaining two syndromic presentations constitute the majority of the problematic psychiatric presentations associated with abuse and addiction, and will be examined separately.

Depressive syndromes seen in substance use are identical to the depressive syndromes produced by affective illness; they are characterized by:

- Sad mood
- Guilt, hopelessness, worthlessness
- Agitation or psychomotor retardation
- Anhedonia
- Sleep disturbance (increased or decreased)
- Delusions
- Suicidality

They may be associated with all forms of abuse and addiction, but are frequently associated with:

- Chronic sedative use
- Chronic stimulant use
- Intoxication and withdrawal

Paranoid syndromes seen in substance use are also clinically indistinguishable from those produced by "pure" psychiatric illness. They are characterized by:

- Suspiciousness
- Delusions
- Hallucinations
- Clear sensorium
- Hypervigilance

Hypervigilance is a syndrome which (in the absence of psychotic symptoms) may characterize this type of presentation. It includes:

- Irritability
- Suspiciousness
- Hyperarousal

Hypervigilance can be conceived of as the affective and emotional tone of an agitated paranoid state *without* psychotic process. These paranoid types of presentations may also be associated with all forms of abuse and addiction and are frequently associated with:

- Chronic stimulant use
- Hallucinogen use
- Intoxication and withdrawal

Let us apply the proposed methodology to alcohol- and drug-involved patients being seen in a mental health or addiction clinic, presenting with a new onset of one of the previously described syndromes.

TREATMENT

Steps for Application of Treatment Plan

1. Treat Life Threatening Complications. Is the patient suicidally depressed, combative due to delusions, dangerously agitated due to hearing voices? Are they so depressed or disorganized that they are unable to feed, clothe or care for themselves? If so, they require hospitalization (or, at least, a supervised setting in the last instance). If not, they can continue to attend the outpatient clinic. These criteria, it should be noted, are standard psychiatric evaluation criteria. The one significant difference in evaluating the acute drug-involved patient is the use, when available, of a safe holding area since even the acute syndromes noted may clear rapidly (e.g., a few hours) in many instances.

2. Support Abstinence. Once the decision whether to hospitalize is made, the next step is therapeutic confrontation. The relationship between psychoactive drug use and the difficulties they are experiencing (life problems, symptoms) is pointed out to the patient. The process does not require negative, provocative, or hostile interaction. Rather, it is the contrasting of the adverse consequences of use with the alternative of avoiding these consequences through a program leading to abstinence.

A treatment plan, however, rudimentary, should be developed to help achieve abstinence. Patients cannot be expected to stop use without help. While they must not be blamed for their substance use, they should be held responsible for treating their addiction. The plan must include real external supports such as referral to treatment programs, safe residential arrangements, and AA and/or NA and/or "Double Trouble" groups.

Participation in the 12-step organizations should be part of every treatment plan. Clinicians often assume that psychiatrically disturbed patients cannot tolerate, or be tolerated by, self-help groups. Except in the case of floridly bizarre behavior, such assumptions are unwarranted. Many mental health professionals erroneously believe that the Twelve-Step Fellowships are confrontational and intrusive. They are not. Clinicians also frequently underestimate the capacity of patients to adapt (especially outside of standard treatment settings).

This ability to "pull it together" can be aided and augmented by providing careful preparation, education, and encouragement to the patient. Such preparation can be done individually or in groups, and should include role-playing as well as clear statements to the patients about what they may expect at meetings. "Double Trouble" groups are currently proliferating and are specifically designed to meet the needs of psychiatrically disturbed addicted individuals.

Patients unwilling to accept such a plan, who deny addiction and report they can stop "on their own," should be supportively encouraged to attempt to do so, while being carefully monitored; if unable to stop using, they are then confronted with the fact that their plan has been unsuccessful and that it must be modified to include treatment.

Although supporting abstinence can be quickly described, it is often a long and difficult process. Denial and minimization, as well as frank psychotic symptoms, can often block acceptance of the need for treatment. This step, supporting abstinence through education and supportive confrontation, continues while the subsequent steps of the methodology are implemented. Acceptance may fluctuate over time, as will the success of attempts to achieve abstinence. It is clinically vital, however, to keep in mind that providing medications and financial benefits in the absence of such education and confrontation, can give the message that addiction is "secondary." This constitutes *enabling*, which can be described as supporting denial and deflecting attention from the addictive process. Once the support of abstinence (not necessarily is attainment) is established, the methodology should be continued.

3. Use Indicated Psychiatric Medications If Symptoms Persist and Impair Function and Recovery. Whether in or out of hospital, patients may experience symptoms that prevent their engagement in neces-

sary life activities, including addiction treatment. An inpatient, who after several days in an alcohol or drug detoxification unit, gets more depressed and begins to exhibit significant vegetative symptoms (such as the inability to get out of bed, concentrate, or bathe) due to profound depression, should be evaluated carefully for antidepressant therapy. If supportive counseling and nutrition do not rapidly improve the clinical picture, medications should be started. As much as the patient deserves medication, the patient also deserves *not* to have a definitive diagnosis other than an affective episode (e.g., organic affective disorder). There would be no reason at that point in time to assume that the patient has an affective illness.

Similarly, a patient suffering from the other common syndrome presentation, the paranoid syndrome, might be delusionally suspicious and fearful, or simply distracted by a hallucinosis and unable to attend a community or AA meeting. If these symptoms do not improve rapidly (within a few days), or if they grow worse, the patient should receive antipsychotic medications to permit safe, effective, and comfortable functioning. Again, an *episode* of psychosis should be diagnosed (e.g., organic hallucinosis, organic delusional disorder), and not an ongoing psychotic illness.

Anxiety symptoms in addicted individuals are common and usually self-limited; however, some report anxiety disorders to be increased in this population. Anxiety may be more treatable than addiction.[8] Its management, when it is truly disabling and not reduced by supportive measures, should include behavioral therapy, beta blockers, tricyclic antidepressants, and serotonergic drugs such as buspirone and fluoxetine. Again, the diagnosis of a temporary disturbance (i.e., organic anxiety disorder) should be made. While the last examples cited here were for inpatients, the identical criteria (the inability to engage in necessary activities, especially recovery-oriented ones) should be used when evaluating outpatients attending a mental health or addiction clinic. Similarly, initial diagnoses should be of temporary conditions, with issues of "primacy" best deferred,[9-11] in favor of engaging the patient into treatment as soon as possible.[12]

4. Do Not Use Cross-Tolerant Medication Except for Detoxification.

Except for acute detoxification or emergency sedation, the use of cross-tolerant sedatives (i.e., benzodiazepines, meprobamate, barbiturates, etc.) should be avoided in both outpatient and inpatient settings. The anxiety symptoms for which these medications are used should be managed as noted in the previous section. Sleep disturbance should be managed behaviorally, or with bedtime doses of sedating antidepressants if the disturbance is profound.

Various issues in medicating the addicted patient have been raised in the psychiatric literature.[13] The use of sedatives, however, is not contraindicated for philosophical reasons, but for practical clinical ones. Addicted individuals develop rapid and extreme tolerance to these medications, thus becoming refractory to the therapeutic effects while experiencing an exacerbation of anxiety (and insomnia) due to withdrawal phenomena. This reduction in efficacy and increase in symptoms often leads to increased dosage, possible addiction to these drugs and more likelihood of relapse to their drugs of choice. The motivation and honesty of patients are not at issue—merely their constitutional inability to control the effects of these substances. Their use is countertherapeutic and inhumane in this population.

5. Discontinue Medications and Observe Patient for Recurrence of Psychiatric Symptoms. Assuming major psychiatric symptoms have ceased, or at least have been very significantly reduced for a period of months, medications should be discontinued and the patient observed over time. This approach coincides with the appropriate response to individuals with other psychiatric disorders (e.g., major depression, etc.).

6. Make Psychiatric Diagnoses Based on Reappearance of Symptoms in the Absence of Alcohol/Drug Use. If symptoms recur, and the patient is verifiably abstinent, a definitive nonorganic psychiatric disorder can be diagnosed. For example, if three months after tricyclics are discontinued, an abstinent patient becomes clinically depressed and meets DSM criteria, a major depressive episode can be diagnosed. Similarly, the reappearance of delusions in such a patient would warrant a diagnosis of a delusional disorder. If hallucinations were also present, schizophrenia (or schizophreniform psychosis) would be diagnosed. If, however, as is often the case, abstinence has not been reliably demonstrated (or even unreliably demonstrated), the methodology should be reapplied (or rather, should be continued to be applied) with no new or definitive diagnosis. Continued support of abstinence and recovery coupled with appropriate periods of medication use will reduce hospital-

ization and improve function even in the absence of achieving abstinence or arriving at a "final" diagnosis.

7. Provide Appropriate Psychiatric Medications and Management Based on Diagnosis. When definitive psychiatric diagnoses, independent of addiction are made, patients should receive the standard accepted psychiatric treatment in addition to treatment for addiction. Clinical inference dictates that receiving both treatments in a unified program works best. Studies are, in fact, underway to test this hypothesis.[14] However, when dual diagnosis or (so-called) MICA (mentally ill clinical abuser) programs are not available, tandem or parallel treatments should occur. Patients should be educated as to their need to take medications and how this differs from abuse and addiction. Information and education should also be provided to the treatment people on "both sides of the street," with the understanding that neither psychiatric care nor addiction treatment will be successful unless both are successful. Addiction counselors should understand the importance of medications and not perceive them as drugs of abuse, while psychiatrically oriented therapists must recognize the significance of active addictive use and relapse, and how it blocks effective psychiatric treatment. In addition to staff education, the confusing course of these patients, their primitive distortions, and "splitting" behaviors necessitate good communication between treatment personnel. Appropriate liaisons and mechanisms for the exchange of clinical information must be developed.

PROGNOSIS

Patients manifesting psychiatric symptoms and addiction or abuse should be managed acutely based on clinical presentation and standard psychiatric evaluation criteria. They should then be supported and encouraged to attain abstinence through addiction treatment and self-help programs, while receiving necessary psychiatric medication and treatment, but with provisional diagnosis only. Definitive diagnosis is made only if abstinence is achieved and it can be expected that this type of management will result in improved clinical outcomes even in the absence of a final diagnosis or attainment of ongoing abstinence.

REFERENCES

1. Blunt G, Galanter M, Lifshutz H & Castanedo R (1990). Cocaine/Crack dependence among psychiatric inpatients. *Am J Psych* 147(11):1542–1546.
2. Regier DA, Farmer ME, Rae DS, Locke BZ, Keith SJ, Judd LL & Goodwin FK (1990). Comorbidity of mental disorders with alcohol and other drug abuse: Results from the epidemiologic catchment area (ECA) study. *J Am Med Assoc* 264(19):2511–2518.
3. Keisler CA, Simpkins CG & Morton TL (1991). Prevalence of dual diagnosis of mental and substance abuse disorders in general hospitals. *Hosp Commun Psych* 42(4):400–403.
4. Crowne DB, Rosse RB, Sheridan MJ & Deutsch SI (1991). Substance abuse diagnoses and discharge patterns among psychiatric inpatients. *Hosp Commun Psych* 42(4):403–405.
5. Kosten TR & Kleber HD (1988). Differential diagnosis of psychiatric co-morbidity in substance abusers. *J Subst Abuse Treat* 5(4):201–206.
6. Fine J & Miller NS (1993). Evaluation and acute management of psychotic symptomatology in alcohol and drug addictions. *J Addict Dis* 12(3):59–72.
7. Helzer JE & Pryzbeck TR (1991). The co-occurrence of alcoholism with other psychiatric disorders in the general population and its impact on treatment. *J Stud Alc* 49:219–224.
8. Brody SL (1990). Violence associated with acute cocaine use in patients admitted to a medical emergency department. *NIDA Res Monog Ser* 103:44–59.
9. Weser RB (1990). Alcohol use and abuse secondary to anxiety. *Psych Clin N Am* 13(4):699–713.
10. Lehman AI, Myers EP & Corty E (1989). Assessment and classification of patients with psychiatric and substance abuse syndromes. *Hosp Commun Psych* 40(10):1019–1025.
11. Schuckit MA & Montiero MG (1988). Alcoholism, anxiety, and depression. *Br J Addict* 83:1373–1380.
12. Weiss RD & Mirin SM (1989). The dual diagnosis alcoholic: and treatment. *Psychiatric Annals* 19(5):261–265.
13. Hanson M, Kramer TH & Gross W (1990). Outpatient treatment of adults with coexisting substance use and mental disorders. *J Subst Abuse Treat* 7:109–116.
14. Rosenthal R (1991). Unified treatment program studies for dual diagnostic patients. Department of Psychiatry, Beth Israel Hospital, personal communication.

14

Affective and Anxiety Disorders

OVERVIEW

Anxiety and depression are the most common comorbid conditions in alcoholics and drug addicts. Addiction, anxiety, and depressive disorders are among the most prevalent psychiatric diagnoses in the general population.[1] According to data from the ECA study, it is estimated that about 15% of individuals will develop alcoholism at some point in their lifetime and 6% will develop drug addiction. Anxiety syndromes including phobic, panic, and obsessive-compulsive disorders are seen in about the same percentage across a life-span. About 5–10% of men and women will suffer a major depressive episode at some point during their lives.[2] Because there is no evidence that having one of these disorders protects an individual from suffering a second illness, then, minimally, one should see dual disorders (i.e., a major psychiatric illness and a substance-use disorder) in the general population occurring at a base rate consistent with that of the most prevalent single disorder.

As pharmacological effects, alcohol and other drugs can cause signs and symptoms of both anxiety and depression. Alcohol and other drugs can mimic signs and symptoms of nearly all of the major anxiety and depression syndromes.[3-5] Patients seldom offer information about their alcohol and drug use patterns when they present their psychological complaints, and the cooccurrence of a psychiatric and drug problem is more likely to bring the individual into the clinic seeking treatment.[2] Unless evaluated for use of drugs, the patient's denial and minimization of her or his substance-related problems will omit this important information, making proper diagnosis and treatment more difficult.

There is a predictable relationship between anxiety and depressive disorders on the one hand, and addiction disorders on the other.[6] All these drugs cross the blood–brain barrier and produce changes in mood and behavior.[5] These alterations occur in a variety of conditions. For example, intoxication with brain stimulants (cocaine, amphetamine, etc.) can produce signs and symptoms of anxiety with anxious mood, rapid heart rate and, at higher doses, even panic attacks.[6,10]

Similar anxiety symptom patterns may be produced during the withdrawal phase from alcohol and other brain depressants, while intoxication with these agents can cause depression that takes on the severity of major depression, with changes in mood, self-attitude, and psychovegetative state.[6]

The major psychiatric illnesses specified in the DSM-III-R as major depression, generalized anxiety disorder, or panic disorder have more or less distinct course, prognosis, and response to treatment. The drug-related conditions appear to have different courses, prognoses, and treatment indications. Most improve or completely resolve within weeks of stopping the use of drugs.

Because anxiety and depression symptoms/signs commonly occur with alcohol/drug use, it is important for clinicians to include an evaluation the patients' drug and alcohol histories in all complaints of anxiety and depression. It is also important to devise an approach through which patients who have multiple problems can be evaluated in a way most likely to arrive at the correct diagnosis or diagnoses.

DIAGNOSIS

Depression and Alcohol Addiction

Alcohol, benzodiazepines, and barbiturates are capable of producing symptoms of depression.[3,5,7,8,11,12] This dysphoria worsens at higher dose ranges or as the blood alcohol concentration falls, and a number of studies in alcoholics have demonstrated that these mood changes occur despite expectations that the drug will have mood elevating effects.[3,11,13] In addition to these "direct" depressant effects, the life-stress crises caused by alcohol use and addiction can produce depression. Misuse of drugs and alcohol and their impact on the alcoholic's lifestyle (e.g., difficulties with relationships, employment and legal problems, etc.) can be so demoralizing that many individuals will seek psychiatric treatment for "depression."

Cross-sectional evaluations of depressive symptoms in alcoholics can lead to inflated estimates of the cooccurrence of these two conditions or independent depression and addiction. Estimates using self-report data in recently detoxified alcoholics reveal symptoms of major depression in 98% of their histories.[4]

Prolonged use of alcohol can produce serious states of depression. There is consistent evidence that these mood changes are likely to improve markedly with abstinence.[3,5,14] A study of 191 carefully diagnosed primary alcoholic inpatients revealed that even after more than a week of abstinence, 42% of the subjects had a Hamilton Depression Rating Scale score that fell in the moderately to severely depressed range.[14]

However, with the supportive treatment provided on the alcoholism rehabilitation unit and continued abstinence alone, the percentage of subjects showing Hamilton scores above 20 dropped to 12% by week two and only 6% by week four. Interestingly, a follow-up 3 months after discharge demonstrated no increased recurrence rates in depressive symptoms except among those individuals who returned to the use of alcohol or other drugs.

These studies emphasize that the course of these "drug-induced depressions" differs from the usual course of an uncomplicated major depressive episode because most depressive symptoms resolve within 2–4 weeks without treatment and without antidepressant medications.[2,14]

Thus, the rate of depressive symptoms in alcoholics is quite high, depending on the sample selected, the criteria used, the time sequence in which subjects are studied (i.e., recently detoxified versus after weeks or months of abstinence), and the duration over which the cooccurrence of symptoms is evaluated (in the last month or over a lifetime). Limiting the definition of depression to only persistent affective disturbances in the setting of drinking that interfere with functioning over a period of two or more weeks, about one-third of alcoholics suffer severe depressions at some point in their drinking careers.[3,11] However, it appears that after 2–4 weeks of abstinence, perhaps only 5% of men and about 10% of women with alcoholism are likely to still meet criteria for the diagnosis of a major depressive episode[11]—a rate similar to that of depression in the general population.

There remains a minority of patients who will present with both an independent substance use and depressive disorder. In the next sections, we briefly discuss the relationship between other drugs of abuse and depression and then describe how the clinician can begin to disentangle these issues and outline a plan for managing these patients.

Depression and Other Drugs of Addiction

Stimulant (e.g., cocaine and amphetamines) use and addiction are also frequently associated with affective disturbances. These symptoms predominate during the withdrawal phase when perhaps as many as 50% or more of chronic stimulant users are affected.[5,10] As with alcohol-related depressions there is evidence that these mood changes are likely to decrease in intensity within 1–4 weeks of abstinence.

Opiate addiction is also associated with high rates of depressive disorders. Lifetime prevalence rates of depression among opiate addicts and individuals on methadone maintenance approximately 50–70% in most patient samples seeking treatment.[9] Similarly, although less data are available, affective disturbances are also reported to be more common during repeated, heavy intoxication with cannabinols.[5]

TREATMENT

The clinician should distinguish between symptoms and syndromes, their duration and severity, and establish the sequence of their occurrence. It would be misleading to diagnose a patient as having a major depression if the mood changes appeared only during periods of intoxication or withdrawal or if they were of insufficient severity and duration to warrant such a diagnosis.[19,20]

Clinical experience and knowledge of data from studies indicating the relatively rapid improvement in depressive symptoms in most early abstinent alcoholics dictates that antidepressant medications be administered conservatively in this population. It is usually advisable that a 2–4 weeks observation period be administered before considering the use of these medications, emphasizing instead supportive and cognitive/behavioral treatments.

This conservative approach ensures that the patient will not be committed to a 6–9 month course of unnecessary pharmacotherapy and minimizes the risk of potential drug interactions.[15] Moreover, there is little convincing evidence that the standard antidepressant medications are effective in the treatment of alcohol-related mood changes. Antidepressant medications may be indicated in the case of the abstinent alcoholic with an independent major depressive episode.

DIAGNOSIS

Anxiety and Alcohol Addiction

As the data presented above indicate, there is emerging evidence that when anxiety occurs in the setting of heavy alcohol or other drug use, the course of these drug-induced disorders tends to be self-limited, in contrast to the independent major anxiety disorders themselves. Similarly, family and genetic studies of alcoholism and anxiety provide results that substantiate the independence of these disorders.

Symptoms and signs of anxiety are very common during alcohol and drug use and the acute and protracted withdrawal states following periods of alcohol and drug intake. As for depressive symptoms, if one measures the occurrence of these symptoms among recently detoxified or newly abstinent alcoholics (e.g., perhaps following 2–3 months of abstinence), almost all of these individuals will report signs and symptoms of anxiety during the months preceding detoxification.[3,16,17]

In a recent investigation of 171 male inpatients with primary alcoholism, 98% had experienced multiple symptoms of mild anxiety during withdrawal, and 80% reported shortness of breath or cardiac awareness soon after stopping drinking, including 50% with both somatic complaints.[16] However, the course of these alcohol-induced anxiety symptoms improved with abstinence and supportive and behavioral techniques alone during the month-long index hospitalization. Whereas 40% of these men scored in the 75th percentile or higher on the Spielberger State Anxiety Inventory (STAI) scale during their first week of abstinence, by week two the self-report anxiety measures returned to within the normal range for the vast majority.[18]

Similarly, at 3-months follow-up, the 41% of alcoholics who had returned to drinking were more likely to show elevated scores on the STAI, with only 5% of the abstainers scoring above the 75th percentile on this measure.[18] Thus, alcohol-induced anxiety symptoms are common during the acute and protracted withdrawal phase following drinking, but have a different course and response to treatment than do independent anxiety disorders.

Comparisons of anxiety scores and diagnoses of anxiety disorders in sons of alcoholics with scores from matched controls showed no increased prevalence of either anxiety symptoms or diagnoses in the group at high risk for alcoholism.[17] Combining this with the results of adoption and long-term follow-up studies demonstrating no firm link between anxiety and alcoholism, there is little consistent evidence to indicate a very high rate of independent anxiety disorders among alcoholics.

Anxiety and Other Drugs of Addiction

Depressant drugs (e.g., benzodiazepines, barbiturates, etc.) are likely to provide anxiety symptoms during intoxication and acute and protracted withdrawal. These drugs can provide symptoms of panic attacks and phobic symptoms. Although the majority of these signs and symptoms usually improve within the first week or two of abstinence, changes in autonomic nervous system functioning and sleep disturbances may persist in a diminished form for up to several months.[5,17]

Intoxication with stimulants (e.g., cocaine and amphetamines) can also produce marked symptoms and signs of anxiety, including feelings of nervousness, palpitations, and even frank panic attacks.[5] Individuals using these drugs may present with complaints that resemble generalized anxiety, panic, or obsessive-compulsive disorder.[5,17] However, if the anxiety developed in the setting of drug use, symptoms are likely to improve with abstinence alone.

Chronic stimulant users exhibit numerous symptoms of anxiety, usually mixed with depression, during the intoxication and withdrawal. Although the majority of these problems improve over the first 2–4 weeks, occasionally some individuals experience a more protracted course over several months.[5] Cannabinols (marijuana, hashish, etc.) and opiates (heroin and methadone) are capable of producing intense feelings of anxiety and panic-like states during acute and chronic intoxication and withdrawal.[5]

TREATMENT

When anxiety disorders are seen either before the onset of alcohol-related life problems, or during an abstinence period of 2–3 months, it is possible that the patient will have independent disorders, each of which may require treatment. But if the anxiety symptoms occur almost exclusively in the setting of alcohol or other drug intake, then it is likely that the anxiety is induced by the drugs and that it will improve with the combination of abstinence and supportive and behavioral measures, showing signs of improvement within the first 2–4 weeks.

It is important to carefully observe the patient over time and reevaluate her or his condition. With this approach, one avoids missing the possibility that the patient has two independent disorders requiring more aggressive treatment. However, at the same time, this approach decreases the probability that medications are started prematurely when the course of the disorder might show improvement with abstinence alone.

Even in individuals with an independent anxiety disorder, it is important to educate the patient that alcohol and other drug use only makes their condition worse, and that these agents are equally poor as long-term anxiolytics as they were as antidepressants. In treating patients with anxiety and addictive disorders, the mainstay of treatment rests with education, supportive therapy, and cognitive/behavioral techniques (see reference 17 for a more comprehensive discussion). Medications should be used sparingly; however, patients with independent anxiety disorders might require pharmacotherapy in addition to other forms of therapy. In addition, chronic use of benzodiazepines should be avoided. Use of antidepressants may be indicated, but their use should be reevaluated periodically, such as every 3–6 months, and discontinuation considered.

REFERENCES

1. Regier DA, Boyd JH & Burke JD, et al. (1988). One-month prevalence of mental disorders in the United States: Based on five Epidemiologic Catchment Area sites. *Arch Gen Psych* 45:977–986.
2. Helzer JE & Pryzbeck TR (1988). The co-occurrence of alcoholism with other psychiatric disorders in the general population and its impact on treatment. *J Stud Alc* 49:219–224.
3. Anthenelli RM & Schuckit MA (1993). Affective and anxiety disorders and alcohol and drug dependence: Diagnosis and treatment. *J Addict Dis.* 12(3):73–87.
4. Schuckit MA, Monteiro MG (1988). Alcoholism, anxiety and depression. *Br J Addict.* 83:1373–1380.

5. Schuckit MA (1989). *Drug and Alcohol Abuse: A Clinical Guide to Diagnosis and Treatment.* 3rd ed. New York: Plenum.

6. Goodwin DW & Guze SB (1989). *Psychiatric Diagnosis.* 4th ed. New York: Oxford University Press.

7. Schuckit MA (1985). The clinical implications of primary diagnostic groups among alcoholics. *Arch Gen Psych* 42:1043–1049.

8. Powell BJ, Read MR & Penick EC, et al. (1987). Primary and secondary depression in alcoholic men: An important distinction? *J Clin Psych* 48:98–101.

9. Rounsaville BJ, Weissman MM & Kleber H, et al. (1982). Heterogeneity of psychiatric diagnosis in treated opiate addicts. *Arch Gen Psych* 39:161–166.

10. Gawin FH & Ellinwood EH (1988). Cocaine and other stimulants: Actions, abuse, and treatment. *N Engl J Med* 318:1173–1182.

11. Schuckit MA (1986). Genetic and clinical implications of alcoholism and affective disorder. *Am J Psych* 143:140–147.

12. Anthenelli RM & Schuckit MA (1991). Alcohol and cerebral depressants. In: Glass IB (ed.), *The International Handbook of Addiction Behavior.* London: Routledge.

13. Tamerin JS, Weiner S & Mendelson JH (1970). Alcoholics' expectancies and recall of experiences during intoxication. *Am J Psych* 126:1697–1704.

14. Brown SA & Schuckit MA (1988). Changes in depression among abstinent alcoholics. *J Stud Alc* 49:412–417.

15. Gawin FH, Kleber HD & Byck R, et al. (1989). Desipramine facilitation of initial cocaine abstinence. *Arch Gen Psych* 46:117–121.

16. Schuckit MA, Irwin M & Brown SA (1990). The history of anxiety symptoms among 171 primary alcoholics. *J Stud Alc* 51:34–41.

17. Schuckit MA. (1990). Treatment of anxiety in patients who abuse alcohol and drugs. In: Noyes Jr. R, Roth M & Burrows GD, (eds.), *Handbook of Anxiety, vol. 4: The Treatment of Anxiety.* New York: Elsevier.

18. Brown SA, Irwin M & Schuckit MA (1991). Changes in anxiety among abstinent male alcoholics. *J Stud Alc* 52:55–61.

19. Weissman M (1988). Anxiety and alcoholism. *J Clin Psych* 49(10S):17–19.

20. Thevkos AK, Johnston AL & Latham PK, et al. (1991). Symptoms of anxiety in inpatient alcoholics with and without DSM-III-R anxiety disorders. *Alc Clin Exp Res* 15:102–105.

15

Psychotic Disorders

OVERVIEW

Psychotic symptoms may be: 1) induced by drug use in the absence of an independent psychotic disorder, 2) induced by drug use in the presence of independent psychotic disorder, or 3) aggravated by drugs in preexisting independent psychotic symptoms. There has been an attempt to use the primary/secondary distinction in order to establish whether the psychiatric disorder (e.g., schizophrenia) or the drug use (e.g., cocaine) existed first.[1,2] Many have largely abandoned the primary/secondary differential, stating that in the clinical forum the historical information needed to establish which came first is usually 1) unavailable; 2) unreliable; 3) does not often lead to major differential assessment or treatment of the acute patient who has active combined psychosis and substance use, especially if both have been going on for years, as is often the case; and/or 4) may have little relevance, i.e., past independent major depression is not necessarily operative in a current alcohol/drug induced depression.[3-5]

DIAGNOSIS

Alcohol and Psychosis

A number of psychiatric disorders that can be induced by alcohol are listed in DSM-III-R. They include alcohol intoxication, idiosyncratic intoxication, withdrawal delirium, hallucinosis, amnestic disorder, and dementia associated with alcoholism. However, because most comorbid patients use a variety of drugs either at the same time or serially, it is sometimes difficult to single out the cause of psychotic symptoms in such individuals. It can be difficult to distinguish alcohol hallucinosis from alcohol, marijuana, and/or cocaine intoxication.[6-8]

Alcohol is the most available addictive drug, and thus is the most common drug found in comorbid populations. Its acute and chronic effects are most often seen in the context of 1) suicide attempts, 2) acting-out behavior, such as property destruction, threats to others, etc., and 3) alcohol use in place of the patient's medication. In the last case, the person with schizophrenia or bipolar disorder may decompensate into aggravated psychosis because of consuming alcohol rather than antipsychotic medication.[7] Often, psychotic patients are admitted in an intoxicated condition and require treatment for alcohol withdrawal, confounding the diagnosis and treatment of the psychosis.

Cocaine and Psychosis

After alcohol, marijuana and cocaine are the most commonly used drugs in comorbid populations. Cocaine and other potent stimulants have long been associated with the induction of psychotic and/or paranoid symptoms.[9] However, most of these patients have also been using alcohol and often other drugs such as marijuana. In hospital settings, patients with cooccurring cocaine use and psychosis usually present in one of the following ways: 1) A brief, but aggressive drug-induced paranoid psychosis in a chronic multiple-drug addict who has been using crack and other forms of cocaine along with alcohol. These patients are admitted for being a danger to others or self and usually respond within hours or a day or two to unit structure and brief use of antipsychotic and/or benzodiazepine sedatives if needed. 2) Another common pattern is the young, often homeless, chronically psychotic person with either schizophrenia or unstable bipolar disorder, who episodically uses cocaine, alcohol, and marijuana. If such patients are able to obtain or be able to afford the use of crack for a few days, they often decompensate with an aggravation of their baseline psychotic and/or mood symptoms. In this kind of patient, three things are going on simultaneously: 1) the patient usually stops using baseline therapeutic psychiatric medications; 2) the patient's use of crack and alcohol aggravates the patient's baseline psychiatric disorder; and 3) the patient often skips appointments while in treatment.

Marijuana and Psychosis

Numerous case reports and studies indicate that cannabis can cause psychotic symptoms that last for hours or even weeks.[10] While such case studies exist, it is not general experience to see classic psychotic symptoms induced solely by cannabis. More commonly, cannabis use distorts perceptions and thoughts and exacerbates independent psychotic symptoms, or promotes medication noncompliance in patients with major psychotic disorders such as schizophrenia, bipolar disorder, or other psychiatric conditions (see below). A few pronounced cases of mania which followed heavy marijuana use have been reported.[10] A small but regular number of patients admitted for depression and suicidal overdose are chronic marijuana users. These patients have often used marijuana for 5, 10, or 20 years and over a period of time have become less and less functional in their relationships, jobs, and other activities.

Hallucinogens and Psychosis

As indicated by their very name, hallucinogens can induce psychotic symptoms. In recent years, few patients with acute psychoses due to hallucinogens are being seen. More common are 23- or 24-year-old patients with a history of heavy marijuana and hallucinogen use throughout their teenage years. These patients are admitted with a schizophrenic-like presentation, however they often have better social skills than patients with organic schizophrenia. Their symptoms may appear more "schizotypal," that is less florid and more likely "eccentric" or magical than a typical schizophrenic presentation.

Other Drugs and Psychosis

While multiple drug addicts will use virtually anything, the bulk of patients currently use alcohol, marijuana, and cocaine.[6-8] Few psychotic patients use heroin on a regular basis. It appears that for patients with chronic unstable psychoses such as schizophrenia the complex behavior requires to obtain money, obtain drugs, shoot up drugs, and repeat the cycle regularly is too difficult.

There is little evidence to show that use of opiates leads to psychotic symptoms. In methadone clinics, there are patients who manifest psychotic symptoms once their methadone dose decreases to a certain point; however these patients are not found in comorbid disorders programs.

Recently, benzodiazepines have been used increasingly in the management of psychoses and mania and it is likely that more cases will be seen of psychotic patients who have become addicted to benzodiazepines or who may use them by increasing dose, and/or combining them with other drugs of addiction.[11,12] Also, psychotic delirium can occur during benzodiazepine withdrawal.

DRUG USE MAY CONTRIBUTE

Psychoses may and do exist separately from induced symptoms from drugs of addiction. Those psychiatric disorders most commonly seen in comorbid diagnosed programs include schizophrenia, mania, depression, brief reactive psychosis, dissociative disorders, and brain damage.

Schizophrenia

Schizophreniform disorder (a schizophrenic-like condition lasting less than 6 months), schizo-affective disorder (schizophrenic-like disease with prominent mood symptoms), and schizophrenia will be discussed. Schizophrenia is characterized by a) psychotic symptoms, hallucinations, and delusions, b) disturbance of functioning in work, social relationships, etc., c) not being due to another mental disorder, and d) continuous signs of the disturbance for at least 6 months. In schizophrenia "positive" psychotic symptoms are those such as auditory hallucinations and bizarre delusions, while negative symptoms are those that involve social withdrawal, flat affect, and passivity.

Because of the relatively fragile mental status and instability of most people with schizophrenia, it is difficult to determine to what degree use of or addiction to drugs destabilizes an already unstable condition. These patients are known to use alcohol, marijuana, and cocaine frequently.[6,13–15] If such use leads to destabilization, increased psychotic symptoms, hospitalization, etc. in schizophrenics, then why do schizophrenics use drugs and alcohol? There is no evidence of self-medication. Similar questions can be asked of alcoholics who use alcohol. A schizophrenic who continues to use despite adverse consequences because of addiction is one of the key criteria for the diagnosis of addictive disorders dependence. Schizophrenics may state that they use alcohol/drugs because of hallucinations/delusions but these are post hoc rationalizations (part of addictive illness).

Despite some reports indicating that schizophrenics prefer stimulants to alcohol or vice versa, none of the research findings are so robust as to be clinically helpful for any individual clinical case.[6,13,14] Experience suggests that schizophrenics tend to use the drugs that are most readily available to them and thus environment and opportunity tend to determine use patterns. It is also rare to find patients who are "only schizophrenic" (clear evidence of established schizophrenia separate from any drug use or addiction) to be heavy users of any drug or alcohol regularly for long continuous periods of time. It appears that schizophrenics who attempt to use heavily and regularly tend to decompensate and end up in the hospital in which a forced period of abstinence occurs. Thus, most comorbid addicted schizophrenic patients have drug and alcohol histories that are variable and episodic. Drugs and alcohol are most implicated in episodes of decompensation in which patients stop taking regularly prescribed medications, stop attending psychiatric or community mental health therapy, and end up admitted in a psychotic decompensated state.[8] Even in patients who do not decompensate so profoundly it is often the use of drugs or alcohol that leads to patients missing their appointments or other responsibilities.

Because a significant part of the schizophrenic picture is abnormal and/or bizarre communication, special considerations regarding their addiction treatment are indicated.[16–19] Also, because most schizophrenics will be maintained on a psychiatric medication, special issues regarding the use of medications will also be discussed.

Mania

Core features of mania are: 1) mood elevation, 2) hyperactivity, i.e., problematic behaviors, including drug abuse, spending, and sex, and 3) delusional thinking. While these symptoms and signs may be drug induced, some manics will use alcohol/drugs as a part of their overall hyperactivity/hedonistic behavior.

Depression

Whereas depression combined with drug use is probably the most common comorbid diagnosis overall, psychotic depression combined with active drug use appears infrequently. Research on this set of disorders is lacking. In the absence of documented research, the clinical impression is that patients who have developed psychotic depressions generally cease to use drugs (including alcohol) in the same manner in which they usually decrease or stop food intake and other activities. Patients with histories of addiction who have later developed psychotic depressions exist, but there appear to be very few patients diagnosed with psychotic depression who have concurrent addictive disorders (not cocaine induced psychotic depression).

Brief Reactive Psychosis

Brief reactive psychosis is a psychosis induced by a well-defined, severe stress causing a temporary psychosis whose content usually involves some aspect of the stress. Brief reactive psychosis is a relatively rare phenomenon, and poorly studied with regard to substance use disorders.

Dissociative Disorders

Dissociative disorders and Post Traumatic Stress Disorder (PTSD) have received increasing attention in the last 10–15 years.[20] Many of the more severe dissociative conditions are found in persons who have been abused as children, and among multiproblem urban patients with significant histories of sexual and physical abuse as children.[20,21] Dissociative disorders may mimic active psychosis in certain patients.[20] Patients who complain of "voices" or thoughts of control who otherwise have nearly normal mental status examinations and who were abused as children are likely candidates for having dissociative disorders versus schizophrenia or other kinds of psychoses. Dissociative patients do not respond to neuroleptics very well and may have many other "personality" kinds of presentations such as borderline personality disorder.

Brain Damage

Organic brain damage may occur as a result of trauma, drug or alcohol ingestion, or other medical disorder. Frequently organic brain damaged patients have difficulties with cognition and impulse control, thus making rational decisions about drug use difficult. The psychotic symptoms in such a patient will often be disorganized and confused, resembling more of a delirium than a schizophrenic or manic picture. Such patients may appear to be in a state of extreme toxicity that is resistant to treatment.

REFERENCES

1. Lehman AF, Myers CP & Corty E (1989). Assessment and classification of patients with psychiatric and substance abuse syndromes. *Hosp Commun Psych* 40(10):1037–1040.
2. Shuckit M (1985). Clinical implications of primary diagnostic groups among alcoholics. *Arch Gen Psych* 42:1043–1049.
3. Wallen M & Weiner H (1988). The dually diagnosed patient in an inpatient chemical dependency treatment program. *Alcoholism Treat Q* 5(1/2):197–218.
4. Ries RK & Miller NS (1993). Dual diagnosis: concept, diagnosis, and treatment. In Dunner DL (ed.), *Current Psychiatric Therapy* pp. 131–138. Philadelphia: WB Saunders.
5. Ries RK (1993). Clinical treatment matching models for dually diagnosed patients. *Psychiatric Clinics of North America* 16(1):167–176.
6. Schneier FR & Siris SG (1987). A review of psychoactive use and abuse in schizophrenia: Patterns of drug choice. *J Nerv Ment Dis* 175(11):641–652.
7. Galanter M, Castaneda R & Ferman J (1989). Substance abuse among general psychiatric patients. *Hosp Commun Psych* 40(10):1041–1045.
8. Drake RE & Wallach MA (1989). Substance abuse among the chronic mentally ill. *Hosp and Commun Psych* 40(10):1041–1045.
9. Mirin SM & Weiss RD (1991). Substance abuse and mental illness. In: Frances RJ & Miller S (ed.), *Clinical Textbook of Addictive Disorders* pp. 282–286. New York: Guilford.
10. Tien AY & Anthony JC (1990). Epidemiological analysis of alcohol and drug use as risk factors for psychotic experiences. *J Nerv Ment Dis* 178(8):473–480.
11. Wolkowitz OM & Pickar D (1991). Benzodiazepines in the treatment of schizophrenia: A review and reappraisal. *American Journal of Psychiatry* 148(6):714–726.
12. Cohen S, Khan A & Johnson S (1987). Pharmacological management of manic psychosis in an unlocked setting. *J Clin Psychopharmacol* 7(4):261–264.
13. Dixon L, Haas G, Weiden P, Sweeney J & Frances A (1990). Acute effects

of drug abuse in schizophrenic patients: Clinical observations and patients' self-reports. *Schizo Bull* 16(1):69–79.

14. Castaneda R, Galanter M & Franco H (1989). Self-medication among addicts with primary psychiatric disorders. *Compre Psych* 30(1):80–83.

15. Brady K, Anton R, Ballenger JC, Lydiard RB, Adinoff B & Selander J (1990). Cocaine abuse among schizophrenic patients. *Am J Psych* 147(9):1164–1167.

16. Minkoff K (1989). An integrated treatment model for dual diagnosis of psychosis and addiction. *Hosp Commun Psych* 40(10):1031–1036.

17. Osher FC & Kofoed LL (1989). Treatment of patients with psychiatric and psychoactive substance abuse disorders. *Hosp Commun Psych* 40(10):1025–1030.

18. Evans K & Sullivan JM (1990). *Dual Diagnosis: Counseling the Mentally Ill Substance Abuser.* New York: Guilford.

19. O'Connell DF (1990). Managing the dually diagnosed patient. In: O'Connell DF (ed.), *Current Issues and Clinical Approaches.* New York: Haworth Press.

20. Kluft RP (1987). First-rank symptoms as a diagnostic clue to multiple personality disorder. *Am J Psych* 144(3):293–298.

21. Brown GR & Anderson B (1991). Psychiatric morbidity in adult inpatients with childhood histories of sexual and physical abuse. *Am J Psych* 148(1):55–61.

16

Personality Disorders

OVERVIEW

The role of personality disorders in addictive disorders is often debated. The question of which came first—the alcohol and other drug addiction or the personality disorder—is confounded by the limitations in studying personality. A longitudinal perspective is mandatory but obviously difficult to achieve, and instruments used to assess personality have their respective drawbacks.[1]

What we do know from a longitudinal study over decades by Vaillant is that personality does not predict the onset of alcoholism. We know that MMPI profiles do not predict who will become an alcoholic or drug addict, and that there is no "addictive personality" prior to the onset of addiction to alcohol and other drugs. We also know that of the total sphere of people addicted to alcohol and other drugs, no single personality type is representative prior to the onset of addiction. However, certain personality types appear to have disproportionately high rates of addiction, namely antisocial and borderline personality disorders.[2,3]

Clinical and epidemiological studies show that personality disturbances are associated with the addictive use of alcohol and other drugs.[4,5] The personality characteristics most representative of an acquired "addictive personality" are narcissistic, antisocial, and histrionic. These personality types appear to achieve dominance in what is described otherwise as a self-centered, egocentric, willful, immature, and grandiose individual.[6,7]

Typically, as with people with personality disorders, they do not accept responsibility for their state. They attribute blame to others for shortcomings and wrongdoings. They see themselves more as victims than as contributors or originators of their problems.[8,9]

Perhaps most importantly, the treatment of addictive disorders, including abstinence, will often result in an improvement in personality, no matter what the type.[12,13] A dramatic reversal of narcissistic, antisocial, and histrionic states will be seen. Addicted people will accept responsibility for their addiction and other aspects of their personality and lifestyle. They become less self-centered and blaming of others for their problems. They develop a more realistic appraisal of their assets and liabilities. The process of change in their personality begins with initially becoming honest with themselves and others.

Role of Personality

Historically, the concept of the "addictive personality" has proven elusive, though this concept has now reappeared as the "self-medication hypothesis."[10] While researchers have underplayed the relevance of personality in drug and alcohol addiction, personality factors actually dominate treatment planning conferences and patient-progress reviews. Thus, clinicians have not abandoned the role of personality in addiction treatment, simply because of the clinical utility such an approach brings to the treatment process.[10]

INTERACTIONS

"Addictive Personality"

It is now clear that there is no "addictive personality." No individual trait or cluster of traits predispose an individual to become addicted before being exposed to drugs/alcohol. There are studies that do find certain traits commonly seen among drug addicts,[1-3] but they fail to substantiate or replicate a consistent pattern of traits among all addicts. Also of significant methodological importance is that our research in this area has been done after the individual has become addicted. Thus, addict traits in personality appear to be acquired from using drugs and alcohol rather than a predisposition to use.

The concept of the "addictive personality" seems to have evolved into a more contemporary version popularly known as the "self-medication hypothesis." This concept has actually been around for some time,[8-10] but has more recently been popularized.[10,11] The theory asserts that addicted persons are predisposed to addiction because they suffer painful affective states associated with underlying psychiatric disorders. The "selection" of stimulant or depressant drugs is not random, not based on social network considerations, not simply based on mere availability, and not due to drug trends. Rather, it is due to a pharmacodynamic interaction between drug of choice and underlying affect.[10]

While many drugs may be tried, the drug that is finally selected is done so unconsciously, based on the drug's ability to manage specific painful affects. Stimulants and cocaine are used, so the theory says, because they have the ability to relieve depression and dysphoria. Heroin and narcotics are selected because they have the ability to manage the affects of anger, rage and aggression.[14,15] Arguments to support this theory generally are based on case reports from psychoanalysts, and from studies of psychiatric comorbidities among substance abusers that report an increased prevalence of anxiety disorders, depression, and dysthymia, and antisocial, narcissistic and passive–aggressive personality disorders.[13-22]

Evidence against the "addiction personality" is convincing.[16] There are many patients who are addicted to both opiates and cocaine, or both alcohol and cocaine. The simultaneous addiction of drugs that are both stimulants and depressants is not easily explained by the theory. The theory proposes a predisposition of underlying affects that are satisfied and managed by the respective drug, but then uses as supporting evidence for the theory psychological states and disorders that may have appeared *as a consequence of* drug use. These theorists have not offered any evidence that these psychic states are not due to induced drug effects. Empirical research is at variance with the self-medication hypothesis. The theory postulates that heroin addicts would be more alike in personality structure than cocaine addicts. Studies show that there is little difference between these addict groups, and that they are more alike in personality manifestation than they are different.[1,28,29]

Finally, this theory would postulate that the successful treatment of the underlying psychiatric condition implies eventual cessation of addiction. This has yet to be demonstrated in controlled, clinical trials. In short, adherents of this theory support it in the absence of confirming scientific evidence.

The concept of an addictive personality and the self-medication hypothesis, which stress a central role for underlying personality factors in the development of addiction, are perhaps the two most well-known theories that implicate personality, but they are by no means the only ones. Actually, there have been several published works on psychodynamic theory and personality functioning to explain addiction.[2,10,11,22,23] These theories often use a paradigm that is psychoanalytically derived or psychoanalytically based. Most of these formulations consider addiction as an attempt to deal with intense, repressed depression relating to feelings of perceived infantile deprivation by seeking either some type of symbiotic experience, or by seeking relief from excessively punitive parental standards that create feelings of inadequacy and worthlessness. Addicts prefer to withdraw from these painful states and from the stress of interpersonal relationships into drug-induced grandiosity, omnipotence and a narcissistic relational style.[24] Addiction has been theorized to represent pathological mourning from intrapersonal and narcissistic losses.[25] Chemical abuse retards the completion of the normal mourning process. Successful therapeutic intervention, from this perspective, would require the addict to complete the stages of grieving. Others have theorized that addicts are characterized by excessive needs for power combined with low inhibition, and some empirical support has been found for this position.[23,24] These theories have proliferated because no single theory can account for all known facts, and because the actual etiology of addiction remains a matter of theory.[17,18]

DIAGNOSIS

Antisocial Personality Disorder (ASP)

The antisocial personality is one of the most common personality disorders seen in alcoholics and addicts.[26,27] This is a lifetime diagnosis and, as defined by the DSM, cannot be made unless the individual has demonstrated antisocial behavior before the age of 15. Yet even this diagnosis can change over time.[3] Another researcher emphasized the importance of dividing ASP's into a primary and secondary group.[28] The primary group has the underlying ASP disorder as a result of genetic and early childhood experiences. The secondary group manifests antisocial behavior as a result of drug use, or fears of loss, or narcissistic injury, but does not have the underlying personality disorder.

The primary group has three major underlying personality defects, e.g., the inability to 1) empathize, 2) experience guilt, or 3) develop meaningful relationships. Obviously they would have a poorer prognosis in therapy than the secondary group.

These characteristics are well described in DSM-III-R and should also be present in DSM-IV. Before the age of 15, people with ASP are often truant, run away, fight frequently (often with weapons), are physically cruel to people and animals, destroy property (for example, through arson), have early sexual experiences (including use of force), lie often, steal with or without physical confrontation, and abuse drugs or alcohol. Some of these behaviors will be highly rewarded by peers so that these preantisocial youths may receive a great deal of acclaim.

Some behaviors such as drug addiction, charming ingratiation, ability as a fighter, early sexual prowess, getting away with forbidden pleasures and defiance of authority can bring great popularity to youths in most cultures so that their potentially self-destructive behaviors are minimized or overlooked.[26]

They may have distinguished themselves either through a military act requiring emotional self-control and/or bravery or the ability to perform a single or brief series of acts of brilliance not requiring follow-through. People with ASP readily rationalize their behavior based on past injustices done to them or the idea that everyone else gets away with worse travesties of society, e.g., under the guise of big business or government intervention. At times the projective focus can seem quite paranoid and immutable to psychotherapy.

Their motivation may range from straight financial gain to the bizarre (one severely disturbed ASP patient of mine fondled the money wrappers of cash he stole from banks just before intercourse to enhance his sexual potency). Because of their inability to incorporate the existence of future consequences, they have difficulty postponing gratification, and thus punishment is often not an effective deterrent. People with ASP and addiction generally avoid violent crimes to get their drugs unless they do not have successful con games or are neurophysiologically overactivated by stimulants—cocaine, particularly smokable "crack," amphetamines, particularly smokable "ice"—or withdrawal from sedatives. Vaillant[26] emphasizes that in outpatient settings, people with ASP commonly lack anxiety, depression, and motivation. However, when appropriate limits are set in residential environments, people with ASP begin to manifest depression and anxiety and become more motivated.

As adults, people with ASP may be sufficiently cunning so that even the most experienced therapist can be fooled initially, particularly without information from relatives, friends, or authorities. The therapist may be conned and enthralled or, on the other hand, disgusted. Competitiveness or fear is more likely to be seen in the same-sex clinician.

The psychotherapy of antisocial personality disorders cannot begin until firm limits are set. Patients can rapidly terminate a therapeutic relationship that feels too intense, or if the therapist demands the implementation of limits that they feel they cannot follow. Thus, limits often must be reinforced by external factors such as threat of loss of job, loss of income, conservatorship or loss of family (not effective with more damaged people with ASP unless they are materially dependent), or threat of incarceration. Often these controls are best implemented by persons other than the therapist. When enforcing the controls is mainly the therapist's responsibility, the patient may experience the controls as being too punitive to be therapeutic.[25,28,29]

The behavior of the person with ASP must also be controlled in order to prevent self-destruction and to provide a contained environment that does not facilitate flight from therapeutic intimacy. Yet it is often critical to separate control from punishment. Most often the therapy of the person with ASP needs to begin in a totally controlled environment, such as a residential treatment community, long-term hospital, or flexible penal institution. This is because sufficient limits can only take place in these types of controlled settings.[28,29]

At times a less restrictive environment, such as a comprehensive 20–40 hours a week outpatient program, can provide sufficient control and stabilization. Some people with ASP who successfully work a 12-step program do so with the zeal of religious conversion. Other comprehensive long-term outpatient environments and/or intensive 12-step programs (AA, CA) when participated in fully, can accomplish similar stabilization. These approaches have the advantage of not limiting the psychotherapy to one person or one hour per day, but rather provide structure and psychotherapy for up to 24 hours daily.[28,29]

The therapist may share his or her own anxiety, particularly as it relates to this patient or his or her projective identifications, but only after a therapeutic alliance has been established.

Once limits have been set and most manipulative defenses removed, the nurturing, reparenting part of the therapy can take hold. New, more adaptive defenses and coping mechanisms are gradually taught and practiced.

Identification with healthy role models gradually takes place and peer group support reinforces new skills and identifications. Practicing helping others (step 12 of AA), jobs and therapeutic roles of long-term members of therapeutic communities are also critical to developing healthier egos and building self esteem.[28,29]

Many of the above therapeutic techniques are appropriate and indicated for narcissistic and borderline personalities who have severe personality pathology, particularly those who act out. Thus, these will not be repeated but differences will be emphasized.[28,29]

Narcissistic Personality Disorder (NPD)

Individuals with NPD present with grandiosity, extreme self-involvement, and a lack of interest in and empathy with others.[30] However, they pursue others for admiration and approval. They seek perfection, wealth, glory, power and beauty, and seek others who will admire their grandiose achievements in a mirroring way.

They may function at three different levels ranging from 1) effective functioning, with neurotic problems (the phallic narcissistic character), 2) to severe object-relation difficulties, to 3) borderline functioning with weak ego strength.[30]

Other common NPD traits are emphasized, including excessive self-absorption, intense ambition, grandiosity, and inordinate need for tribute from others.[30] Underneath these compensations is an emotional shallowness, defective empathy, and inability to tolerate mourning and sadness when faced with loss.

Clinically, addicted people with narcissism may present as one of five types: 1) self-absorption in the physical aspects of addiction, such as withdrawal symptoms and related somatic disorders; 2) manipulative and antisocial but in a grandiose way; 3) needy, clinging, and demanding; 4) phallic–narcissistic (the latter is seen in flashy, wealthy cocaine addicts whose wealth may be inherited, obtained from selling large quantities of cocaine or who are extremely successful in legitimate business yet need to use cocaine to drive themselves even harder to achieve more and more); and 5) closet narcissists who present themselves as timid, shy and ineffective but who reveal themselves later in therapy as having a richly grandiose fantasy life. These fantasies may also be acted out during intoxications, particularly on stimulants. Thus they often present with other "codependent" relationships.

Addicted people with NPD expect to be noticed as special. They feel their problems are unique and would be appreciated if only they could find the right person to understand and mirror them. They feel justified in exploiting others to meet their needs and alleviate their frustrations (DSM-III-R). Since all addicted people in an intense state of addiction or withdrawal will demonstrate many of the narcissistic behaviors described above, it is important to take a careful history of prior behavior, particularly receiving and giving empathy, and to observe the patient over time after withdrawal is complete. DSM-III-R notes that many features of the other disorders in this cluster are often present (histrionic, borderline, and antisocial) and multiple diagnoses may be warranted.

Eventually the NPD drives everyone away who can provide gratification, or devalues those who remain. This real-life emptiness reinforces their empty internal world, which is devoid of positive object relations, and leads to their experiencing their internal void. They then desperately attempt to fill up the emptiness by gaining endless admiration from others and by controlling others to avoid feeling envy[31] for their successes.

Borderline Personality Disorder (BPD)

Borderline personality is often considered as a problem related to personality organization rather than a true disorder. Thus people with BPD may present a rather broad range of maladaptive behavior on "general dimensions of impulsivity, affect turbulence, and inconsistent self-representations."[32] Borderline personality organization includes most infantile, narcissistic personalities, schizoid, paranoid, and hypomanic personalities and all antisocial personalities.[21]

These patients share the use of primitive defenses such as splitting, denial, projective identification and omnipotent idealization. They also manifest an unstable self-identity and impaired reality testing, based to some extent on field dependence.

Thus, BPD is most often seen in association with other concurrent personality disorders. There is good evidence that many alcoholics/drug addicts who are diagnosed as borderline are really "pseudoborderline." This occurs because characteristics inherent in alcohol/drug abusers such as 1) unstable and intense interpersonal relationships, 2) inappropriate, intense, out-of-control anger, 3) affective instability, and 4) physically self-damaging acts, when combined with alcohol/drug abuse, will achieve the five criteria necessary to diagnose BPD.[33]

This will occur even in the absence of such basic BPD characteristics as identity disturbance, intolerance of being alone, and chronic feelings of emptiness or boredom.

DSM-III-R emphasizes a "pervasive pattern of instability of self-image, interpersonal relationships and mood." The comorbidity of BPD with other personality disorders has been discussed previously. However, brief psychotic episodes and major depression are also both quite common, particularly in reaction to drugs of abuse.

Often the person with NPD is viewed as having a similar, disturbed, underlying core but is able to present a cohesive, grandiose self that hides the inner identity diffusion. It has been noted that there is a commonality of narcissistic traits in borderline patients, e.g., envy, attention seeking, exploitativeness, oversensitivity to criticism, and preoccupation with compensatory fantasies of power and success. These are basically sufficient to diagnose most borderlines as narcissists as well, yet the two present quite differently.

REFERENCES

1. Craig RJ (1988). A psychometric study of the prevalence of DSM-III personality disorders among treated opiate addicts. *Intern J Addict* 23(2):115–124.
2. Rounsaville BJ, Weissman MB & Kleber HD, et al. (1982). Heterogeneity of psychiatric diagnosis in treated opiate addicts. *Arch Gen Psych* 39:161–166.
3. Kosten TR, Rounsaville BJ & Kleber HD (1982). DSM-III personality disorders in opiate addicts *R. Comp Psych* 23:572–591.
4. Meyer RE (1986). How to Understand the Relationship between Psychopathology and Addictive Disorders. In: Meyer RE (ed.), *Psychopathology and Addictive Disorders,* pp. 3–16. New York: Guilford.
5. Helzer JE & Pryzbeck TR (1988). The co-occurrence of alcoholism with other psychiatric disorders in the general population and its impact on treatment. *J Stud Alc* 49(3):219–224.
6. Nace EP (1989). Personality disorder in the alcoholic patient. *Psych Ann* 191(5):256–260.
7. Koenigsberg HW, Kaplan RD & Gilmore MM, et al. (1985). The relationship between syndrome and personality disorder in DSM-III: Experience with 2,462 patients. *Am J Psych* 142:207–212.
8. Khantzian EJ & Treece C (1985). DSM-III Psychiatric Diagnosis of Narcotic Addicts. *Arch Gen Psych* 42:1067–1071.

9. Kleinman PH, Miller AB & Millman RB (1990). Psychopathology among Cocaine Abusers Entering Treatment. *J Nerv Ment Dis* 178:442–447.

10. Khantzian E (1985). The self medication hypothesis of addictive disorders: Focus on heroin and cocaine dependence. *Am J Psych* 142:1259–1264.

11. Weiss RD & Mirin SM (1986). Subtypes of cocaine abusers. *Psych Clin N Am* 9(3):491–501.

12. Griffin MC, Weiss RD, Mirin SM & Lange V (1989). A comparison of male and female cocaine abusers. *Arch Gen Psych* 46:122–126.

13. Hesselbrock MN, Meyer RE & Keener JJ (1985). Psychopathology in Hospitalized Alcoholics. *Arch Gen Psych* 42:1050–1055.

14. Kosten TR & Rounsaville BJ (1986). Psychopathology in Opioid Addicts. *Psych Clin N Am* 9(3):515–532.

15. Widiger TA & Rogers JH (1989). Prevalence and comorbidity of personality disorders. *Psych Ann* 19(3):132–136.

16. Oldham JM & Skodol AE (1991). Personality disorders in the public sector. *Hosp Commun Psych* 42(5):481–387.

17. Stone MH (1980). *The Borderline Syndrome.* New York: McGraw Hill.

18. *Diagnosis and Statistical Manual of Mental Disorders.* 3rd ed., rev. (1987). Washington, DC: American Psychiatric Association.

19. Kernberg O (1975). *Borderline Conditions and Pathological Narcissism.* New York: Aronson.

20. Cadoret RJ, Troughton E & Widner RB (1984). Clinical differences between antisocial and primary alcoholics. *Compre Psych* 25:1–8.

21. Goldsmith SJ, Jacobsberg LB & Bell R (1989). Personality Disorder Assessment. *Psych Ann* 19:139–142.

22. Millon T (1981). *Disorders of Personality, DSM III.* New York: Wiley.

23. Freeman PS & Gunderson J (1989). Treatment of personality disorders. *Psych Ann* 19(3):147–153.

24. Gerstely L, McLellan T & Alterman AI, et al. (1900). Ability to form an alliance with the therapist: A possible marker of prognosis for patients with antisocial personality disorder. *Am J Psych* 164(4):508–512.

25. Woody GE, McLellan AT & Luborsky L, et al. (1984). Sociopathy and psychotherapy outcome. *Arch Gen Psych* 42:1081–1086.

26. Vaillant GE (1975). Sociopathy is a human process: A viewpoint. *Arch Gen Psych* 32:178–188.

27. Glueck S & Glueck E (1970). *Toward a Typology of Juvenile Offenders.* New York: Grune & Stratton.

28. Kaufman E (1989). The psychotherapy of dually diagnosed patients. *J Subst Abuse Treat* 6:9–18.

29. Kaufman E & Remx J (1988). Guidelines for the successful psychotherapy of substance abusers. *Am J Drug & Alc Abuse* 14:199–209.

30. Kernberg OF (1989). An ego psychology object relations theory of structure

and treatment of pathologic narcissism. In: Kernberg OF (ed.), *The Psychiatric Clinics of North America.* Philadelphia: Saunders.

31. Hurt SW & Clarkin JF (1990). Borderline personality disorder prototypic typology and the development of therapy manuals. *Psych Ann* 20(1):13–18.

32. Stone MH (1989). Long term follow-up of narcissistic/borderline patients. *Psych Clin N Am* 12(3):621–651.

33. McGlashan TH & Heinssen RK. Narcissistic, antisocial and non-comorbid subgroups, 653–670.

17

Neuropsychopharmacology of Abstinence

OVERVIEW

It is often assumed that once the user of a drug ceases self-administration, all effects of the drug diminish and resolve within hours to days. In fact, there is a growing body of clinical evidence suggesting that some effects caused by alcohol and other drugs may persist for months and sometimes years beyond the immediate effects of intoxication and acute withdrawal.[1-8]

Various terms have been used to describe these persistent effects, such as protracted abstinence, subacute withdrawal, and prolonged effects of alcohol and other drugs. The commonality through all the states is that despite abstinence, effects directly or indirectly related to the intoxication continue to be observable and have a bearing on the clinical course and treatment management.[9-11]

The reasons for the symptoms during the initial stages of recovery are many and varied and include: 1) manifestations of end-organ damage; 2) persistent changes in receptor-mediated function; 3) the prolonged presence of the drug in storage sites in the body; 4) the influence of conflict created by the addictive behaviors; and 5) personality skills and maturity.[1,12-17]

INTERACTIONS

The end-organ damage from alcohol and other drugs occurs throughout the body. The brain is especially vulnerable to the effects of drugs such as alcohol. Studies show that cerebral atrophy with a decrease in volume of brain matter and an increase in ventricular size is present in chronic alcoholics. These changes reflect some yet to be identified pathological process that may include actual neuronal dropout, neural fiber degeneration or astrocytic death, or a combination of these that lead to reduced brain volume.[18]

In several studies, the cerebral atrophy, as measured by computerized tomography (CT), was reversed over months of abstinence in many of the chronic alcoholics studied. The brain matter volume returned and the ventricular size diminished. These findings have been correlated with changes in IQ in some studies. The IQ function of alcoholics of all ages were reduced, particularly in those that showed cerebral atrophy. Both the IQ improved and the cerebral atrophy resolved over months of abstinence.[18]

Many investigators have demonstrated lowered IQ in chronic alcoholics. It is a well-established clinical observation that the cognitive deficits of the actively drinking alcoholic improve with abstinence. These cognitive defects are global and represent a dementia syndrome in which memory, attention and concentration, cognitive and other measures of higher cortical function are reduced. All of these changes improve with abstinence over time, and in some studies improvement is noted as long as two years or longer postcessation of alcohol consumption.[19]

Other studies have shown that chronic alcohol intake produces measurable central nervous system changes that persist long after alcohol is withdrawn. These changes are in the form of neural hyperexcitability, most marked in the reticular formation, hippocampus, and frontal and parietal cortex. Following induced alcohol dependence in rats, abnormal locomotor and REM sleep patterns persisted after six months of abstinence from alcohol. In another study, nearly half of acutely abstinent alcoholics revealed increased metabolites of noradrenergic release as measured by increased levels of 3-methoxy-4-hydroxyphenyl-glycol (MHPG) in the cerebrospinal fluid. These increased levels of MHPG declined over several weeks of abstinence and correlated with a diminution of clinical symptoms of irritability and grandiosity and changes in auditory evoked potentials.[20–22]

Cannabis (marijuana) intoxication has been shown in monkeys to produce persistent changes in electrical activity and brain size. Recorded activity by septal electrodes persisted many months after the monkey smoked the equivalent of three marijuana cigarettes a day. Ventricular enlargement with reduction in brain volume was found in monkeys administered daily THC for 5 years. In humans, abrupt discontinuation of marijuana is followed by irritability, restlessness, hypotension, tachycardia, anxiety, depression, insomnia that may persist for months after abstinence.[23-25]

Examples of possible receptor changes and persistence of drugs in storage sites in the body are available, particularly with lipid-soluble drugs such as cannabis and benzodiazepines. Studies have shown that metabolites of THC may be found in the urine months after cessation of use. Also, in animal studies, one injection of THC in the peritoneal cavity of a naive rat resulted in the detection of cannabis in the fat stores two months later.

Anecdotal clinical reports commonly report that human chronic marijuana users will experience a "rush" or "high" months after a dose of marijuana, particularly during exercise or following a diet with weight loss and mobilization of fat stores. It appears that THC may be released slowly over time, as it is known that there is constant turnover of fat stores.[25]

The storage phenomenon may also be true for benzodiazepines. Clinical studies have demonstrated that benzodiazepines may be detected in the urine months after discontinuation of use. Benzodiazepines, like THC, are highly lipid soluble. There is considerable evidence that a severe, protracted benzodiazepine withdrawal may persist for months and years after last use. The symptoms are anxiety, depression, tinnitus, involuntary movements, paresthesia, hypersensitivity to sensory stimuli, perceptual distortions, tremors, headaches, irritability, anhedonia, lack of energy, impaired concentration, derealization, and depersonalization. These symptoms diminish imperceptibly in the individual and can be difficult to tolerate, however, they do eventually subside.[26,27]

Mood disturbances in alcoholics and drug addicts, including those using benzodiazepines, stimulants, and opiates, may persist for months after cessation of use. A small proportion of alcoholics and stimulant and benzodiazepine users will show persistent depression with lowered mood, anhedonia, and sleep disturbances. Also, anxiety and a lack of motivation and mood modulation are evident for months and years in these alcohol and drug users. However, substantial improvement in mood occurs in the first year or two.[28,29]

The bases of these persistent drug effects during abstinence may reflect changes in receptor structure and function. Chronic stimulation by the agonist drugs leads to up- and down-regulation, with changes in receptor numbers and subsequent hypersensitivity and hyposensitivity of post-synaptic receptors. The actual changes induced by the drugs depend on the neurochemical mechanism of action. Chronic cocaine administration results in a presynaptic dopamine depletion and a postsynaptic hypersensitivity whereas chronic opiate administration leads to a reduced receptor response to opiates and, perhaps, a reduction in the endogenous ligand.[30,31]

Studies have not clearly demonstrated how long these persistent effects of drug in storage sites and receptor changes last, and how closely they correlate with clinical symptoms in the abstinent state. More studies, particularly in humans, need to confirm these preliminary results that show a protracted drug effect during abstinence.[32,33]

A study that illustrates these persistent effects investigated psychiatric symptomatology over 10 years in a sample of alcoholics drawn from Alcoholics Anonymous. The study found on measures of severity of psychopathology that there was overall lessening of these measures in the 312 subjects studied over the 10-year period. The initial scores for those alcoholics abstinent less than 6 months showed an extreme severity comparable to only 2.5% of the population. The results after 10 years of abstinence approximated the general population. The recovered alcoholics resembled the norms for the population on most measures.[1]

The items relating to CNS hyperexcitability, such as restlessness and disturbances in sleep, depression, and interpersonal sensitivity, anxiety and obsessive–compulsive symptoms, are common in early abstinence, but are diminished or extinguished over time, whereas memory problems also improve but remain above population norms after 10 years of abstinence.[28,29]

TREATMENT

Time is the essential factor in treatment of these drug-induced persistent effects. In some ways, these troublesome symptoms can serve as reminders of the drug-induced effects and motivate the drug user to continue to abstain from alcohol and drugs.

Persisting symptoms such as anxiety and depression can serve as strong motivators for involvement in a treatment strategy such as the twelve-step self-help programs of Alcoholics Anonymous. The alcoholic or drug addict may be more apt to take the necessary actions to abstain from these drugs and make the necessary changes in attitude and lifestyle if the individual's present state is not a comfortable one.[34] However, there are times when the severity of the symptoms may be too overwhelming for the alcoholic or drug addict to abstain, i.e., intense anxiety, depression, or insomnia. The judicious use of antidepressants and antipsychotic medications may be useful in these instances. As a rule of thumb, if the symptoms persist for more than a few weeks and significantly interfere with function or jeopardize abstinence, or are incapacitating from the onset of abstinence, these medications may be instituted.[35–37] The doses must be titrated but generally are similar to those used for other disorders that are nondrug-related depressions. The duration of use is also similar in that they can be tapered and discontinued after 6 months to observe if the drug effects have subsided.

It is important to note that antidepressants and antipsychotic medications also have withdrawal syndromes that are similar to other drugs; this must be considered if symptoms are still present. The withdrawal syndromes from antidepressants and antipsychotics include anxiety, depression, insomnia, malaise, and other manifestations.[38,39]

Because the typical alcoholic and drug addict in current clinical populations is addicted to and dependent on multiple drugs and alcohol simultaneously and concurrently, the withdrawal syndrome will be influenced accordingly. Studies show that alcohol addiction in multiple-drug-addicted alcoholics is more severe than in those not addicted to drugs, and the withdrawal may be as well. It is important to recognize that the abstinence period may be marked by multiple-drug effects.

The treatment of multiple-drug addiction is similar to that of the single-drug addiction. The symptoms of anxiety, depression, insomnia and others are nonspecific manifestations of drug effects on the brain. The same principles apply in the use of medications for multiple-drug effects as with the single drugs.[1]

It is also important to bear in mind that the alcoholic or drug addict has a vulnerability to drug effects from any origin, whether a drug of addiction or medication. The drug effect is nonspecific and may impair the alcoholic's or drug addict's ability to think clearly and experience changes in the psychodynamic and affective states that are critical to recovery. Also, the same loss of control over addictive drug and alcohol use extends to medications. Reports are available that suggest that several medications may be used with loss of control by addicts, such as anticholinergics, clonidine, monoamine oxidase inhibitors, naltrexone, and others.[33] The clinician must exert control for the addicted patient, and always be alert to evidence of compulsion, drug hunger, drug-seeking behavior, and changes of thinking and behavior that may represent relapse or prerelapse problems.[1]

REFERENCES

1. Geller A (1991). A protracted abstinence. In Miller NS (ed.), *Comprehensive Handbook of Drug and Alcohol Addiction,* pp. 905–914. New York: Marcel Dekker.
2. Hidrosis CK (1942). Clinical studies of drug addiction. *Arch Int Med* 69:766–772.
3. Kay DC (1975). Human sleep and EEG through a cycle of methadone dependence. *Electroenceph Clin Neurophysiol* 38:35–43.
4. Kissin B, Schenker V & Schenker A (1959). The acute effects of ethyl alcohol and chlorpromazine on certain physiological functions in alcoholics. *Q J Stud Alc* 20:481–493.
5. Begleiter H & Porjesz B (1977). Persistence of brain hyperexcitability following chronic alcohol exposure in rats. *Adv Exp Med Biol* 85B:209–222.
6. Gitlow SE, Dziedzic SW & Dziedzic LM (1977). Tolerance to ethanol after prolonged abstinence. *Adv Exp Med Biol* 85A:511–591.
7. Begleiter H, Denoble V & Porjesz B (1980). Protracted brain dysfunction after alcohol withdrawal in monkeys. In H Begleiter (ed.), *Biological Effects of Alcohol,* pp. 231–249. New York: Plenum.
8. Begleiter H & Porjesz B (1979). Persistence of a subacute withdrawal system following ethanol intake. *Drug Alc Depend* 4:353–357.
9. Khan A, Ciranlo DA & Nelson WH (1984). Dexamethasone suppression test in recently detoxified alcoholics. *J Clin Psychopharm* 4:94–97.
10. Brown SA & Schuckit MA (1988). Changes in depression among abstinent alcoholics. *J Stud Alc* 49:412–417.
11. Snyder S & Karacan I (1985). Sleep patterns of sober chronic alcoholics. *Neuropsychobiol* 13:97–100.
12. Smith DE & Wesson DR (1983). Benzodiazepine dependency syndromes. *J Psychoact Drugs* 15:85–89.
13. Busto V, Fornazzari L & Naranjo CA (1988). Protracted tinnitus after discontinuation of long-term therapeutic use of benzodiazepines. *J Clin Psychopharm* 8:359–362.

14. Golombok S, Moodley P & Lader M (1988). Cognitive impairment in long term benzodiazepine users. *Psychol Med* 18:365–374.

15. Ricaurte GA, Schuster CR & Seiden IS (1980). Long-term effects of repeated methylamphetamine administration on dopamine and serotonin neurons in the rat brain. *Brain Res* 193:153–163.

16. Ricuarte GA, Bryan D & Strauss L, et al. (1985). Hallucinogenic amphetamine selectively destroys brain serotonin nerve terminals. *Science* 229:986–988.

17. Cala LA & Mastaglia FL (1981). Computerized tomography in chronic alcoholics. *Alcoholism: Clin & Exp Res* 5(2).

18. Parsons DA & Leber WR (1981). The relationship between cognitive dysfunction and brain damage in alcoholics: Causation or epiphirnomendal. *Clin & Exp Res* 5(2):326–343.

19. Bonnet MH (1985). Effects of sleep disruption on sleep, performance and mood. *Sleep* 8:11–19.

20. Borg S, Kvande H & Sedvall G (1981). Central norepinephrine metabolism during alcohol intoxication in addicts and healthy volunteers. *Science* 213:1135–1137.

21. Alling C, Balldin J & Bokstrom K, et al. (1982). Studies on duration of a late recovery period after chronic abuse of ethanol. *Acta Psych Scand* 66:384–397.

22. Jones RT (1983). Cannabis and health. *Am Rev Med* 34:247–258.

23. McGraham JP, Dublin AB & Sassenrath E (1984). Long-term 9-tetra-hydro-cannabinol treatment: Computed tomography of the brains of rhesus monkeys. *Am J Dis Child* 138:1109–1112.

24. Heath RA, Fitzjarrell AT & Garey RE, et al. (1979). Chronic marijuana smoking: Its effects on function and structure of the primate brain. In: Nahas GC, Patton WDM (eds.), *Marijuana: Biological Effects.* New York: Plenum.

25. Ashton H (1984). Benzodiazepine withdrawal: An unfinished story. *Br Med J* 288:1135–1140.

26. Ashton H (1986). Adverse effects of prolonged benzodiazepine use. *Adverse Drug Reaction Bulletin* 118:440–443.

27. DeSoto CB, O'Donnell WE & Alfred LJ, et al. (1985). Symptomatology in alcoholics at various stages of abstinence. *Alcoholism Clin Exp Res* 9:505–512.

28. DeSoto CB, O'Donnell WE & DeSoto JL (1989). Long-term recovery in alcoholics. *Alcoholism Clin Exp Res* 13:693–697.

29. Elinwood EH (1974). The epidemiology of stimulant use. In: Josephson F, Carroll E (eds.), *Drug Use: Epidemiology and Sociological Approaches,* pp. 303–309. Washington, DC: Hemisphere.

30. Gawin FH & Kleber HD (1986). Abstinence symptomatology and psychiatric diagnoses in cocaine abusers. *Arch Gen Psych* 43:107–113.

31. Wikler A (1948). Recent progress in research on the neurophysiological basis of morphine addiction. *Am J Psych* 105:328–338.

32. Dole VP (1988). Implications of methadone maintenance for theories of narcotics addiction. *J Amer Med Assoc* 260:3025–3029.

33. Miller NS (1987). A primer of the treatment process for alcoholism and drug addiction. *Psych Lett* 5(7):30–37.

34. Garwin FH, Kleber HD & Byck R, et al. (1989). Desipramine facilitation of initial cocaine abstinence. *Arch Gen Psych* 46:117–121.

35. Weiss RD (1988). Relapse to cocaine abuse after initiating desipramine treatment. *J Amer Med Assoc* 260:2545–2546.

36. Little HJ, Dolin S & Halsey MJ (1986). Calcium channel antagonists decrease ethanol withdrawal syndrome. *Life Sci* 39:2059–2065.

37. Charney DS, Heninger GR & Sternberg DE, et al. (1982). Abrupt discontinuation of tricyclic antidepressant drugs: Evidence for noradrenergic hyperactivity. *Brit J Psych* 141:377–386.

38. Overall JE, Reilly EL & Kelley JT, et al. (1985). Persistence of depression in detoxified alcoholics. *Alc Clin Exp Res* 9(4):331–333.

39. Higgit AC, Lader MH & Fonagy P (1985). Clinical management of benzodiazepine dependence. *Br Med J* 291:688–790.

PART VI

Treatment Approaches

18

Abstinence-Based Treatment

OVERVIEW

The history of addiction treatment as generally practiced has not been well recorded in the psychological and medical literature. There is a striking dichotomy between actual clinical methods and experimental investigations. The former have determined the standards for trends in clinical practice while the latter have generated the majority of controlled studies in the literature. While there are multiple explanations for the lack of documentation of addiction treatment as practiced, the most compelling is that the contemporary treatment of alcohol and drug disorders, with few notable exceptions, has developed outside of mainstream medicine, psychiatry, and psychology. The exceptions pertain to pharmacological treatments of alcohol and drug withdrawal and methadone maintenance. Moreover, the vast majority of clinically relevant, specific addiction treatments that have evolved over the past half century are nonpharmacological.[1-3]

The twelve-step form of treatment has been largely arbitrarily excluded from the reviews on addiction treatment either because of the small number of studies in the literature or because the studies on the abstinence-based method were not "controlled," i.e., random assignment of patients to different treatments or no treatments despite large evaluation studies available for abstinence-based treatment.[4] However, it has only been recently that the abstinence-based method has begun to be examined in systematic studies.[5,6]

The abstinence-based method was derived from the principles of Alcoholics Anonymous (AA), which was founded in 1935 by two alcoholics, a stockbroker and a physician. The AA program is based on the fundamental concept that alcoholism is an addiction to alcohol, and as such is an independent "disease" or disorder. The first known treatment center to employ this method arose in Center City, Minnesota in the 1950's and the form of treatment has come to be known as the "Minnesota Model."[7,8]

While the Minnesota Model borrowed heavily from AA, it added important practices that distinguish this treatment from membership in Alcoholics Anonymous. In fact, AA's traditions preclude any official association with treatment facilities, and contrary to popular notions, AA does not employ treatment providers. On the other hand, treatment providers have incorporated principles of AA into their treatment approach, hold AA meetings on site, and refer patients to AA on discharge. However, they have no official connection with AA as a whole.[9]

The principal alternative treatment methods that have challenged the AA model have been derived from behavioral techniques and "learning theory." The labels attached to these methods are social learning and motivational and controlled drinking, reflecting the emphasis on behavioral approaches. While studies have demonstrated short-range effectiveness in small, controlled studies, there is little evidence that these methods have wide-range or long-term applications to the treatment of addictive disorders.[4] However, these techniques are being incorporated into various treatment settings in adjunctive ways.

Because the abstinence-based method of treatment has only recently (over the past decade) been studied with rigorous methods, critics have been slow to acknowledge that it is an effective treatment. Rather, its favorable outcome has been attributed to the general factors inherently contained in the stability of the middle class, psychologically integrated, and socially adjusted alcoholic or drug addict that would predict a favorable treatment response. In such populations, evaluation studies of large samples (10,000 patients) have demonstrated high abstinence rates and other associated outcomes that indicate an effective treatment response from an abstinence-based treatment approach.[5,6]

TREATMENT

Current Methodologies for the Study of Treatment Outcome

There are three major study designs currently employed for the study of the effectiveness of treatment outcome: epidemiological, evaluation, and experimental. All are legitimate forms of study and employ rigorous statistical designs for testing significance. Each provides a perspective on the study of treatment outcome that is unique. Because no one type of study can be used to answer all the questions of treatment outcome and effectiveness, the combination of all three is ultimately necessary to fully assess a response to various forms of treatment. No one approach is always better than the others; for each research question a judgement must be made as to which design is the most efficient way to get a satisfactory answer. Inexplicably, the randomized trial (experimental study) is often held up as the ultimate standard, but there are many situations for which an observational study is a better choice. The relatively low cost of observational studies makes them particularly attractive for questions they can answer satisfactorily.[5]

Epidemiological studies, a form of observational study, attempt to assess the prevalence of certain phenomena and their relationship to various factors. There is no attempt to control variables and the most fundamental aspect is to stand apart from the events taking place in the study subjects. The measurements may be made on a single occasion or over a period of time, with either retrospective or prospective techniques.[5]

Evaluation research seeks to explore relationships without experimental manipulation. The setting is naturalistic, in the clinical setting where the particular treatment takes place, without external alterations for controlling variables. Without the randomization of experimental studies, strict comparisons to other forms of treatment, particularly no treatment, are difficult to make. However, statistical approaches can be used to control for the lack of randomized assignment of subjects by partialing-out differences to compare treatment approaches. Evaluation research requires larger sample sizes to compensate for the lack of external control in experimental design. Importantly, because of the naturalistic setting and large sample size, generalization as to the effectiveness of treatment method is possible. The evaluation method allows for a continuous assessment of a treatment method in a clinical setting as the treatment is practiced, with progressively larger samples. Statistical inference is still possible regarding relationships within the treatment practices.[5]

Experimental designs allow for randomization of subjects to various treatment options in order to compare treatments or no treatment. The experimental design involves the manipulation of the environment or clinical practices so that the capacity is diminished to generalize the effectiveness of the treatment method to other clinical settings beyond the limitations of the design. Because of the randomization, statistical inference regarding the effectiveness of one treatment relative to another is possible according to a probability, i.e., significance, level. However, often a particular method is studied at a point in time with a particular method that may or may not resemble the current or future clinical practice. The samples studied are typically small and the expense of the study is high.[5]

Abstinence-Based Treatment

Evaluation Studies. In a natural survey of alcohol and drug inpatient treatment centers data were collected in interviews on site with treatment center administrators, program directors, clinical supervisors, marketing personnel, and other employees. The total sample consisted of 125 private, hospital-based, and freestanding centers. Sampling regions were chosen in such a way that the overall sample would approximate a representative composite of treatment programs across the country.

According to most center administrators (97.6%), treatment center ideology was based on a strong belief in the disease concept of alcoholism. Ninety-five percent of the administrators reported that their treatment programs were based on the "twelve-step program" of Alcoholics Anonymous. With regard to beliefs about treatment goals, 90.4% of the administrators reported that a treatment goal other than complete abstinence was not acceptable for any patient in recovery.[10]

In an evaluation study a sample of an entire population of 8,087 inpatients and 1,663 outpatients was taken for assessment of effectiveness of the abstinence-based treatment method. The contact rate was 70% at one year follow-up for 4166 inpatients and 898 outpatients. The results showed that abstinence rates were strongly associated with attendance at continuing care and regular attendance at meetings of Alcoholics Anonymous postdischarge.[6] These results are shown in Table 8.1.

TABLE 8.1 One-year Abstinence by Continuum of Care and Self-help Support

Variable	Inpatients ($n = 4166$)		Outpatients ($n = 898$)	
	% Attending	% Abstinent	% Attending	% Abstinent
Months of aftercare attended in year:				
0	38	55	23	58
1–3	25	50	27	60
4–11	29	70	33	74
12	8	88	17	93
AA attendance:				
Non-attender	54	49	49	57
Regular attender	46	75	51	82

Survey Studies. While AA is not treatment, it is linked to most forms of treatment. Since 1968 the membership of AA has been surveyed triennially by systematic statistical procedures according to established epidemiological techniques. Questionnaires were sent to a stratified random sample of 3% of the AA members from each delegate's area in the United States and Canada or to approximately 10,000 members in the 1989 survey. The survey has found consistently over the years a high drop-out rate (50%) in the first 3 months with a gradual leveling off to a plateau by 1 year.[11]

The results of the survey can be summarized accordingly: 1) of those sober less than a year, about 41% will remain in the AA Fellowship another year; 2) of those sober less than 5 years, about 83% will remain in the Fellowship another year; and 3) of those sober 5 years or more, 91% will remain in the Fellowship another year.[11]

The attendance at AA has been very stable; the average number of meetings per week is three. In the 1989 survey, the number of women members had increased to almost one-third of the total membership. Those members under 30 years old represent more than one-fifth of the total membership and those over 50 years old represent just under one-fourth of the total. An increasing number of members are also addicted to other drugs (46%).[11]

Controlled Studies. Controlled studies also find significant treatment outcomes for abstinence-based programs, particularly when combined with referral to AA. The first randomized clinical trial of abstinence-based treatment showed significant improvement in drinking behavior as compared to a more traditional form of treatment.[12] One hundred forty-one employed alcoholics were randomized to the abstinence-based program (*n* = 74) or to traditional-type treatment (*n* = 67). The abstinence-based treatment was significantly more involving, supportive, encouraging to spontaneity, and oriented to personal problems than the traditional-type treatment. The drop-out rate was 7.9% for abstinence and 25.9% for traditional, and participation in outpatient treatment was significantly better after the former treatment modality. Overall the abstinence-based treatment obtained a greater one-year abstinence rate than a more traditional-type treatment.[12]

In a second controlled study, a random assignment of 227 workers newly identified as alcoholics was made to one of three treatment regimens: compulsory inpatient treatment, compulsory attendance at AA meetings, and a choice of options.[13] The hospitals for inpatient treatment were abstinence-based, with eventual referrals to AA at discharge.[13] Inpatient back-up was provided if needed. On seven measures of drinking and drug use the hospital group fared best and that assigned to AA the least well; those allowed to choose a program had intermediate results. The estimated costs of inpatient treatment for the AA and choice groups averaged only 10% less than the costs for the hospital group because of their higher rates of additional treatment. The conclusion was that inpatient care was more costly but an initial referral to AA or choice of programs involved more risk than compulsory inpatient treatment.

REFERENCES

1. Longabaugh R (1988). Longitudinal outcome studies. In: Rose R & Barrett J (eds.), *Alcoholism: Origins and Outcome,* pp. 267–280. New York: Raven Press.
2. Goodwin DW (1988). Alcoholism: Who gets better and who does not. In Rose R & Barrett J (eds.), *Alcholism: Origins and Outcome,* pp. 281–292. New York: Raven Press.
3. Emerick CD (1975). A review of psychologically oriented treatment of alcoholism: II. *Q J Stud Alc* 36(1):88–103.
4. Miller WR & Hester RK (1989). The effectiveness of alcoholism treatment methods: What research reveals. In: Miller WR & Heather N (eds.), *Treating Addictive Behaviors: Processes of Change.* New York: Plenum.

5. Hoffmann NG & Miller NS (1992). Treatment outcomes for abstinence-based programs. *Psych Ann* 22(8):402–408.

6. Harrison PA, Hoffmann NH & Streed SG (1991). Drug and alcohol treatment outcome. In Miller NS (ed.), *Comprehensive Handbook of Drugs and Alcohol Addiction,* pp. 1163–1200. New York: Marcel Dekker.

7. Miller NS & Chappel J (1991). History of Disease Concept. *Psych Ann* 21(1):1–8.

8. Laundergan JC (1982). *Easy Does It: Alcoholism Treatment Outcomes, Hazelden and the Minnesota Model.* Center City, MN: Hazelden Foundation.

9. Hoffmann NG, Harrison PA & Belile CA (1986). Alcoholics Anonymous after treatment: Attendance and abstinence. *J Addict* 218:311–318.

10. Roman PM (1989). Inpatient alcohol and drug treatment: A national study of treatment centers. Executive report. Institute for Behavioral Research, University of Georgia 1–22 (supported by NIAAA).

11. Chappel J (1993). Long term recovery from alcoholism. In Miller NS (ed.), *Psychiatric Clinics of North America,* pp. 177–189. Philadelphia: Saunders.

12. Keso L & Salaspuro M (1991). Inpatient treatment of employed alcoholics: A randomized clinical trial on Hazelden-type and traditional treatment. *Alcoholism: Clin & Exp Res* 14(4):584–589.

13. Walsh DC, Hingson RW & Merrigan DM (1991). A randomized trial of treatment options for alcohol-abusing workers. *N Engl J Med* 325(11):775–852.

19

Other Forms
of Treatment

OVERVIEW

In a general review of forms of treatment other than the abstinence-based model, it is surprising to note the large volume of studies reported in recent decades. A major source of confusion is that a large number of these studies pertain to the treatment of alcohol problems, and it is not always clear if they refer to alcoholism, an addiction to alcohol, or problem drinking.[1]

Included in these studies are a vast array of methods and studies that include small numbers of subjects without replication or follow-up beyond a few weeks or months. The results may appear consistent when taken as a whole but, given the uncertainty of diagnosis, small numbers per treatment method, and short follow-up, it is unclear what, if any, relevance these studies may have to the treatment of the alcoholic.[1] Another serious omission is the lack of inclusion of other drugs in addition to alcohol. The contemporary alcoholic, particularly those drinkers under the age of 30, is often addicted to other drugs, including marijuana, cocaine, opiates, and benzodiazepines. The relevance of a particular treatment for only alcoholism is questionable. There is a strong propensity toward other drugs to promote relapse to alcohol in alcoholics, and the reverse, the relapse to drugs after the use of alcohol, by a drug addict.

These methods are very rarely used in the U.S. despite the claims by the investigators of the effectiveness of the treatment methods. Many of these studies were conducted under controlled conditions with random assignment of patients to comparison interventions.

The conclusions regarding the effectiveness of addictions treatment that have evolved based on available studies are 1) one treatment is not superior to another; 2) there is little evidence that treatment is superior to no treatment; 3) patient and psychosocial characteristics and not treatment methods predict treatment outcome; 4) there is little difference between inpatient and outpatient treatment sites; 5) the acute treatment effect is short-lived and longitudinal—continuous treatment is necessary to maintain a treatment effect; 6) there is a need to focus on the active ingredients in treatment and to determine how these interact with patient variables; and 7) the longer the treatment is provided in a continuing, less-intense fashion, the more likely the positive treatment effect will be sustained.[39–42]

However, rarely in these studies is there made a comparison to no interventions or treatment at all. Moreover, the sample assignment is biased because of the patient's selection of one treatment over another or refusal to enter the study. Additionally, the generalizability of the results is limited because of small sample sizes, patient selection bias, lack of replication, and the novelty of treatments (little previous history of the method).

Review of Early Studies

In a lengthy review of over 100 studies for the treatment of alcoholism before 1940, the conclusion was that no treatment had been proven effective for alcoholism.[39] In a subsequent review of 49 psychotherapeutic studies of alcoholism, only two studies employed methods that were interpretable, and these results were equivocal.[40] In a review of nearly 400 studies, the conclusion was that the motivation state of the alcoholic was the greatest predictor of treatment response.[41] Moreover, the studies did not control for patient characteristics nor did they compare treatment to no treatment. Comparisons of inpatient to outpatient in studies did not reveal significant differences in treatment outcome.[42]

However, studies support the view that the alcoholic or addict is better off overall after treatment.[39–42] The type of treatment has little effect, and specificity of treatment beyond abstinence has little predictive value. Moreover, the treatment effect may last up to 2 years if continued treatment is included. Subtypes of alcoholics or addicts may more accurately predict a response to any treatment.[36–38]

These early studies were largely a collection of heterogenous methods that examined different aspects of addiction treatment in cross-sectional views or short-term follow-up in small numbers of patients in controlled and uncontrolled ways. Little can be concluded regarding the common elements of treatment that represent effective treatment.

Newer Measures of Treatment Effectiveness

The question of what to measure to validate treatment outcome has undergone considerable change. In earlier studies the emphasis was on abstinence as the gold standard for the effectiveness of treatment. More recently, the standard has been raised to include other benefits such as psychosocial adjustments and quality of life.

The importance of treatment "process" has evolved. The suggestion to identify active ingredients in treatment in order to determine the factors that lead to change is increasingly being made. This can be regarded as a step toward sophistication of treatment research and as an attempt to identify critical components of treatment that will lead to causal links and specific modifications to improve treatment responses. The recent development of treatment protocols for standardization of the components of a treatment intervention tests a particular treatment's efficacy.[43]

Future Research

Beyond the treatment of withdrawal, the history of pharmacological treatments for addictive disorders is still preliminary. Whatever form or route the research may take, the necessity to base the pharmacological research on biological theory and not psychosocial factors appears plausible at this point.[44]

The posttreatment environment, including continuing participation in treatment modalities, has not been examined in studies. The immediate posttreatment environment (i.e., use of a halfway house for several months) can lead to significant increases in positive treatment outcome and needs to be studied.[45]

TREATMENT

Psychotherapy and Counseling

Despite the results of selected studies, psychotherapy and counseling are acknowledged as very important and essential to the overall treatment of alcohol and drug addiction.

The studies in general do not examine psychotherapy alone, but rather in conjunction with other forms of treatment such as inpatient or outpatient treatments. The studies do not reveal consistently positive results despite clinical intuition that individual attention to the alcoholic or addict is valuable. The studies show that adjunctive psychotherapy or counseling resulted in no differences or, contrary to the expectations of the investigators, the trends favored the patients who did not receive the additional therapies.[2-7]

Confrontation

While confrontation is considered a mainstay in the treatment of the alcoholic or drug addict, studies that examine the effectiveness of this particular technique are lacking. The few available studies show that confrontation can have a substantial impact on the eventual treatment response, particularly with respect to drinking behavior.[8,9] One study reporting on the subjective states of denial did find a positive benefit from confrontation.[10]

Aversion Therapy

The principal goal of aversion therapy is to produce an aversive reaction to alcohol by establishing a conditioned response in an individual. The ingestion of alcohol is paired with a negative stimulus in order to produce an automatic negative response when exposed to alcohol alone. The four major types of aversive stimuli are nausea, apnea, electric shock, and imagery.[11-13]

There is a large body of research into this modality of therapy. Aversive conditioning strategies appear to show effectiveness for a period of a few months. However, the studies report a reduction in consumption rather than total abstinence, so that the success of these approaches is not as great if continuous abstinence is used as a criterion. Another major confounding variable is that many centers utilizing the aversive methods refer their patients to Alcoholics Anonymous following the aversive treatments. To what extent the attendance at AA meetings independently influence the overall results from aversive therapy remains unknown.[14,15] However, together they may be effective.

Controlled Drinking

The studies that examine "problem drinkers" find improvement in drinking behavior at one-and two-year follow-up. Of interest is that the group that does consistently the best in most studies is the group that abstains the most or has the greatest days of abstinence. Further problems in these studies are that the criteria used for the consequences of alcohol consumption lack sensitivity and specificity. The threshold for what is considered problem drinking determines the effectiveness of outcomes. Given the propensity for rationalization and minimization by active alcoholics for the reasons why they drink, in addition to quantity and frequency, the self-reports by them must be critically examined.

At the same time, the results from studies on controlled drinking involving actual alcoholics (those with alcoholism and alcohol dependence) indicate alcoholics cannot drink without loss of control. In large studies involving over 1600 alcoholics less than 1% of the alcoholics were able to return to "normal" drinking without adverse consequences.[16] It is important to bear in mind that the loss of control experienced by the alcoholic may take more than a few weeks or months, and in some cases years, to manifest itself. Vaillant and others have shown that the natural history of alcoholism is one of chronic remissions and exacerbations to drinking with attendant adverse consequences.[17] In a study of controlled drinking, those alcoholics who appeared to receive benefit at 1 and 2 years later showed severe relapse into fatal alcoholism.[18,19] In this particular study these alcoholics had significantly greater numbers of abstinent days than controls, indicating that abstinence rather than controlled drinking led to better outcomes early on. Most of the other studies are anecdotal, small in numbers (<10), and short in duration of follow-up (months). A recent study showed, as did previous studies, that those who abstain continue to do the best in terms of adverse consequences from drinking.[20,21]

Operant Methods

The idea that operant conditioning techniques can alter drinking behavior through behavior modification has been studied extensively. While there are few controlled studies, the abundance of the studies claim effectiveness for this form of treatment for alcoholism. Overall, as expected perhaps, reinforcement and punishment contingencies can be used to enhance program compliance, but the ultimate impact on drinking behavior depends on the effectiveness of the program itself.[22,23]

Broad-Spectrum Approaches

Social Skills Training. The studies investigating social skills training are based on the assumption that alcoholics are deficient in social skills. The studies investigate social skills training as an independent and adjunctive method of treatment for alcoholism. The studies tend to contain small numbers of highly selected subjects who are followed for brief periods of time. Also, confounding variables such as participation in other aftercare programs such as AA are not well controlled.[24,25]

Stress Management. These studies are based on the techniques of relaxation management training. As with social skills training, stress management is frequently combined with other forms of treatment such as aversion therapy. The technique of biofeedback relaxation training is often combined with other forms of alcoholism treatment.[26,27]

Community Reinforcement Approach. This method has promise but has not been extensively studied. The concept is to change or restructure family, social, and vocational activities for the alcoholic in his or her habitat in the community. This is akin to "changing people, places, and things" in its fullest meaning. Studies to date tend to examine smaller components such as job finding or disulfiram compliance.[28,29]

All three methods focus on coping mechanisms as a treatment for alcoholism. The studies show that the methods are effective for those who are deficient in coping skills. While these approaches may be intuitively appealing, studies also show that much of the difficulties in coping result from the drinking that caused the stress and subsequently improve post-drinking during abstinence. However, the basic problem of alcoholism or uncontrolled drinking is left unaddressed or untreated, so that any gains from this method are subject to ultimate failure.

Relapse Prevention

The major proponent for this method of treatment has been Marlatt.[30] The principal ingredient is a behavioral approach to relapse prevention. The emphasis is on the outside influences on the alcoholic or addict. The goal is to reduce the "precipitants" in the relapse to alcohol and drugs. Abstinence or reduced consumption are seen as the measures for positive behavioral changes.[30,31]

The major drawback is the lack of attention to the root causes of addictive behavior in regard to alcohol and drugs, namely, the mind and brain. Ultimately, chemical experience strongly suggests that without changing the "inside," the rearranging of the exterior, i.e., geographical cures, will result in relapse to alcohol and drugs. The variance between the relapse-prevention model and the disease approach is clearly seen in these opposing strategies. Some of the ideas are compatible with the disease model, such as a recommendation for changing "people, places, and things," in addition to a recommendation for making fundamental changes in attitudes and behaviors.[32]

Length and Setting of Treatment

These studies are basically flawed by the lack of inclusion of the form of treatment employed by the vast majority in the U.S. namely abstinence-based treatment. Despite this compelling omission, perhaps some lessons may be learned from evaluating the available studies. Perhaps the greatest lesson is that it is important to compare apples to apples, as many of the studies assess the length of stay by comparing apples to oranges. The results indicate that a greater length of stay does not translate into a better treatment outcome. The level of intensity of treatment does not correlate with success in treatment in some methods. Moreover, in these studies the methods are diverse and the levels of treatment varied, so that comparisons from one treatment setting to another are difficult.[33,34]

A recent study of multicenters using similar modalities and settings for treatment of addiction found that the greater the number of services, the better the treatment outcome. In this study it appeared that the level of intensity correlated with better outcome when units of service of comparable forms of treatment are examined.[35]

REFERENCES

1. Miller WR & Hester RK (1989). The effectiveness of alcoholism treatment methods: What research reveals. In: Miller WR & Heather N (eds.), *Treating Addictive Behaviors: Processes of Change*. New York: Plenum.
2. Tomsovic M (1970). A follow-up study of discharged alcoholics. *Hosp & Commun Psych* 21:94–97.
3. Levinson T & Sereny G (1969). An experimental evaluation of "insight therapy" for the chronic alcoholic. *Canad Psych Assoc J* 14:143–146.
4. Ogborne AC & Wilmot R (1979). Evaluation of an experimental counseling service for male Skid Row alcoholics. *J Stud Alc* 40:129–132.
5. Zimberg S (1974). Evaluation of alcoholism treatment in Harlem. *Q J Stud Alc* 35:550–557.
6. McCance C & McCance PF (1969). Alcoholism in North-East Scotland: Its treatment and outcome. *Br J Psych* 115:189–198.
7. Ends EJ & Page CW (1957). A study of three types of group psychotherapy with hospitalized inebriates. *Q J Stud Alc* 18:263–277.
8. Schaefer HH, Sobell MB & Mills KC (1971). Some sobering data on the use of self-confrontation with alcoholics. *Behav Ther* 2:28–39.
9. Faia C & Shean G (1976). Using videotapes and group discussion in the treatment of male chronic alcoholics. *Hosp & Commun Psych* 27:847,851.
10. Lieberman MA, Yalom ID & Miles MB (1973). *Encounter Groups: First Facts*. New York: Basic Books.
11. Boland FJ, Mellor CS & Revusky S (1978). Chemical aversion treatment of alcoholism: Lithium as the aversive agent. *Behav Res Ther* 16:401–409.
12. Jackson TR & Smith JW (1978). A comparison of two aversion treatment methods of alcoholism. *J Stud Alc* 39:187–191.
13. Glover JH & McCue PA (1977). Electrical aversion therapy with alcoholics: A comparative follow-up study. *Br J Psych* 130:279–286.
14. Cannon DS, Baker TB & Wehl CK (1981). Emetic and electric shock alcohol aversion therapy: Six- and twelve-month follow-up. *J Consul Clin Psychol* 49:360–368.
15. Vogler RE, Lunde SE & Martin PL (1971). Electrical aversion conditioning with chronic alcoholics: Follow-up and suggestions for research. *J Consul Clin Psychol* 36:450.
16. Helzer TE, Robins LN & Taylor JR (1985). The extent of long-term moderate drinking among alcoholics discharged from medical and psychiatric treatment facilities. *N Engl J Med* 312:1679–1682.

17. Vaillant GB (1983). *Natural History of Alcoholism.* Cambridge: Harvard Press.

18. Sobell MB & Sobell LC (1973). Individualized behavior therapy for alcoholics. *Behav Ther* 4:49–72.

19. Pendery ML, Maltzman TM & West LJ (1982). Controlled drinking by alcoholics? New findings and a re-evaluation of a major affirmative study. *Science* 217:169–175.

20. Alden L (1978). Evaluation of a preventative self-management programme for problem drinkers. *Canad J Behav Sci* 10:258–263.

21. Miller NS (1991). Special problems of the alcohol and multiple-drug dependent: Clinical interactions and detoxification. In Frances RJ & Miller SI (eds.), *Clinical Textbook of Addictive Disorders,* pp. 194–220. New York: Guilford.

22. Rosenberg SD (1979). Relaxation training and a differential assessment of alcoholism. Unpublished doctoral dissertation, California School of Professional Psychology, San Diego CA: (University Microfilms No. 8004362).

23. Smart RG (1974). Employed alcoholics treated voluntarily and under constructive coercion: A follow-up study. *Q J Stud Alc* 35:196–209.

24. Chaney EF, O'Leary MR & Marlatt GA (1978). Skill training with alcoholics. *J Consult & Clin Psychol* 46:1092–1104.

25. Oei TPS & Jackson P (1980). Long-term effects of group and individual social skills training with alcoholics. *Addict Behav* 5:129–136.

26. Blake BG (1967). A follow-up of alcoholics treated by behaviour therapy. *Behaviour Res & Theory* 5:89–94.

27. Sisson RW (1981). The effect of three relaxation procedures on tension reduction and subsequent drinking of inpatient alcoholics. Unpublished doctoral dissertation, Southern Illinois University at Carbondale, Carbondale IL (University Microfilms No. 8122668).

28. Azrin NH (1976). Improvements in the community-reinforcement approach to alcoholism. *Behav Res Ther* 14:339–348.

29. Azrin NH, Sisson, RW, Meyers R & Godley M (1982). Alcoholism treatment by disulfiram and community reinforcement therapy. *J Behav Ther Exp Psych* 13:105–112.

30. Marlatt GA (1973, April). A comparison of aversive conditioning procedures in the treatment of alcoholism. Paper presented at the annual meeting of the Western Psychological Association, Anaheim, CA.

31. Miller WR, Hedrick KA & Taylor CA (1983). Addictive behaviors and life problems before and after behavioral treatment of problem drinkers. *Addict Behav* 8:403–412.

32. Miller NS & Chappel J (1991). History of Disease Concept. *Psych Ann* 21(1):1–8.

33. Edwards G & Guthrie S (1966). A comparison of inpatient and outpatient treatment of alcohol dependence. *Lancet* 1:467–468.

34. Edwards G & Guthrie S (1967). A controlled trial of inpatient and outpatient treatment of alcohol dependence. *Lancet* 1:555–559.

35. McLellan T. Presented at the Meeting of the American Society of Addiction Medicine (ASAM), April 16, 1994, New York, NY.

36. Miller WR & Hester RK (1989). The effectiveness of alcoholism treatment methods: What research reveals. In: Miller WR & Heather N (eds.), *Treating Addictive Behaviors: Processes of Change.* New York: Plenum Press.

37. Harrison PA, Hoffmann NH & Streed SG (1991). Drug and alcohol treatment outcome. In Miller NS (ed.), *Comprehensive Handbook of Drugs and Alcohol Addiction* pp. 1163–1200. New York: Marcel Dekker.

38. Miller NS & Chappel J (1991). History of Disease Concept. *Psych Ann* 21(1):1–8.

39. Voegtlin W & Lemere F (1942). The treatment of alcohol addiction: A review of the literature. *Q J Stud Alc* 2:717.

40. Hill MJ & Blane HT (1967). Evaluation of psychotherapy with alcoholics. *Q J Stud Alc* 28:76–104.

41. Emerick CD (1974). A review of psychologically oriented treatment of alcoholism: I. The use and interrelations of outcome criteria and drunken behavior following treatment. *Q J Stud Alc* 35:523.

42. Baekeland F, Lundwall L & Kissin B (1975). Methods for the treatment of chronic alcoholism: A critical appraisal. In Isreal Y (ed.), *Research Advances in Alcohol and Drug Problems,* vol. 2. New York: Wiley.

43. Nowinski J & Baker S (1992). *The Twelve-step Facilitation Handbook.* New York, NY: Lexington Books.

44. Gorelick DA (1993). Overview of pharmacological treatment approach for alcohol and other drug addictions: Intoxication, withdrawal, and relapse prevention. In Miller NS (ed.), *Psychiatric Clinics of North America* pp. 141–156. Philadelphia: Saunders.

45. Collins GB (1993). Contemporary issues in the treatment of alcohol dependence. In Miller NS (ed.), *Psychiatric Clinics of North America* pp. 33–48. Philadelphia: Saunders.

20

Treatment in Psychiatric and Addiction Settings

OVERVIEW

The Problem—Dichotomous Systems

Traditionally, we have had predominantly dichotomous systems for the treatment of addictive and psychiatric disorders. Although each side has recently moved towards the acknowledgment of the benefits of combined treatment for addictive and psychiatric disorders, the progress thus far in treatment practices is only in the initial stages. As a result, many patients do not yet receive adequate attention and treatment for either addictive or psychiatric disorders depending on which setting they might seek treatment from.[1-3] Those with identified addictive disorders but without a chronic mental illness tend to be admitted to addiction programs without receiving psychiatric evaluations and treatment for other psychiatric disorders in addition to the addictive disorder.[4-10] Because identified psychiatric patients with addictive disorders, particularly those with a chronic mental illness, tend to utilize psychiatric services, they are underdiagnosed and generally do not receive comprehensive treatment for addictive disorders.

The Need—Prevalence of the Problem

The overall prevalence rates in clinical populations for addictive disorders in private and public psychiatric settings are approximately 50%; in other words, the likelihood of finding a diagnosis of substance use disorder in a psychiatric patient is one in two. The actual prevalence rates for addictive disorders, according to psychiatric diagnostic categories, vary accordingly in inpatient and outpatient settings: 30% in depressive disorders, 50% in bipolar disorders, 50% in schizophrenic disorders, 80% in antisocial personality disorders, 30% in anxiety disorders, and 25% in phobic disorders.[11-17]

On the other hand, studies reveal that the prevalence rates for psychiatric disorders in addiction populations are considerably lower, similar to those rates found in the general population for psychiatric disorders. The prevalence rates for psychiatric disorders in addiction populations are 4% for depressive disorders, 0.8% for bipolar disorders, 1.1% for schizophrenic disorders, 2.0% for antisocial personality disorders, 2% for anxiety disorders, and 6% for phobic disorders.[18-21]

DIAGNOSIS

Traditional Diagnostic and Treatment Methods

Diagnosis in Addiction Settings. Typically, there is a selection process that takes place before an admission to an addiction facility. The screening is usually more stringent than that which occurs in psychiatric settings where pervasive criteria tend to govern admission policies. Besides possessing an addictive disorder and willingness to undergo a structured treatment program, the overriding criterion is whether or not the patient can withstand confrontation and close interactions with other patients and staff. The capacity for an addiction setting to withstand behaviors deviant from a defined norm is limited. The tolerated behavior norms for membership in the addiction milieu are well defined whether or not the behaviors are deemed under the control of the individual.[22]

Because of behavioral expectations within the addiction milieu, patients with chronic mental illnesses and those with severe depressive, acute mania, and anxiety (obsessive–compulsive) disorders, among others, tend to be excluded or extruded unless they meet rather strict behavior controls.[20] Moreover, identification of these problems may be delayed until the patient has been discharged and in recovery for a substantial period.

TREATMENT

In addiction-treatment settings, the use of medications in addictive disorders has gained increasingly more acceptance for legitimate independent psychiatric disorders; however, the use of medications for "underlying causes" of addictive disorders continues to be discouraged. There is usually a "waiting period" for the pharmacological and addictive effects from alcohol and drugs to subside before initiating pharmacotherapies.[28,29] The exceptions to this practice include a documented history of major psychiatric illnesses such as schizophrenia or mania where medications are generally continued or initiated until a full evaluation and observations of the interactions between the psychiatric and addictive disorders over time can be undertaken.[28–31]

There is a de-emphasis on "uncovering" or making retrospective diagnoses in order to focus on the "here and now" and what are the sources of the current symptoms (commonly attributed to the addictive disorder). Moreover, because the techniques used in addiction treatment are cognitive/behavioral, their employment may be effective for symptoms arising from either the addictive or other psychiatric disorders (commonly anxiety and depression). In general, the use of medications in the addiction population carries a relative contraindication because of a deficiency in control of a drug effect by those who are drug addicted. Prominent examples are medications whose addiction propensity among alcoholics and drug addicts is known, such as benzodiazepines or anticholinergics.[32,33]

Anxiety, depression, and maladaptive behaviors are viewed as signals or warnings to make constructive changes without which the alcoholic/addict would not have motivation to recovery from addictive disorders.[32,34] Anxiety, depression, and personality disorders are indicative of psychopathological addictive states that the alcoholic or drug addict must first acknowledge and then take therapeutic actions to treat. It is often a poor prognostic sign if the alcoholic/drug addict does not show some affect in response to real-life events and problems. The aim is to avoid suppressing anxiety, depression, or destructive behaviors and to take corrective actions.[32] In fact, learning how to regulate one's own mood is a crucial developmental milestone that involves feeling the affect over a period of time.

Diagnosis in Psychiatric Settings

While increasing numbers of reports of "comorbid" psychiatric and addictive disorders have appeared in recent years, clinical experience and studies show that addictive disorders continue to be underdiagnosed in psychiatric settings.[35]

Alcohol and drugs can produce virtually any psychiatric symptom or syndrome, including mood, thought, and personality disturbances. Specifically, stimulant drugs can produce anxiety, hallucinations, delusions during intoxication, and depression during withdrawal. Depressant drugs can produce depression during intoxication, and anxiety, hallucinations, and delusions during withdrawal. Both acute and chronic use of stimulants and depressants can produce pathological changes in personality. In general, the earlier and the longer the use in chronological years, the more delayed and prolonged are the effects on personality.[20,36]

Generally, a period of abstinence or of being "drug free" is required before definitive psychiatric diagnoses can be made *in addition to* the addictive disorder. Recommendations range from waiting a few days to years before making other psychiatric diagnoses and instituting treatments.[20,36] Generally, psychotic, affective, and anxiety symptoms from drugs and alcohol will remit in days to weeks, whereas personality disturbances may take months to years to remit.

Treatment in Psychiatric Settings

Central to the philosophy of traditional psychiatric treatment, whether pharmacological or nonpharmacological, is the "self-medication hypothesis."[37] A corollary of the hypothesis states that alcohol and drug use, including addictive use, is secondary to another condition. Therefore, it is essential to treat the "reasons" (i.e., anxiety or depression) for using alcohol and drugs to provide some kind of medicinal relief. Despite the widespread acceptance of this hypothesis in clinical psychiatric practice and research methods, controlled and uncontrolled studies have failed to provide evidence for the validity of self-medication.[35] What studies actually show is that treatment of the underlying psychiatric disorder does not alter the addictive use of alcohol and drugs. Generally, psychiatric symptoms worsen with continued alcohol and drug use.[37]

Contemporary Treatment Models

Addiction Treatment Settings. *Dual Focus Programs.* Addiction treatment programs are increasingly adding trained psychiatric staff to treat psychiatric disorders that appear to be independent of the addictive disorder and often require medications or other psychiatric approaches such as brief, supportive psychotherapy. There are additional tracks for "dual-focused" patients in a specialized psychiatry setting within the addiction milieu.[1-3]

Psychiatric Treatment Settings. The treatment of addictive disorders is currently available in limited ways in psychiatric settings to reach the patients (the chronic mentally ill) who "fall between the cracks" because they are not easily managed in addiction settings.[38-40] The three approaches that are currently advocated in psychiatric settings are the serial, parallel, and integrated models. The serial model has been the most commonly employed, while the others are only in limited use.

The Serial Treatment Model. The serial model is the oldest model in which one form of treatment follows another form. The psychiatric milieu and staff are physically separate from the addiction milieu and staff so that the patient is transferred sequentially from one to the other. Typically, a patient is stabilized on the psychiatric unit or outpatient clinic before transfer to addiction settings, often with the use of medications, and given psychiatric explanations for alcohol and drug use that are sometimes in contradiction to the clinical approaches used in the addiction setting.[41] Psychiatric populations contain the chronic mentally ill who cannot be transferred because they cannot tolerate the confrontive milieu and are not tolerated by the more integrated alcoholics and addicts found in addiction settings. The basic defect of splitting of affect from thought may make it difficult for the schizophrenic to conform to a principal goal of addiction treatment that involves joining feelings with thoughts. Other negative symptoms of schizophrenia, e.g., poverty of emotions and being overwhelmed by the emotions of others, make full participation in group addiction settings difficult. Moreover, any paranoid delusions and thoughts lead to further isolation from peers in the addiction setting.[8,42]

In the serial treatment model, neither the staff nor the patient participates in the combined treatment, and the psychiatric and addiction approaches remain apart and in apparent conflict. The staff from either side are neither knowledgeable nor skilled in the other staff members' approaches, and treatment is fragmented and antagonistic. Turf issues emerge regarding treatment practices, and the patient becomes caught in the middle.

The Parallel Treatment Model. In the parallel model of treatment, the patient undergoes concurrent treatment in a separate milieu and by different staff members. In this respect, the parallel and serial treatment models are similar. Also, the limitations of the serial model generally apply to the parallel model. While the patient is hospitalized or primarily attending an outpatient clinic in one setting, he or she is "sent" to another setting for the other treatment. The parallel model works best in settings where both psychiatric and addiction-treatment programs are available and cooperation is possible between disparate staff.[1,2] Inversely, where one or the other treatment setting is missing, the patient can be further fragmented by "commuting" from one treatment setting to the other and being treated by staff who are "foreign" to each other. Also, the treatment experience can be taxing and stressful on particularly vulnerable and fragile patients, namely the chronic mentally ill. Relapse to use of alcohol and drugs and drop-out rates from addiction treatment can be high. Perhaps what is most significant is the fact that the two treatment "systems" remain separate and run the risk of conflict because of the different treatment paradigms.[1,2] Moreover, patients do receive addiction treatment in addition to their psychiatric treatments.

The Integrated Treatment Model. In the integrated treatment model, the core treatment program provides the therapeutic modalities from both psychiatric and addictive settings in the same milieu. The staff are trained in both psychiatric and addiction methods of diagnosis and treatment, and the patient receives an approach from a unified staff in an integrated milieu.[1,2] In the integrated model, splitting of staff and patients is less pronounced, and therefore denial is better confronted and treated. The patients benefit from the integrated approach in which both psychiatric and addictive disorders are seen as priorities in the treatment methods employed by staff.[1,2]

In the integrated setting, the diagnosis and treatment for both the psychiatric and addictive disorders often can be instituted simultaneously. The staff will continue to learn effective and advanced techniques for diagnosing and treating both disorders. The patient will receive referrals for continuing treatment postdischarge for both the psychiatric and addictive disorders. Importantly, both staff and patients will be able to better maintain a dual focus on the independent statuses of the psychiatric and addictive disorders.[1,2]

One of the major limitations to the integrated model is that it may lead to undertreatment of addictive disorders and overtreatment of psychiatric symptoms in those patients who have only or predominately an addictive disorder.[1,2] Typically, these are alcoholics and drug addicts who have been hospitalized or sought outpatient treatment for the psychiatric consequences of their addictive disorders, i.e., transient anxiety/depression, suicidal thoughts and behaviors, or psychotic symptoms associated with use of drugs and alcohol.

The integrated model appears to work best for those with true "dual diagnoses," such as the chronic mentally ill. Patients who are schizophrenic, manic, or have severe personality disorders that require relatively intensive psychiatric care can better utilize a less-intensive addiction program. The staff can incorporate the knowledge and skill for both psychiatric and addictive disorders in a core treatment program to give total therapy to the patient. The patient can benefit from the integrated attitudes and perspectives of the staff and the confrontive and supportive approaches to addictive and other mental disorders.

INTERACTIONS

Treatment Outcome Results for Comorbidity

Only a few studies in either addiction or psychiatric settings are available for the treatment outcome of comorbid addictive and psychiatric disorders. The reasons are mainly due to the lack of addiction treatment in psychiatric settings and the lack of the severely psychiatrically ill in addiction settings.

Treatment of Major Depression in Addiction Settings

The predictive value of a lifetime diagnosis of major depression on the outcome following treatment in abstinence-based programs for alcohol and drug disorders has been examined.[43] The sample consisted of 6355 subjects from inpatient and outpatient programs in 41 independent sites. The subjects received structured interviews for lifetime diagnoses of major depression and current alcohol and drug disorders (DSM-III-R) in association with treatment outcome. The evaluation of subjects was conducted prospectively in a personal interview on admission and by telephone contacts at 6 and 12 months postdischarge.[43]

The majority of the subjects attended an inpatient treatment site (78.4%), were middle-aged (35.7 years of age), male (70.6%), white (88.9%), high school educated (84.6%), employed (73.3%), and married (43.3%). The prevalence rate of a lifetime diagnosis of major depression was 56.3%.[43]

A lifetime diagnosis of major depression did not predict the abstinence rates at one year in depressed and nondepressed males with alcohol and/or drug disorders (54.9% versus 54.4%) and females (58.0% versus 56.0%). Attendance at continuing care and AA meetings was associated with significantly better abstinence rates (72.2% for regular attenders versus 38.6% for nonattenders).[43] (Depressed patients were more likely to be regular attenders.)

Treatment of Comorbidity in "Two-Track" Settings

A three-month outcome study was conducted in a psychiatric unit that provided two "tracks" (integrated model) for the treatment of addictive disorders: one for the chronic mentally ill ($n = 12$) and one for those without mental illness ($n = 16$).[44] There were no differences in treatment outcome between the two groups in the five outcome variables studied (abstinence, employment, taking medication, compliance with community treatment, and major untoward events).[44]

Initially, the modality of treatment was described as a modified therapeutic community in which patients provided feedback to each other about behavioral patterns. However, many patients, particularly the chronic mentally ill, were unable to tolerate the intense interpersonal interactions generated by such a system. A second track was developed for the chronic mentally ill patients, and consisted of a smaller, more relaxed group, with a more concrete, experimental approach to improving maladaptive behaviors.[44]

REFERENCES

1. Ries R (1993). Clinical treatment matching models for dually diagnosed patients. *Psych Clin N Amer* 16(1):1–9.
2. Minkoff K (1989). An integrated treatment model for drug dual diagnosis of psychosis and addiction. *Hosp Commun Psych* 40:1031–1036.
3. Drake RE & Wallach MA (1989). Substance abuse among chronic mentally ill. *Hosp Commun Psych* 40:1041–1045.
4. Galanter M (1985). Substance abuse among general psychiatric patients: Place of presentation, diagnosis, and treatment. *Am J Drug Alc Abuse* 14:211–235.
5. Evans K & Sullivan JM (1990). *Dual Diagnosis: Counseling the Mentally Ill Substance Abuser.* New York: Guilford.
6. Kofoed L, Kania J & Walsh T (1986). Outpatient treatment of patients with substance abuse and coexisting psychiatric disorders. *Am J Psych* 143:867–872.
7. Lehman AF, Meyers CP & Lehman AF (1989). Assessment and classification of patients with psychiatric and substance abuse syndromes. *Hosp Commun Psych* 40:1019–1025.
8. Pepper B, Kirshner MC & Ryglewicz H (1981). The young adult chronic patient: Overview of a population. *Hosp Commun Psych* 32:463–474.
9. Rosenheck R, Massari, Astrachan B (1990). Mentally ill chemical abusers discharged from VA inpatient treatment. *Psych Q* 61:237–249.
10. Regier DA, Farmer ME & Rae DS (1990). Comorbidity of mental disorders with alcohol and other drug abuse: Results from the epidemiological catchment area (ECA) study. *J Am Med Assoc* 264:2511–2518.
11. Alterman AL, Erdlen FR & Murphy E (1981). Alcohol abuse in the psychiatric hospital population. *Addict Behav* 6:69–73.
12. Brady K, Casto S & Lydiard RB (1991). Substance abuse in an inpatient psychiatric sample. *Am J Drug Alc Abuse* 17:389–398.
13. Canton CL, Gralnick A & Bender S (1989). Young chronic patients and substance abuse. *Hosp Commun Psych* 40:1037–1040.
14. Drake RE, Osher EC & Wallach MA (1989). Alcohol use and abuse in schizophrenia 1989; A prospective community study. *J Nerv Ment Disord* 177:408–414.
15. Drake RE & Wallach MA (1989). Substance abuse among the chronic mentally ill. *Hosp Commun Psych* 40:1041–1046.
16. Hekimian LJ & Gershon S (1968). Characteristics of drug abusers admitted to a psychiatric hospital. ??? 205:75–80.
17. Drake RE, Osher EC & Wallach MA (1989). Alcohol use and abuse in schizophrenia: A prospective community study. *J Nerv Ment Disord* 177:408–414.

18. Robbins LN, Helzer JE & Przybeck TR (1988). Alcohol disorders in the community: A report from the Epidemiologic Catchment Area. In: Rose RM, Barret J (eds.), *Alcoholism: Origins and Outcome.* New York: Raven Press.

19. Meyers JK, Weissman MM & Tschler GL (1984). Six-month prevalence of psychiatric disorders in three communities. *Arch Gen Psych* 41:959–967.

20. Schuckit MA (1983). Alcoholism and other psychiatric disorders. *Hosp Commun Psych* 34:1022–1027.

21. Miller NS & Fine J (1992). Epidemiology of comobridity of psychiatric and addiction disorders. *Psych Clin N Am,* In press.

22. Miller NS & Mahler JC (1991). "AA" Treatment Methods, Advances in Alcohol and Substance Abuse. *Alcoholism Treat Q* 8:39–51.

23. Harrison A, Hoffmann NS & Sneed SG (1991). Treatment Outcome. In: Miller NS (ed.), *Comprehensive Handbook of Drugs and Alcohol Addiction.* New York: Marcel Dekker.

24. Keso L & Salaspuro M (1991). Inpatient treatment of employed alcoholics: A randomized clinical trial on Hazelden-type and traditional treatment. *Alcoholism: Chem Exp Res* 14(4):524–589.

25. Walsh DC, Hingson RW & Merrigan DM (1991). A randomized trial of treatment options for alcohol-abusing workers. *N Engl J Med* 325(11):775–782.

26. Hoffmann NG & Miller NS (1992). Treatment outcome for abstinence based programs. *Psych Ann.*

27. Roman PM (1989). Inpatient alcohol and drug treatment: A national study of treatment centers. Executive Report. Institute for Behavioral Research. University of Georgia, 1–22. Supported by National Institute of Alcohol Abuse and Addictions.

28. Kosten TR & Kleber HD (1988). Differentiated diagnosis of psychiatric comorbidity in substance abusers. *Subst Abuse Treat* 5:201–206.

29. Blankfield A (1986). Psychiatric symptoms in alcohol dependence: Diagnostic and treatment applications. *J Subst Abuse Treat* 3:275–278.

30. Ries RK (1989). Roy-Byrne PP (ed.), *Alcoholism and Anxiety: New Findings for the Clinician.* Washington, DC: American Psychiatric Association Press.

31. Kay SR, Kalanthara M & Meinzer AE (1986). Diagnostic and behavioral characteristics of psychiatric patients who abuse substances. *Hosp Commun Psych* 143:867–872.

32. Miller NS & Gold MS (1992). The psychologist's role in unbridging pharmacological and non-pharmacological treatments for addiction disorders. *Psych Ann* 22(8):436–440.

33. Miller NS & Gold MS (1989). Identification and treatment of benzodiazepine abuse. *Am Fam Phys* 40(4):175–183.

34. Tiebout HM. The act of surrender in the therapeutic process. The National Council on Alcoholism, Inc., pp. 1–15.

35. Khantzian EJ (1985). The self medication hypothesis of addiction disorders from heroin and cocaine dependence. *Am J Psych* 142:1259–1264.

36. Miller NS, Mahler JC & Belkin BM, et al. (1991). Psychiatric Diagnosis in Alcohol and Drug Dependency. *Ann Clin Psych* 3(1):79–89.

37. Miller NS & Gold MS (1991). Dependence syndrome: A critical analysis of essential Lectures. *Psych Ann* 21(5):282–290.

38. Simon R (1989). Young chronic patients and substance abuse. *Hosp Commun Psych* 40:1037–1040.

39. Miller NS & Ries RK (1991). Drug and alcohol dependence and psychiatric populations: The need for diagnosis intervention and training. *Comp Psych* 3:268–276.

40. McCarrick AK, Manderscheid RW & Bertolucci DE (1985). Correlates of acting-out behaviors among young adult chronic patients. *Hosp Commun Psych* 36:848–853.

41. Sheets JL, Prevost JA & Reihman (1982). Young adult chronic patients: Three hypothesized subgroups. *Hosp Commun Psych* 33:197–203.

42. Schwartz SR & Goldfinger SM (1987). The new chronic patient: Clinical characteristics of an emergency subgroup. *Hosp Commun Psych* 470–474.

43. Miller NS, Hoffmann NG & Astrachan BM (1994). Major depression as a predictor of treatment response in abstinence-based programs. *Arch Gen Psych* (resubmitted for publication).

44. Hoffman GW, Rito DC & McGill EC (1993). Three month follow-up of 28 dual diagnosis inpatients. *Am J Drug Alc Addict* 19(1):79–88.

21

The Integrated Model

OVERVIEW

The integration of pharmacological and nonpharmacological treatments for addictive disorders is extending beyond the pharmacological treatment of withdrawal in addictive disorders. As a group, psychiatrists are beginning to take a leadership position in the diagnosis and treatment of addictive disorders. They are extending their focus of interest from the psychiatric disorders associated with addictive disorders to the diagnosis and treatment of addictive disorders themselves.

The relationship between psychiatry, addiction treatment, and self-help programs such as Alcoholics Anonymous (AA) is undergoing an integration. Psychiatrists are developing treatment programs with an integrated dual-disorders treatment focus in which psychiatrists have an integral role within the context of a multidisciplinary, biopsychosocial approach.

More commonly, psychiatrists are increasing their practice to include treatment of patients with addictive disorders. Psychiatrists are more often being employed in the primary treatment of addictive disorders. Their role is changing from that of adjunct clinician who provides assessment and medical management of psychiatric problems in the addiction treatment populations. Moreover, the notion that the psychiatrist can play no role in the long-term recovery from addiction is changing. Recovering addicts utilize psychiatric and psychological services and view them as helpful.

Resolution for Integration

There is substantial movement towards resolution of tension between traditional methods for understanding, diagnosing, and treating psychiatric and addictive disorders. The traditional psychiatric perspective is based on the self-medication hypothesis, which proposes that the addictive use of alcohol and drugs is the result of an underlying psychiatric disorder. The addiction-medicine perspective is based on the premise that addiction is an independent or primary disorder that can cause psychiatric symptoms.

In reality, the relationships between alcohol and other drug use and psychiatric symptoms and disorders are complex. Some of the relationships can be described as follows:

- Alcohol and other drug use can cause psychiatric symptoms.
- Withdrawal from alcohol and other drug use can cause psychiatric symptoms.
- Alcohol and other drug use can provoke the emergence or worsen the severity of preexisting psychiatric disorders.
- Alcohol and other drug use can mask psychiatric symptoms.
- Psychiatric disorders can cause behaviors and distortions in thinking that mimic those associated with addiction.[1]

In current practice, the decision whether to use pharmacological or nonpharmacological therapies (or both) in comorbid addictive and psychiatric disorders may be influenced by the perspective of the clinician and whether the addictive or psychiatric disorder is viewed as independent or secondary to the other disorder.

Another stage for integration is the use of pharmacological agents in conjunction with nonpharmacological treatments in the chronic management of addictive disorders that are often lifelong. Because addiction is characterized by relapse to the active use of alcohol and other drugs, pharmacological agents are being tested for relapse prevention beyond the withdrawal period. At any stage, however, progress towards an integration will depend on the acceptance of independent statuses for both categories of disorders, addiction and psychiatric, and knowledge and competence in their diagnosis and treatment.

INTERACTIONS

Exclusionary Criteria for Substance-Use Disorders

In the DSM-III-R, many Axis I diagnoses require exclusion of alcohol and other drug use. These diagnoses include schizophrenia, somatization disorder, cyclothymia, panic disorder, insomnia, hypersomnia, generalized anxiety, obsessive–compulsive disorder, Tourette's disorder, chronic motor or vocal motor disorder, transient tic disorder, intermittent explosive disorder, and psychogenic amnesia. Also, organic factors, including specific mention of intoxication and withdrawal from alcohol or other drugs are to be excluded for symptoms related to schizophrenia, delusional disorder (paranoid disorder), brief reactive psychosis, schizophreniform disorder, schizo-affective disorder, atypical psychosis, manic episodes, dysthymia, psychogenic fugue, dream anxiety disorder, sleep-terror and sleepwalking disorders, and alcohol-related blackout or cannabis dependence. There are also categories with general exclusions for any Axis I disorder.[2,3]

Self-Medication Hypothesis

The self-medication hypothesis states that alcohol and drug use is secondary to, or because of, an "underlying" condition, or that a psychological state, at times psychopathological, causes or motivates alcohol or drug use to alleviate or alter the emotional or cognitive state. The evidence for a self-medication hypothesis as an etiology or genesis of addictive use of alcohol and drugs is lacking. This is an assumption often based on retrospective diagnoses and dogmatic speculation. There are few objectives studies that support the common interpretation that psychiatric disorders are responsible for causing and sustaining addictive use. Controlled studies show that alcoholics drink despite alcohol-induced depression and that drinking and depression are negatively correlated in nonalcoholics.[4–6] Controlled and longitudinal studies further show that anxious or depressed people do not prefer to drink more than nonanxious or nondepressed people.[2,7]

While alcoholics report drinking because of anxiety and depression, under laboratory conditions they become increasingly anxious and depressed in a dose-dependent manner as they drink and not before. Similar findings have been reported for cocaine use. Addicted people rationalize the consequences to the antecedent position, and their self-reports can be a source of confusion to the clinician who takes addicted people literally.[5,6]

A study relating to the interactions of schizophrenia and alcohol or drug use was done by Bernadt and Murray in the United Kingdom.[8] Patients were diagnosed according to the Research Diagnostic Criteria, and increase or decrease in alcohol use in the month prior to admission was carefully studied. The only group of patients who increased alcohol use in a significant fashion in the month prior to admission were those with a diagnosis of alcoholism. Patients with disorder such as bipolar, mania, depression, anxiety, and schizophrenia were found to have a different pattern: 1) the bulk of patients did not change their drinking, and 2) about as many decreased their use of alcohol as increased their alcohol use prior to admission.

Thus, if the 20% of manics who increased their drinking prior to admission are called "self-medicators," should the 25% of manics who decreased their drinking prior to admission as their mania was developing be called "antiself-medicators" and should the ones who did not change their use of drugs be called "nonself-medicators"? What differentiates the "self-medicators" from the "antiself-medicators" and/or the "nonself-medicators"? It appears from the work of Bernadt and Murray and others that those patients who drink more as they are getting worse (drinking despite adverse consequences?) are those who qualify as having an alcohol or drug use disorder.[8,9] One wonders what purpose the "self-medication" hypothesis might serve, other than to rationalize (by the clinician and/or patient) a drug use condition without recognizing it as a problem needing specific addiction interventions.

Clinicians uncomfortable with addictive intervention or treatment may prefer to believe that drug-use disorders will disappear if they treat the "core" condition of mania, schizophrenia, or other more familiar psychiatric diagnoses. This perception is not borne out by the substantial body of research showing that specific interventions for both the psychiatric and the addictive disorders must be designed.[10-17] Drug interventions developed by such programs usually mimic those that have been developed within the addiction-treatment field.

TREATMENT

Psychiatric Comorbidity in Addictive Disorders

Principles from Studies. Studies employing both pharmacological and nonpharmacological agents for depression occurring in the context of addiction have indicated that traditional forms of therapy are not efficacious in reducing either the depression or the addiction.[2,3] Antidepressants, antianxiety agents, and psychotherapy do not relieve the depression and anxiety induced by alcoholism or drug addiction or the overall course of the addictive use of alcohol and drugs. Similarly, hallucinations and delusions induced by the addictive use of alcohol and other drugs have a different course, timeline, and prognosis than these psychiatric problems not induced by drugs, and do not have the same response to conventional psychiatric pharmacological or nonpharmacological therapies.[2,3]

Specific Treatment of Addiction. Studies confirm that the specific treatment of the addictive disorders will alleviate the addictive use of alcohol and other drugs and the consequent psychiatric comorbidity. A period of observation of several days to several weeks may be necessary to examine important causal links in the genesis of psychiatric symptoms from addictive disorders and to establish independent psychiatric disorders.[2-4]

Medications for Comorbid Psychiatric and Addictive Disorders. Most psychotropic medications can be used to treat independent psychiatric symptoms and disorders in alcoholism and drug addiction. Generally, beyond the detoxifying period in the abstinent state, there is little evidence that patients with addictive disorders respond significantly differently than the nonaddicted to most psychotropic medications. The caveat is that addicted people are more likely to overuse and lose control of psychoactive medications—especially psychoactive medications that have abuse and addiction potential—than nonaddicted patients.[2,18]

The Power of Medications versus the Power of the Individual

The physician views medications as powerful and inherently good despite the potential for toxicity and abuse potential. However, clinicians skilled in the treatment of addictive disorders often hold that addicted people need a clear sensorium and access to feelings in order to make fundamental changes in attitudes and behaviors for continued abstinence. Medications may impair cognition and blunt feelings, albeit sometimes subtly. Psychotherapists often advise only the judicious use of mood-altering chemicals that might interfere with the process of psychotherapy.

Recovering people must assume a proactive role regarding the changing of attitudes and feelings. They must abandon their often long-held belief that alcohol and other drugs can successfully fix, treat, or medicate life problems and uncomfortable psychological states. Clinically acknowledged, anxiety and depression can be motivating experiences that promote introspection and change. A commonly used expression to explain this interrelationship among recovering individuals is "no pain, no gain." Pharmacotherapy can indeed suppress symptoms such as suppressed or unconscious anxiety and depression among recovering people; but the emergence of these symptoms is often vital to their recovery and survival. Enormous misunderstanding has arisen from a divergence in purpose and perspective towards medications between the physician and the addicted patient.

INTEGRATION

Medication

There are relative contraindications for the use of pharmacological agents in patients with addictive disorders. However, some agents can be used as indicated with additional psychiatric disorders. The treatment of addictive disorders can be difficult without adequate treatment of the psychiatric disorder. For instance, a schizophrenic who is hallucinating and delusional and using alcohol and other drugs cannot enter treatment for addiction without having adequate control over the psychotic symptoms. The same can be true of a manic who is euphoric, delusional, and alcoholic or of a depressive or phobic who is also addicted to alcohol and/or benzodiazepines.[22] The integration of pharmacological and non-pharmacological treatments for addictive disorders and attendant psychiatric comorbidity lies in securing an independent status for each disorder, and utilizing the indicated therapies according to the diagnoses.[19,20]

At the same time, nonpharmacological treatment of an addictive disorder is indicated for a schizophrenic, manic, depressive, or phobic disorder in order to ultimately comply with medication treatments. Poor control of the addictive disorder bodes unfavorably for the prognosis of the psychiatric disorder. The prognosis of a combined psychiatric and addictive disorder follows that of the addictive disorders, so its treatment is mandatory to affect the course of either disorder.[8,18,23]

Treatment and Alcoholics Anonymous

Available data demonstrate abstinence rates of 60–80% after 2 years for addicted people in treatment programs that refer to AA. AA surveys also show recovery rates of 44% at less than 1 year, 83% between 1 and 5 years, and 90% at greater than 5 years of membership (44% of alcoholics in AA are addicted also to other drugs).[24] A recent study revealed that the best treatment outcome is obtained when professional treatment and AA membership are combined.[25] Studies are not yet available that examine the efficacy of psychiatric treatments in enhancing treatment outcome in addicted people with psychiatric comorbidity.

Roots of the Solution

Psychiatry as a specialty is establishing a commitment to integrate addictive disorders into the mainstream of clinical practice and education. More faculty members in psychiatry departments of medical schools are becoming skilled in the diagnosis and treatment of addictive disorders. However, role models skilled in addictive disorders are still in short supply for psychiatric resident trainees in psychiatric departments across the country. Psychiatrists are endorsing in greater numbers the standard of care that is used in over 90% of current addiction-treatment centers, namely, abstinence-based, multidisciplinary, biopsychosocial, twelve-step oriented programs for the treatment of addictive disorders.[7,26,27]

Minimum requirements for training in psychiatric residency for addictive disorders are being defined in order to begin the process of preparing trainees in the diagnosis and treatment. The "Catch 22" of not having role models among faculty can best be broken by training tomorrow's faculty now. Clearly defined minimum requirements will provide the catalyst for psychiatry departments to hire those already trained in addictive disorders as well as encouraging interested faculty members to step forward and to obtain specialized training in order to incorporate addictive disorders into the mainstream of psychiatry.[26]

REFERENCES

1. Landry MJ (1994). *Understanding Drugs of Abuse: The Processes of Addiction, Treatment, and Recovery.* Washington, DC: American Psychiatric Press.
2. Miller NS, Mahler JC, Belkin BM & Gold MS (1990). Psychiatric diagnosis in alcohol and drug dependence. *Ann Clin Psych* 3(1):79–89.
3. Schuckit MA (1983). Alcoholism and other psychiatric disorders. *Hosp Commun Psych* 34:1022–1027.
4. Blankfield A (1986). Psychiatric symptoms in alcohol dependence. Diagnosis and treatment implications. *J Subst Abuse Treat* 3:275–278.
5. Tamerin JS & Mendelson JH (1969). The psychodynamics of chronic inebriation. Observations of alcoholic during the process of drinking in an experimental group setting. *Am J Psych* 125(7):886–899.
6. Mayfield DG (1979). Alcohol and affect: Experimental studies. In: Goodwin DW, Erickson CK (eds.), *Alcoholism and Affective Disorders,* pp. 99–107. New York: SP Medical and Scientific Books.
7. Vaillant GE & Milofsky EP (1982). The etiology of alcoholism: A prospective viewpoint. *Am Psychol* 37:494–503.
8. Bernadt MW & Murray RM (1986). Psychiatric disorder, drinking and alcoholism: What are the links? *Br J Psych* 148:393–400.
9. Miller NS (1991). Drug and alcohol addiction as a disease. In: Miller NS (ed.), *Comprehensive Handbook of Drug and Alcohol Addiction,* pp. 295–309. New York: Marcel Dekker.
10. Shuckit M (1985). Clinical implications of primary diagnostic groups among alcoholics. *Arch Gen Psych* 42:1043–1049.
11. Wallen M & Weiner H (1988). The dually diagnosed patient in an inpatient chemical dependency treatment program. *Alcoholism Treat Q* 5(1/2):197–218.
12. Ries RK & Miller NS (1993). Dual diagnosis: Concept, diagnosis, and treatment. In Dunner DL (ed.), *Current Psychiatric Therapy,* pp. 131–138. Philadelphia: WB Saunders.
13. Ries RK (1993). Clinical treatment matching models for dually diagnosed patients. *Psychiatric Clinics of North America* 16(1):167–176.
14. Minkoff K (1989). An integrated treatment model for dual diagnosis of psychosis and addiction. *Hosp Commun Psych* 40(10):1031–1036.
15. Osher FC & Kofoed LL (1989). Treatment of patients with psychiatric and

psychoactive substance abuse disorders. *Hosp Commun Psych* 40(10):1025–1030.

16. Evans K & Sullivan JM (1990). *Dual Diagnosis: Counseling the Mentally Ill Substance Abuser.* New York: Guilford.

17. O'Connell DF (1990). Managing the dually diagnosed patient. In: O'Connell DF (ed.), *Current Issues and Clinical Approaches.* New York: Haworth Press.

18. Ries RK & Samson H (1987). Substance abuse among inpatient psychiatric patients. *Subst Abuse* 8:28–34.

19. Halikas J, Kuhn K & Carlson G (1992). The effect of Carbamazepine on cocaine use. *Am J Addict* 1(1):30–39.

20. Kosten TR, Gawin FH & Kosten TA, et al. (1992). Six month follow-up of short-term pharmacotherapy for cocaine dependence. *Am J Addict* 1(1):40–49.

21. Naranjo CA, Sellers EM & Lawrin MO. Modulation of ethanol intake by serotonin inhibitors. *J Clin Psych* 47;41(Suppl):16–22.

22. Dackis CA, Gold MS, Pottash ALC & Sweeney DR (1986). Evaluating depression in alcoholics. *Psych Res* 17:105–109.

23. Woodruff RA, Guze SB & Clayton PH (1973). Alcoholism and depression. *Arch Gen Psych* 28:97–100.

24. Alcoholics Anonymous Membership 1989 Survey. New York: Alcoholics Anonymous World Services.

25. Walsh DC, Hingson RW & Merrigan DM, et al. (1991). A randomized trial of treatment options for alcohol-abusing workers. *N Engl J Med* 325(11):775–782.

26. Group for the Advancement of Psychiatry, Committee on Alcoholism and the Addictions (1991). Substance abuse disorders: A psychiatric priority. *Am J Psych* 148(10):1291–1300.

27. Harrison A, Hoffman NG & Streed SG (1991). Treatment outcome. In: Miller NS (ed.), *Comprehensive Handbook of Drug and Alcohol Addiction.* New York: Marcel Dekker.

22

Pharmacological Treatment: An Overview

OVERVIEW

The recent advances in the pharmacotherapy for the prevention of relapse in alcoholics has not extended beyond basic research in animals and clinical research in humans. The application of experimental findings to clinical practice awaits further research in many instances. However, enthusiasm in developing pharmacotherapies for alcoholism has stimulated renewed interest in the treatment of alcoholism by physicians. Similar advances have occurred in pharmacotherapies for other drug addictions. Because contemporary alcoholics are generally addicted to other drugs, the search for a pharmacotherapy for alcohol *and* drug addiction is requisite.[1-4]

The pharmacological agents subsumed in the pharmacotherapies for alcoholism (and other drug addictions) can be classified according to these major categories:

1. Intoxication—agents that reverse the active pharmacological effects of alcohol.
2. Withdrawal—agents that suppress the pharmacological withdrawal from alcohol.
3. Desire and compulsion—agents that block the preoccupation with acquiring alcohol and the desire to use or continue to use alcohol.

4. Psychiatric complications—agents that treat or ameliorate the psychiatric symptoms induced by alcohol and other drugs.
5. Psychiatric disorders—agents that are used in patients who have additional independent psychiatric disorders.
6. Concurrent drug addiction—agents used in drug addictions among those with alcoholism.[1-5]

Contemporary Alcoholics—Concurrent Drug Addiction

The contemporary alcoholic, especially the younger alcoholic, is usually addicted to one or more other drugs. The order of drugs of dependence used by alcoholic addicts, in descending frequency of addiction, is nicotine, cannabis, cocaine, benzodiazepines/barbiturates, opiates, and hallucinogens. The nonpharmacological treatment approach is to "lump" together the various drug addictions, including alcohol, for the specific treatment of alcohol/drug addiction.[2,6] Also, the withdrawal from most of the drugs is benign and pharmacological detoxification is not necessary.[2,6] Recent experimental investigations of the use of pharmacological agents have been aimed at the subacute period of the first 3–6 months, when the relapse rate is highest, to improve treatment compliance and retention.[2,3,5,6]

Alcohol

Symptoms of withdrawal from alcohol extend from relatively mild, such as sweating, tachycardia, hypertension, tremors, and anxiety, to more serious phenomena, such as convulsions and delirium.[2,7] Hypothesized origins of the syndrome are disturbances in several neuronal systems throughout the brain. Growing clinical opinion is that clinicians should routinely consider adjunctive pharmacologic therapy for alcohol withdrawal in order to limit the severity of subsequent relapse episodes.[8] The model of "kindling" suggests that repeated withdrawal from alcohol and drugs contributes to future relapse. Kindling is a phenomenon wherein the brain is increasingly sensitized to the effects of alcohol and/or drugs with repeated use.

Benzodiazepines are the most commonly used agents to treat alcohol withdrawal. These agents act by several methods. They bind to a benzodiazepine receptor in order to facilitate the action of gamma-aminobutyric acid (GABA). In addition, benzodiazepines act on both the noradrenergic system and the hypothalamic–pituitary–adrenal axis to diminish the severity of arousal in these systems.[2]

Diazepam is commonly used to treat alcohol withdrawal and can be administered at 5–10 mg, 4 times per day. An alternate method of dosage is the "loading dose" method in with 5 mg diazepam is given every 1–2 hours to a patient until withdrawal symptoms subside, at which time the drug is discontinued.[9] The long half-life of diazepam provides continuing coverage and limits the need for further administration of medication.

Because of the problem of dependency on benzodiazepines in alcoholics, routine use of benzodiazepines should be restricted to treating the alcohol-withdrawal syndrome.[2] Since diazepam and chlordiazepoxide are metabolized in the liver, there may be problematic accumulation. Because of this factor there is growing use of short- and intermediate-acting benzodiazepines such as oxazepam and lorazepam. These agents do not accumulate in the body for as long a period as the long-acting benzodiazepines, and a clinician can readily administer a more specific dose.[2]

β-Adrenergic blockers (atenolol and propranolol) may have a future role in treating alcohol withdrawal. However, a troubling side effect of β-adrenergic blockers is delirium and hallucinations. β-Adrenergic agents block the peripheral manifestations of withdrawal, such as elevated vital signs and tremor.

Other agents being examined in clinical trials for treatment of alcohol withdrawal include the α_2-adrenergic agonists clonidine and lofexidine; a dopamine-2 blocker, haloperidol; calcium channel antagonists or blockers, such as nifedipine; and carbamazepine, a tricyclic anticonvulsant.[2]

Agents for Compulsion

Agents such as serotonin-uptake inhibitors have been studied in social, early, and heavy drinkers, and chronic alcoholics. Results show reduction in number of drinks and increase in abstinent days (10–26%). Animals studies using these agents have substantiated a decrease in alcohol consumption.[2] Naltrexone is another agent that is aimed at reducing alcohol intake by blocking a possible link between alcohol and opiate byproducts from the metabolism of alcohol. Recently, preliminary studies of naltrexone in two controlled studies revealed fewer and shorter relapses than placebo in a three-month follow-up.[2,5,10–14]

Cocaine

Most of the research on pharmacological treatments of cocaine has been directed at the prolonged detoxification stage in the first 3–6 months. Studies have examined desipramine, imipramine, bromocriptine, amantadine, carbamazepine, and flupentixol decanoate.[3,5,15,16] Of these, desipramine has been studied in a double-blind, controlled fashion. In a 6-month follow up of 43 of 72 patients who entered a 6-week randomized clinical trial, self-reported cocaine abstinence during the 6 months was significantly greater in patients treated with desipramine 250 mg (44%—16) than those treated with lithium 900 mg (19%—16) and placebo (27%—11).[3,5,15–17]

Opiates

Opiate detoxification is typically performed with either methadone or clonidine from any opiate including heroin, morphine, or methadone itself. Schedules employing a regular dosing or as needed for withdrawal symptoms may be used with clonidine in the range of 0.1–0.3 mg per dose through the peak period of withdrawal from heroin (1–3 days) and methadone (1–2 weeks). The rate-limiting factors are sedation and hypotension from clonidine, which must be carefully monitored.[3,5] A rate-limiting factor using methadone for withdrawal is its addictiveness, making completing the transition to abstinence problematic. While accepted as a medical treatment, the efficacy of methadone maintenance remains controversial. As with many other forms of pharmacological treatments, the better outcomes with methadone appear to occur with highly motivated patients.

Of clinical interest are the problems of use of other addicting drugs such as alcohol, cocaine, cannabis, and benzodiazepines by those in methadone maintenance, along with the addicting nature of methadone. Also, psychiatric symptoms appear to occur as a result of the pharmacological effects of methadone.[3,5,18]

Another drug of high research interest is buprenorphine, which is a mixed opiate agonist with μ-agonist and κ-antagonist activity. Buprenorphine may be useful in treating opiate withdrawal. Preliminary results suggest buprenorphine produces less pharmacological dependence than methadone, as reflected in a milder withdrawal syndrome while suppressing drug-seeking behaviors.[19]

Naltrexone as an opiate antagonist has been difficult to study. It seems that opiate addicts are reluctant to enter studies and have a high dropout rate if there is participation in a study. Many opiate addicts appear to not choose an abstinence-based approach to treatment. Opiate withdrawal is medically benign, and therefore, much of the pharmacotherapy for detoxification is aimed at the uneasiness that the opiate addict experiences in attempts to achieve an abstinent state.[20]

REFERENCES

1. Liskow BI & Goodwin DW (1987). Pharmacological treatment of alcohol intoxication, withdrawal and dependence: A critical review. *J Stud Alc* 8:356–370.
2. Litten RZ & Allen JP (1991). Pharmacotherapies for alcoholism: Promising agents and clinical issues. Alcoholism: *Clin Exp Res* 15(4):620–633.
3. Weddington WW (1992). Use of pharmacologic agents in the treatment of addiction. *Psych Ann* 22(8):425–429.
4. Miller NS, Belkin BM & Gold MS (1990). Cosynchronous use of alcohol and drugs. *N Y State J Med* 90(12):596–600.
5. Gorelick DA (1993). Overview of pharmacological treatment approach for alcohol and other drug addictions: Intoxication, withdrawal, and relapse prevention. In Miller NS (ed.), *Psychiatric Clinics of North America* pp. 141–156. Philadelphia: Saunders.
6. Miller NS (1991). Special problems of the alcohol and multiple-drug dependent: Clinical interactions and detoxification. In Frances RJ & Miller SI (eds.), *Clinical Textbook of Addictive Disorders* pp. 194–220. New York: Guilford.
7. Miller NS, Belkin BM & Gold MS (1989). Laboratory testing for drug abuse and addiction. *Ann Clin Psych* 1(4):227–236.
8. National Institute on Alcohol Abuse and Alcoholism (NIAAA) (1989). Alcohol withdrawal syndrome. *Alc Alert* 5:1–4.
9. Sellers EM, Naranjo CA, Harrison M, Devenyl P, Roach C & Sykora K (1983). Diazepam loading: Simplified treatment of alcohol withdrawal. *Clin Pharmacol Ther* 34:822–826.
10. Fuller RK & Roth HP (1979). Disulfiram for the treatment of alcoholism: An evaluation in 128 men. *Ann Intern Med* 90:901–904.
11. Meyer RE (1992). New pharmacotherapies for cocaine dependence revisited. *Arch Gen Psych* 49:900–904.
12. Butterworth AT & Watts RD (1974). Double-blind comparison of thiothixene, trifluoperazine, and placebo in chronic alcoholism. *Psychosomatics* 15:85–87.
13. Turek IS, Ota K, Brown C, Massari F & Kurland AA (1973). Thiothixene and thioridazine in alcoholism treatment. *Q J Stud Alc* 34:853–859.

14. Fox V & Smith MA (1959). Evaluation of a chemopsychotherapeutic program for the rehabilitation of alcoholics: Observations over a two-year period. *Q J Stud Alc* 20:767–850.

15. Weiss RD & Mirin SM (1991). Psychological and pharmacological treatment strategies in cocaine dependence. *Ann Clin Psych* 2:239–243.

16. Halikas J, Kuhn K & Carlson G (1992). The effect of carbamazepine on cocaine use. *Am J Addict* 1(1):30–39.

17. Kosten TR, Gawin FH, Kosten TA, Morgan C, Rounsaville BJ, Schottenfeld R & Kleber HD (1992). Six-month follow-up of short-term pharmacotherapy for cocaine dependence. *Am J Addict* 1(1):40–49.

18. Ball JC & Ross A (1991). *The Effectiveness of Methadone Maintenance Treatment.* New York: Springer-Verlag.

19. Kosten TR, Morgan C & Kleber HD (1991). Treatment of heroin addicts using buprenorphine. *Am J Drug Alc Abuse* 17:119–128.

20. Gonzalez JP & Brogen RN (1992). Naltrexone: A review of its pharmacodynamic and pharmocokinetic properties and therapeutic efficacy in the management of opioid dependence. *Drugs* 35:192–213.

23

Pharmacological Treatments: A Practical Guide

HISTORY

The effects of drugs and alcohol may be caused by the stimulation or inhibition of different neurotransmitters, chiefly gamma-aminobutyric acid, acetylcholine, norepinephrine, dopamine, serotonin, and beta-endorphin. The biopsychiatric model focuses on putative neurotransmitter activity to diagnose and treat overdose and addiction. This model explains how different drugs exert their effects and provides a rationale for specific pharmacologic intervention in the drug-dependent patient.

Alcohol and drug addiction are often misdiagnosed because of the multiple signs and symptoms associated with each drug and the varying, complicated presentations that result from drug–drug interactions. Misdiagnosis can result in significant morbidity and even mortality.

The biopsychiatric model may assist physicians in the accurate diagnosis and efficient treatment of drug intoxication and withdrawal. The advantage of this model is that only a few principles must be mastered. These principles can then be applied to most drug-dependency situations.[1]

The biopsychiatric model is based on the principle that drugs of abuse and addiction do not interact uniquely with the brain to produce highly specific symptoms. In fact, they increase or inhibit the rate of release of only a limited number of known neurotransmitters. A basic knowledge of neurotransmitter activity helps physicians recognize drug abuse and addiction. Once the type of drug dependence is diagnosed, treatment can be tailored according to the specific neurotransmitters that have been affected by the drug.[2]

Neurotransmitters

The neurotransmitters—gamma-aminobutyric acid (GABA), acetylcholine, norepinephrine, dopamine, serotonin, beta-endorphin, NMDA, and glutamate—account for most of the symptoms seen with alcohol and other drugs most commonly used in the United States (see Fig. 23.1).[1]

Gamma-Aminobutyric Acid (GABA). GABA is the neurotransmitter most often affected in drug abuse and addiction. This modified amino-acid transmitter system accounts for 20% of all receptor sites in the brain.[3] The major inhibitory neurotransmitter of the central nervous system, GABA acts by opening chloride channels into the neurons. These channels are operated by the fitting of GABA into its proper site on the receptor. The receptor has a second site where barbiturates can fit and facilitate chloride ingress.[4] The GABA receptor also has an auxiliary receptor, the BZ receptor, that boosts the action of GABA. The BZ receptor is named after the benzodiazepines, which function in that location.[5]

Acetylcholine. The most important distribution of acetylcholine is in the nucleus basalis of Meynert and the nigrostriatal tract. Degeneration of the nucleus basalis causes downstream degeneration of projecting cholinergic neurons in the cerebral cortex, resulting in some of the manifestations of Alzheimer's disease. Nigrostriatal acetylcholine acts in rough balance with nigrostriatal dopamine. When there is a relative increase in the acetylcholine portion of this ratio, the symptoms of parkinsonism result.

Most cholinergic receptors in the brain are of the muscarinic type and serve cognitive functions. Nicotinic receptors are peripheral and cause cardiac inhibition and gastric stimulation. At low levels of activation, nicotinic receptors stimulate autonomic ganglia and myoneural junctions, but at higher levels this action is depressed.[6]

Norepinephrine. Norepinephrine is a stimulatory and inhibitory neurotransmitter and is synthesized and stored in the nucleus locus ceruleus. This nucleus is paired and located in the pons, near the floor of the third ventricle. Norepinephrine is a catecholamine that regulates mood and

Neurotransmitter/Central Action

Serotonin
Modulates mood
Initiates sleep
Involved in REM sleep

β-Endorphin
Modulates mood
Modulates pain perception
Inhibits norepinephrine release

Drugs of Addiction that Affect
Neurotransmitter Action

Psychedelic agents
Phencyclidine

Opiates
Phencyclidine

Central Location

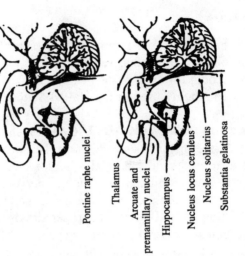

Pontine raphe nuclei

Thalamus
Arcuate and
premamillary nuclei
Hippocampus
Nucleus locus ceruleus
Nucleus solitarius
Substantia gelatinosa

FIGURE 23.1. Drugs of addiction that affect neurotransmitter action in the brain.

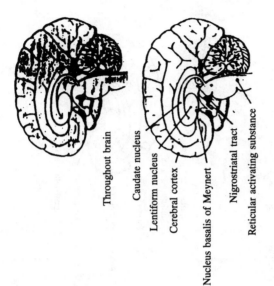

γ-Aminobutyric acid (GABA)
General inhibition of other
neurotransmitters

Acetylcholine
Counterbalance dopamine
Maintains memory
Initiates short-term memory

Alcohol
Barbiturates
Benzodiazepines
Chloral hydrage
Ethchlorvynol
Meprobamate
Methaqualone (?)
Phencyclidine

Phencyclidine

Throughout brain

Caudate nucleus
Lentiform nucleus
Cerebral cortex
Nucleus basalis of Meynert
Nigrostriatal tract
Reticular activating substance

FIGURE 23.1. Continued.

Neurotransmitter/Central Action	Drugs of Addiction that Affect Neurotransmitter Action	Central Location
Norepinephrine Modulates mood Maintains sleeping state	Amphetamines Cocaine Opiates Phencyclidine	Nucleus locus ceruleus
Dopamine Counterbalances acetylcholine Stimulates pleasure center Modulates mood Affects intellectual processes Inhibits prolactin release	Amphetamines Cocaine Phencyclidine	Pontine and medullary cell groups Caudate nucleus Lentiform nucleus Nucleus accumbens Tuberioinfundibular pathway Nigrostriatal tract

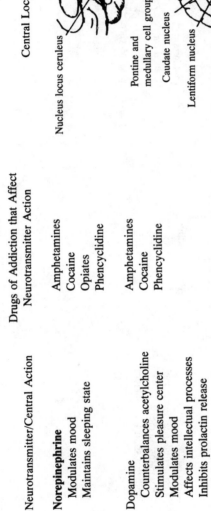

FIGURE 23.1. *Continued.*

arousal. High levels of norepinephrine are associated with mania and anxiety whereas low levels are associated with depression. Norepinephrine also maintains the sleeping state. Peripherally, it acts as a vasoconstrictor.[7]

Dopamine. Another important catecholamine is dopamine, a stimulatory and inhibitory neurotransmitter that affects mood and thought. Abnormally high levels of dopamine are found in schizophrenia and chorea; low levels of this neurotransmitter are associated with depression and parkinsonism. In fact, degeneration of dopaminergic neurons in the nigrostriatal tract is seen in primary Parkinson's disease. Dopamine is also important in the primary pleasure pathway between the nucleus accumbens and the pars compacta.[7] Dopamine inhibits prolactin release from the pituitary gland via the tuberoinfundibular pathway.[8]

Serotonin. Central serotonin is produced at five paired nuclei in the pons—the pontine raphe nuclei. Serotonin is an indolamine that acts to modulate mood and initiate sleep. Low levels of serotonin activity are associated with depression and violent behaviors. Stimulation of serotonin receptors is associated with an electroencephalogram (EEG) pattern similar to that seen in the rapid-eye-movement (REM) or dream phase of sleep.[9]

Beta-Endorphin. Relaxation and analgesia are produced by beta-endorphin, which is an opioid peptide. This peptide is distributed throughout the hippocampus, nucleus solitarious, substantia gelatinosa, thalamus, and nucleus locus ceruleus. By means of this distributory network, beta-endorphin interconnects the perceptions of panic, pain, stress, and affect. In the nucleus locus ceruleus, beta-endorphin acts at μ-receptors to inhibit the release of norepinephrine (see Fig. 23.1).[10]

ACTIONS OF DRUGS OF ABUSE AND ADDICTION

The most common drugs of abuse in the United States are listed in Table 23.1 and are discussed by class in the following sections.

Sedatives and Tranquilizers

Alcohol, the barbiturates, the agents ethchlorvynol (Placidyl), glutethimide (Doriden, Doriglute), and meprobamate (Equanil, Miltown, Neura-

TABLE 23.1 Common Drugs of Abuse

Drug	Class	Street names
Amphetamines	Stimulant	Black beauty Crosses Hearts
Barbiturates	Sedative/tranquilizer	Barbs Blue racers Yellow jackets
Benzodiazepines	Sedative/tranquilizer	"Roches" Tranks Pumpkin
Cocaine	Stimulant	Coke Crack Free base
Ethchlorvynol (Placidyl)	Sedative/tranquilizer	Green jeans Pickles
Fentanyl	Opiate	Six-pack
Glutethimide (Doriden, Doriglute)	Sedative/tranquilizer	Grays Seabees
Heroin	Opiate	Horse Skag Smack
Lysergic acid (LSD)	Psychedelic agent	Acid Blue cheer LSD
Meperidine (Demerol)	Opiate	Banana
Meprobamate (Equanil, Miltown, Neuramate, etc.)	Sedative/tranquilizer	Bams
Mescaline	Psychedelic agent	Cactus Mex Peyote
Methamphetamine (Desoxyn)	Stimulant	Crystal meth Twenty-twenty
3,4-Methylenedioxy-methamphetamine (MDMA)	Psychedelic agent	Adam Ecstasy
Phencyclidine	Phencyclidine	Hog PCP Surfer
Propoxyphene (Darvon, Dolene, Doxaphene, etc.)	Psychedelic agent	Lilies
Psilocybin	Psychedelic agent	Mushroom Purple passion

mate, etc.), and the benzodiazepines suppress brain function by activating the GABA system.[11] This causes slowing and eventual paralysis of CNS and motor function. Sedation, slowed mentation, confusion, loss of consciousness, and coma occur as the effects of the stimulatory transmitters are deactivated by GABA-like effects. Peripherally, the sedatives and tranquilizers cause hypotension, bradycardia, and slowed respiratory rate. As heart conduction slows, arrhythmias emerge. Prolonged slowing of the respiratory rate may lead to acidosis.

According to the biopsychiatric model, sedatives and tranquilizers mimic the action of GABA by opening chloride channels.[12] When a sedative is taken for a prolonged period, the production (and supply) of GABA is progressively decreased. If the sedative is then abruptly withdrawn, the natural inhibitory function of the GABA system is reduced, leading to a rebound excess of neurotransmitter activity formerly under GABA control. Norepinephrine rebound causes increased alertness, hyperglycemia, hypertension, hyperreflexia, nystagmus, and pupillary dilation. Dopamine rebound results in hyperactivity, tremors, hallucinations, delusions and seizures.

Drugs that act directly on GABA receptors cause more severe addiction and withdrawal symptoms than drugs that act indirectly on BZ receptors.[13] Direct-acting agents include all the barbiturates that act specifically at the so-called barbiturate receptor, which is part of the GABA–chloride channel complex. Methaqualone, meprobamate, ethchlorvynol, and glutethimide also act at the barbiturate receptor; in terms of neuroreceptor activity, these drugs are indistinguishable from the barbiturates and offer no distinct therapeutic advantage.

The BZ receptor is not part of the GABA–chloride channel complex and is therefore referred to as the GABA coreceptor. Because the BZ receptor is physically somewhat removed from the channel complex, actions at this receptor are indirect or of reduced intensity. The benzodiazepines, alcohol and alcohol derivatives, including methanol, ethanol, isopropyl alcohol, chloral hydrate (Noctec) and paraldehyde (Paral), also activate the BZ receptor.

Stimulants

Amphetamines and cocaine exert a stimulatory effect on the CNS.[14] Acutely, they increase the release of dopamine and norepinephrine from presynaptic neurons. These drugs have a dual action. First, they increase the release of stored dopamine from the presynaptic vesicles into the synaptic cleft. Second, this enhanced supply of available dopamine is further augmented by amphetamine- or cocaine-induced blockade of pre-synaptic uptake. Thus, an increased supply of dopamine is available for a longer period to stimulate postsynaptic receptors. It is presumed that a similar mechanism operates with norepinephrine and serotonin.[15]

The presynaptic blockade, however, causes the catecholamine depletion associated with chronic stimulant use. Because reuptake is prevented, large amounts of dopamine are degraded in the synaptic cleft by catechol-O-methyltransferase (COMT). The result of COMT metabolism is 5-OH-tyramine. Normally, dopamine, as other catecholamines, would be taken up into the neuron and metabolized into homovanillic acid by monoamine oxidase. While homovanillic acid can be recycled to produce a continuous resupply of dopamine, 5-OH-tyramine cannot be recycled. Therefore, as more stimulants are used, the supply of dopamine and other catecholamines are gradually depleted.[16]

The initial increase in catecholamine levels causes the stimulatory rush of an amphetamine or cocaine "high." Peripheral stimulatory effects include hypertension secondary to vasoconstriction, tachycardia, and pupillary dilation. Tachycardia may progress to heart block due to direct cardiac effects. Central stimulatory effects include anorexia, euphoria, hypervigilance, hypersexuality, and grandiosity.[17]

Major effects occur at the nucleus accumbens, a primary pleasure center. After repeated stimulation of this area, the need for cocaine or amphetamine becomes a pseudodrive. The drive for these drugs takes on the same force as other primary drives that also affect the nucleus accumbens, including thirst, hunger, and sexual desire. Eventually, the drive (craving) for the drug exceeds even the primary drives. A classic example is a cocaine-addicted rat that has been dehydrated but will not turn away from a cocaine supply for even one second to drink water from an easily accessible source. The rat will continue to prefer cocaine to water until it dies of dehydration.[18]

Because the dopamine and norepinephrine supply is constantly depleted by chronic use, ever higher doses of the drug must be taken. When the drug supply is suddenly cut off, deactivation of the nucleus accumbens produces a profound dysphoria. Decreased catecholamine levels then produce vasodilation, muscle cramping, and hypersomnia.[18]

Opiates

Opiates act on the nucleus accumbens like stimulants. Since the opiates have indirect effects on dopamine, mediated through the μ-opioid receptors, the pleasure experience is quantitatively less than the experience derived from stimulants. Although opiates can displace food and sex as primary drives, they do not displace thirst.[19]

The activity at the nucleus accumbens, however, is not related to withdrawal symptoms. During intoxication, opiates stimulate opioid receptors in the nucleus locus ceruleus; this causes a suppression of noradrenergic release. Since the nucleus accumbens is the major source of central norepinephrine, the effects of opiate use are substantial. Mood and affect are inhibited. Pupils are constricted. Peripherally, there is vasodilation and constipation as noradrenergic alpha-receptors and beta-receptors are affected. If large amounts of opiates are acutely abused, noradrenergic suppression can lead to respiratory and cardiovascular suppression.[20]

Withdrawal, although medically benign, is subjectively quite distressing and is marked by an intense drive to use more opiates. When opioid receptors are no longer hyperstimulated by drugs such as morphine or heroin, the inhibition of the norepinephrine system is released. The previous opiate-dependent suppression of norepinephrine is replaced by rebound release of the large amounts of norepinephrine that had accumulated. Since norepinephrine is a natural stimulant and causes muscles to contract, this release produces generalized muscular cramping, pilomotor erection, increased pulse rate, and hot/cold flashes.[21]

Psychedelic Agents

A number of drugs are termed psychedelic or hallucinogenic. All of these drugs produce intense, mind-altering experiences that are related to altering serotonin levels. Excitation of the presynaptic receptors in the pontine rephe nuclei produces visual, proprioceptive, and perceptual distortions. Dissolution of ego boundaries occurs without cognitive or memory impairment, disorientation, or confusion. Psychedelic agents also produce EEG changes similar to those seen during REM sleep, which may account for the dream-like quality of the high reported by those using this class of drugs.

In addition to action at the raphe nuclei, psychedelic agents bind to the auditory and visual areas, the corpus amygdaloideum, the hippocampus, and the hypothalamus. By acting in these sites, psychedelic agents alter the transfer and integration of sensory messages to produce alterations in perceptions and frank hallucinations.[22,23]

Phencyclidine

Phencyclidine (PCP) acts at several neurotransmitter sites. Its actions mimic those of all the drugs previously described. Phencyclidine stimulants release dopamine, norepinephrine, and serotonin.[24] It also inhibits the actions of acetylcholine and, possibly, GABA.[25] Opioids are simultaneously stimulated and inhibited.[26]

Peripheral anticholinergic activity produces hot, dry, flushed skin, as well as tachycardia. Central anticholinergic inhibition in the reticular activating substance is associated with amnesia and confusion. Tachycardia is further increased by the stimulation of peripheral dopamine and norepinephrine. Centrally, dopamine stimulation at dopamine-2 receptors can give rise to hypervigilance, as well as illogical and paranoid thought patterns. Dopaminergic overactivity in the nigrostriatal tract can cause impaired coordination. Stimulation of norepinephrine in the nucleus locus ceruleus produces anxiety and increased activity.[25]

The characteristic superhuman strength of phencyclidine abusers is related to the opioid receptors. Because their perception of pain is reduced, these users can subject their musculoskeletal systems to otherwise intolerable strains. They can bend steel bars, because they are able to ignore muscle tears and stress fractures. Their insensitivity to pain, disturbed thinking and increased motor activity makes phencyclidine addicts dangerous to themselves and those around them. The expected noradrenergic inhibition associated with increased activity is apparently overridden by direct noradrenergic activity.[26,27]

INTERVENTION AND TREATMENT

Sedatives and Tranquilizers

When the daily dose of a barbiturate is known, 50–100 mg of phenobarbital per day is given for each 100 mg of the barbiturate to which the patient is dependent. The phenobarbital dosage is then reduced by 20%

every other day. If withdrawal symptoms appear, 30–100 mg or oral phenobarbital is given immediately and the schedule is revised. By slowly titrating the dosage of this agent downward, the GABA system is gradually reactivated[28] (see Table 23.2).

If the daily dose of the dependent drug is not known, or if the patient is a mixed-drug addict, the phenobarbital challenge test may be useful. The initial test dose is 200 mg. If sleep is induced, it should be assumed that the average daily dose of abused drug is the equivalent of 200 mg of phenobarbital. If the patient is only drowsy, the daily dose of the abused drug is the equivalent of 400–600 mg of phenobarbital. An awake state with nystagmus indicates a daily dose equivalent to 600–1,000 mg of phenobarbital, while an awake state without nystagmus is consistent with a daily abuse dosage equivalent to more than 1,000 mg of phenobarbital.

For alcoholics and benzodiazepine addicts, an indirect GABA agent, such as chlordiazepoxide (Librium, Lipoxide, Mitran, etc.) is recommended. The usual initial dosage is 25–50 mg every 6 hours as needed, titrated downward according to blood pressure elevation, pulse rate, agitation, and psychosis. Thiamine, hydration, and magnesium replacement may be indicated by the severity of the withdrawal symptoms (see Table 23.3).[29]

For benzodiazepine addicts, the detoxification can be simplified and easily applied if basic principles are followed. First, benzodiazepines have cross-tolerance and dependence with each other, alcohol, and other sedative/hypnotic drugs. Any benzodiazepine can be substituted for another benzodiazepine and with barbiturates, so that conversion for equivalent doses can be calculated. Second, a long-acting benzodiazepine is more effective in suppressing the withdrawal symptoms and producing a gradual and smooth transition to the abstinent state. Greater patient compliance and less morbidity will result from the use of the longer-acting benzodiazepines.[30,31]

Third, select a benzodiazepine with lower euphoric properties, such as chlordiazepam, avoiding diazepam as much as possible. Fourth, do not leave as-needed doses as this would give the addict a choice that is beyond control. Withdrawal from benzodiazepines is not usually marked by hypertension and tachycardia as with alcohol so that prn doses are not needed. The anxiety of withdrawal should be controlled with the prescribed taper unless objectively it appears that the doses are too low. Caution is urged at this point, as drug-seeking behavior needs to be differentiated from anxiety of withdrawal and the anxiety of another disorder. Only the anxiety

TABLE 23.2 Benzodiazepine (Barbiturate) Withdrawal and Detoxification

Withdrawal

Signs

1. Increased or decreased psychomotor activity
2. Muscular weakness
3. Tremulousness
4. Hyperpyrexia, sweating
5. Delirium
6. Convulsions
7. Tachycardia and elevated blood pressure
8. Course tremor of tongue, eyelids, and hands
9. Status epilepticus

Symptoms

1. Anxiety
2. Euphoria
3. Depression
4. Thought disorder
5. Hostility
6. Grandiosity
7. Disorientation
8. Euphoria
9. Depression
10. Tactile, auditory, and visual hallucinations
11. Suicidal ideation and thinking

Detoxification

Short-Acting
7–10 Day Taper:
Day 1 Librium 25–50 mg, po, qid with a gradual taper to 10 mg, po, qid on last day.
No prn.

or

7–10 Day Taper:
Calculate benzodiazepine equivalence and give 50% of dose over the taper (if actual
dose is known prior to detoxification)

Long Acting:
10–14 Day Taper:
Day 1 Librium 25–50 mg, po, qid with a gradual taper to 10 mg po, qid on last day.
No prn.

or

10–14 Day Taper:
Calculate benzodiazepine equivalence and give 50% dose over the taper (if actual dose
is known prior to detoxification).

TABLE 23.3 Alcohol Withdrawal and Detoxification

Withdrawal

Signs

1. Hand tremor
2. Diaphoresis
3. Tachycardia and elevated blood pressure
4. Dilated pupils
5. Increase in temperature
6. Seizures
7. Restlessness
8. Hyperactivity, agitation
9. Ataxia
10. Clouding of consciousness

Symptoms

1. Anxiety and panic attacks
2. Paranoid delusions or ideation
3. Illusions
4. Disorientation
5. Hallucinations, either of rapidly moving small animals such as
   snakes or Lilliputian hallucinations (auditory hallucinations are rare)

Detoxification

Mild Withdrawal

Librium 25–50 mg po every 4 hours prn for systolic blood pressure > 150
diastolic blood pressure > 90
pulse > 100
temperature > 101
tremulousness

Librium 25–50 mg p.o. prn for insomnia × 2 days.

Moderate Withdrawal

Librium 25–50 mg po qid day 1
20–40 mg po qid day 2
10–30 mg po qid day 3

(optional)

20 mg po qid day 4
10 mg po qid day 5

May need to adjust based on signs and symptoms of alcohol withdrawal

Severe Withdrawal

Librium 25–50 mg po every hour while awake (to sedate).
systolic blood pressure > 150
diastolic blood pressure > 90
Pulse > 100
Temperature > 101
Tremulousness

of withdrawal, when severe, need be treated with increased doses of benzodiazepines, although this condition is unusual with the long-acting benzodiazepines. Alternative methods to benzodiazepines for treating the anxiety of another disorder and drug-seeking behavior are indicated. The prescriber must be in control of the dispensing of the benzodiazepines for withdrawal, as the addict, by definition, is out of control and cannot reliably negotiate the schedule for tapering.

The duration of the tapering schedule is determined by the half-life of the benzodiazepine that is being withdrawn. For short-acting benzodiazepines such as alprazolam, 7–10 days of a gradual taper with a long-acting benzodiazepine or barbiturate is sufficient; 7 days for low-dose use and 10 days for high-dose use. For the long-acting benzodiazepines, 10–14 days of a gradual taper with a long-acting benzodiazepine or barbiturate is sufficient; 10 days for low-dose and 14 days for high-dose use. The doses should be given in a qid or tid interval. Exact numerical deductions are not needed, as the long-acting benzodiazepines accumulate to result in a self-leveling effect of the blood level of the benzodiazepines over time (see Table 23.2).[30,31]

Stimulants

Cocaine and amphetamines are both CNS stimulants. Their short-term effect is to increase the release of dopamine, but after prolonged use, they deplete the dopamine supply. The key to treatment of acute overdose is catecholamine blockade. After the ingested drug is eliminated with syrup of ipecac, activated charcoal is administered. Hypertensive episodes and cardiotoxicity are both treated with intravenous doses of the beta-blocker propranolol (Inderal) as indicated. Psychosis responds to the dopamine blocker haloperidol (Haldol), 5–10 mg orally or intramuscularly every 1–6 hours as needed (see Table 23.4).[32]

Withdrawal appears to be correlated with depletion of dopamine, norepinephrine, and epinephrine supplies. Signs and symptoms of withdrawal include anhedonia, depression, hyperphagia, hypersomnia, psychomotor retardation, and suicidal ideation. Ordinarily, these signs and symptoms resolve without specific pharmacological therapy. However, at times persistent delusions and/or depression may require the use of pharmacotherapy.

While bromocriptine, a dopamine agonist, acts acutely to neutralize the

TABLE 23.4. Cocaine and Similar-Acting Sympathomimetic Withdrawal (peak period 0–4 days)

History

1. The symptoms and physical signs of withdrawal from cocaine or similar acting substances generally commence within hours of cessation of use and peak within one to three days.
2. Depression and irritability may persist, however, for months and, necessitate the use of antidepressants and neuroleptic medication, or electroshock because of the risk of suicide.

Signs and Symptoms

1. Depression
2. Anxiety
3. Panic
4. Hypersomnambulance
5. Fatigue
6. Disturbed sleep
7. Agitation
8. Suicidal thinking
9. Irritability
10. Apathy
11. Hyperphagia

Detoxification

Desipramine hydrochloride 2.5 mg/kg po loading dose.
Obtain blood level next day to determine dose.

or

150–250 mg (one or divided dose) po every day for 2 weeks or more.

Taper over 2–5 days.

and

Bromocriptine 1.25–2.5 mg, po g 6 hours and taper over one to 3 weeks.

effects of dopamine depletion, desipramine resets noradrenergic auto-receptors so that the remaining supply of norepinephrine is more efficiently utilized. Bromocriptine acts acutely to block withdrawal symptoms, while desipramine works over a longer period to prevent relapse by decreasing cocaine and amphetamine cravings.[33]

Pharmacologic treatment focuses on repleting dopamine and norepinephrine levels. Withdrawal therapy is initiated with bromocriptine (Par-

TABLE 23.5. Cocaine Intoxication

Signs

1. Dilated and reactive pupils
2. Tachycardia
3. Elevated temperature
4. Elevated blood pressure
5. Dry mouth
6. Perspiration or chills
7. Nausea and vomiting
8. Tremulousness
9. Hyperactive reflexes
10. Repetitous compulsive behavior
11. Stereotypic biting causes ulcers around mouth
12. Cardiac arrhythmias
13. Flushed skin
14. Poor self-care and suicide
15. Violence and homicide
16. Seizures

Symptoms

1. Euphoria
2. Hyperarousal
3. Hypervigilance
4. Panic and anxiety
5. Irritability
6. Loquacity and pressured speech
7. Emotional lability
8. Anorexia
9. Aggressiveness and hostility
10. Anxiety
11. Grandiosity
12. Depression
13. Suicidal ideation

Symptoms of Sympathomimetic Cocaine Delusional Syndromes

In addition to the symptoms and physical signs with sympathomimetic intoxication, individuals with a cocaine or similar-acting sympathomimetic delusional syndrome have:

1. Thought disorder
2. Ideas of reference
3. Auditory hallucinations, frequently of voices commenting, criticizing, and accusing the patient of misconduct
4. Paranoid ideation, with delusions of persecution in a clear sensorium
5. Visual hallucinations, sometimes with distortion of faces and disturbances of body image
6. Fornication.

lodel), 1.25–2.5 mg every 6 hours. The dosage is gradually decreased over 1–3 weeks. Desipramine (Norpramin, Pertofrane) is simultaneously initiated at a dosage of 50 mg per day; the dosage is then titrated upward every other day in 50 mg increments until a dosage of 150–250 mg per day is attained. This dosage is maintained for 3–6 months and is then discontinued by gradually tapering the drug over 2 weeks (see Table 23.4).[15]

Opiates

During intoxication, opiates suppress norepinephrine stimulation. This effect can be reversed by naloxone (Narcan), an opiate antagonist. Naloxone is given intravenously in doses of 0.4–0.8 mg every 20 minutes as required. The dose is increased as indicated by symptom response until an upper limit of 24 mg is attained over an 8–12-hour period. Hypotension is treated by volume replacement. Pulmonary edema usually responds to naloxone therapy; if not, the measures usually employed for pulmonary edema are instituted, including diuresis, afterload reduction, and oxygen.[33]

Although not medically dangerous, opiate withdrawal is distressing and sometimes painful. When μ-opioid receptors are no longer hyperstimulated by opiates, a massive release of stored norepinephrine occurs. Clonidine (Catapres), an alpha-2-agonist, acts directly on noradrenergic receptors to reduce norepinephrine release from the nucleus locus ceruleus. An initial dosage of 0.2–0.8 mg per day given during the peak period of withdrawal alleviates the withdrawal discomfort and craving. The dosage is then gradually reduced over the subsequent days for the duration of withdrawal (1–3 days peak, 5–7 days duration for heroin; 7–14 days peak, 14–28 days duration for methadone). Hypotension is the only side effect of clonidine. If hypotension is severe, the dosage can be reduced until blood pressure stabilizes.[34] Methadone may also be used for detoxification from heroin and methadone itself (see Table 23.6).

Naltrexone (Trexan) may help the motivated addict maintain abstinence. This drug is a pure opiate antagonist that blocks the effects of all opium-derived compounds. The usual dosage is 50 mg orally each morning, or three times per week, usually under direct medical supervision, since this is the period of highest motivation. If the patient uses an opiate later that day, the effects of the opiate are blocked. Thus, the psychologic and physical reinforcements of continued opiate use are decreased. Side effects include sedation and liver toxicity (unusual and mild).

TABLE 23.6. Objective Opiate Withdrawal and Detoxification

Signs

1. Pulse 10 beats per minute or more over baseline or over 90 if no history of tachycardia and baseline unknown. (Baseline: vital sign values one hour after receiving 10 mg of methadone.)
2. Systolic blood pressure 10 mm Hg or more above baseline or over 160/96 in nonhypertensive patients.
3. Dilated pupils.
4. Gooseflesh, sweating, rhinorrhea, or lacrimation.

Detoxification

Heroin Morphine Withdrawal (Clonidine)

Clonidine 20 ug/kg/day in three divided doses or 0.1–2 mg po tid for 4–5 days and taper over 4–6 days, or:
Clonidine 0.1 or 0.2 mg po every 4 hours prn for signs and symptoms of withdrawal. (Peak doses are between 2–4 days.)
Check blood pressure before each dose, do not give if hypotensive (for that individual, i.e., 90/60).

Methadone Withdrawal (Clonidine)

Clonidine 20 ug/kg/day in three divided doses or 0.1–0.2 mg po tid × 14 days.
0.1–0.2 mg po did × 3 days.
0.1–0.2 mg po every 4 hours po prn for signs and symptoms of withdrawal (18–20 days).
Check blood pressure before each dose, do not give if hypotensive (for that individual, i.e., 90/60).

Heroin Morphine Withdrawal (Methadone)

Methadone test dose of 10 mg po in liquid or crushed tablet. Additional 10 mg doses are given for signs and symptoms of withdrawal every 4 hours. Average dose is 30 mg in 24 hours. Next day, repeat total first day dose in two divided doses (stabilization dose), then reduce by 3–5 mg a day until completely withdrawn.

Methadone Withdrawal (Methadone)

Methadone test dose of 10 mg po in liquid or crushed tablet. Additional 10 mg doses are given for signs and symptoms of withdrawal every 4 hours. Average dose is 30 mg in 24 hours. Next day, repeat total first day dose in two divided doses (stabilization dose) then reduce by 1–5 mg a day until completely withdrawn.

Nicotine

Nicotine has very specific properties that involve stereospecific receptors and dopaminergic pathways. The nicotine receptors can be blocked with mecamylamine but not with muscarinic, cholinergic, or adrenergic blocking agents. Nicotine causes an increase in hand tremor, an arousal

EEG (low voltage, fast activity), and decreased muscle tone and deep-tendon reflexes. Nicotine causes the release of norepinephrine and dopamine from brain tissue and, depending on the dose, increases or inhibits the release of acetylcholine.[35-37]

Cigarette smoking is reduced following the administration of nicotine intravenously, orally, in a capsule, buccally, nasally, or across the skin.[38] A nicotine substitute commonly used in fading is nicotine polacrilex or gum. This polacrilex preparation is approved by the Food and Drug Administration. Its alkaline pH permits nicotine absorption across the buccal mucosa.

Nicotine gum is prescribed only after the patient completely understands how to use it. Patients should read *How to Use Nicotine Gum and Other Strategies to Quit Smoking.*[39] Correct usage is of paramount importance. Nicotine gum is not chewed like bubble gum; instead, it is gently chewed as one would puff a cigarette and then parked between the teeth and cheek. The amount of nicotine absorbed depends on numerous variables. One factor is the amount of saliva swallowed while chewing. The majority of swallowed nicotine is not absorbed into the bloodstream because of alteration in the first pass through the liver. Therefore, patients who drink fluids while using nicotine gum may absorb less nicotine than patients who retain nicotine longer in the buccal cavity.

A schedule for tapering gum use is planned after the daily maintenance dose is established. For example, a patient using 15 pieces of 2 mg gum each day during the first week of treatment gradually reduces the number of pieces to 10 per day by the end of the first month and 5 per day by the end of the second month. Patients are typically able to discontinue nicotine gum after 3–6 months of treatment. However, they must be reminded not to smoke while using it.

Patients who use polacrilex for nicotine replacement and tapering should be counseled regularly about other aspects of nicotine cessation. Unsupervised patients are more likely to use the gum over an extended period of time and nicotine polacrilex addiction may result.[37] This is especially common with nicotine addicts who suffer from other drug addictions.

Preliminary research with transcutaneous nicotine patches is promising. Nicotine patches are more likely than polacrilex to deliver a steady, predictable, and measurable amount of nicotine. Nicotine patches are manufactured in different diameters. The transcutaneous method involves applying the large-diameter patch to skin for the first week, an intermediate size patch during the second week, and the smallest patch during the third week. One disadvantage to this method is the development of contact dermatitis. Nicotine replacement and fading should be used in conjunction with a recovery program.

Psychedelic Agents

Addiction to psychedelic agents can be misdiagnosed as schizophrenia. The psychedelic effects of these agents are produced by the massive release of serotonin from the raphe nuclei in the pons. The release is localized to the CNS, causing major psychiatric effects but minimal physical changes.[40]

Supportive care in a quiet environment is usually sufficient until the effects of serotonin overload abate. If the patient's condition does not improve within 12 hours or the panic becomes uncontrollable, pharmacologic intervention is indicated. The effects of serotonin can be blocked with an indirect GABA agonist such as lorazepam (Alzapam, Ativan), 1–2 mg intramuscularly.[41]

Phencyclidine

The most important clinical symptoms of phencyclidine intoxication are hyperactivity, paranoia, insensitivity to pain, hypertension, hallucinations, paranoid delusions, and memory loss. Other signs and symptoms include eyelid retraction (producing a wide-eyed stare), dry, erythematous skin, dilated pupils, horizontal nystagmus, and an excitable, angry mood.

Most symptoms are reversed by the dopamine-2 antagonist haloperidol, 5 mg intramuscularly or orally every 20 minutes for three to four doses.[27]

Most of the symptoms of phencyclidine abuse are caused by a combination of the stimulation of catecholamines and the blockade of acetylcholine. Haloperidol restores the dopamine/acetylcholine balance by blocking dopamine receptors. Because phencyclidine is a dopamine-2 agonist and haloperidol is a dopamine-2 antagonist, a specific and therapeutic blockade occurs. (Other antipsychotics are less specific and block dopamine-1 receptors as well as cholinergic receptors, further complicating an already compromised neurochemical interaction.) To intensify the effects of haloperidol and increase the rate of phencyclidine elimination, ascorbic acid, 1 g intramuscularly, may be given.[42] Benzodiazepines may be used for the agitation (see Alcohol). A summary of the treatments for five classes of addicting drugs is provided in Tables 23.2–23.6.

REFERENCES

1. Giannini AJ, Gold MS & Sternberg DE (1989). *Treating Drug Abuse* pp. 73–84. New York: Marcel Dekker.
2. Giannini AJ, Slaby AE (eds.), (1989). *Drugs of Abuse* pp. 111–116. Oradell, NJ: Medical Economics.
3. Tallman JF, Paul SM & Skolnick P, et al. (1980). Receptors for the age of anxiety: Pharmacology of the benzodiazepines. *Science* 207:274–281.
4. Cooper JR, Bloom FE & Roth RH (1988). *Biochemical Basis of Neuropharmacology* p. 94. New York: Oxford University Press.
5. Mohler H & Okada T (1977). Benzodiazepine receptor: Demonstration in the central nervous system. *Science* 198:849–851.
6. Aquilonious SM (1977). Role of acetylcholine in the central nervous system. *Clin Neuro* 29:435–458.
7. Langer S (1978). Modern concepts of noradrenergic transmission. In Legg NJ (ed.), *Neurotransmitter Systems and Their Clinical Disorders* pp. 117–184. New York: Academic.
8. Bird ED, Spokes EG & Iversen LL (1979). Brain norepinephrine and dopamine in schizophrenia [Letter]. *Science* 204:93–94.
9. Ho BT, Schoolar JC, Usdin E (eds.), (1982). *Serotonin in Biological Psychiatry* pp. 69–84. New York: Raven.
10. Lord JA, Waterfield AA & Hughes J, et al. (1977). Endogenous opioid peptides: Multiple agonists and receptors. *Nature* 267:495–499.
11. Krogsgaard-Larsen P, Scheel-Kruger J, Kofod H (eds.), (1979). Gaba-neurotransmitters: Pharmacochemical, biochemical, and pharmacological aspects. *Proceedings of the Alfred Benzon Symposium, Copenhagen* pp. 251–258. New York: Academic.
12. van Kammen DP, Sternberg DE, Hare TA, et al. (1982). CSF levels of gamma-aminobutyric acid in schizophrenia. Low values in recently ill patients. *Arch Gen Psych* 39:91–97.
13. Chang RS & Snyder SH (1978). Benzodiazepine receptors: Labeling in intact animals with [^{3}H]flunitrazepam. *Eur J Pharmacol* 48:123–128.
14. Tecce JJ & Cole JO (1974). Amphetamine effects in man: Paradoxical drowsiness and lowered electrical brain activity (CNV). *Science* 185:451–453.
15. Giannini AJ & Billett W (1987). Bromocriptine-desipramine protocol in treatment for cocaine addiction. *J Clin Pharmacol* 27:549–554.
16. Dackis CA, Gold MS & Davies RK, et al. (1985). Bromocriptine treatment for cocaine abuse: The dopamine depletion hypothesis. *Int J Psych Med* 15:125–135.

17. Dackis CA & Gold MS (1985). New concepts in cocaine addiction: The dopamine depletion hypothesis. *Neurosci Biobehav Rev* 9:469–477.

18. Gawin FH & Kleber HD (1986). Abstinence symptomatology and psychiatric diagnosis in cocaine abusers. Clinical Observations. *Arch Gen Psych* 43:107–113.

19. Tennant FS Jr, Russell BA & Casas SK, et al. (1975). Heroin detoxification. A comparison of propoxyphene and methadone. *JAMA* 232:1019–1022.

20. Cedarbaum JM & Aghajanian GK (1976). Noradrenergic neurons of the locus ceruleus: Inhibition by epinephrine and activation by the alpha-antagonist piperoxan. *Brain Res* 112:413–419.

21. O'Brien CP, Testa T & O'Brien TJ, et al. (1977). Conditioned narcotic withdrawal in humans. *Science* 195:1000–1002.

22. Freedman DX (1964). The psychopharmacology of hallucinogenic agents. *Ann Rev Med* 20:409–415.

23. Bowers MB Jr & Freedman DX (1966). "Psychedelic" experiences in acute psychoses. *Arch Gen Psych* 15:240–248.

24. Giannini AJ, Giannini MC & Price WA (1984). Antidotal strategies in phencyclidine intoxication. *Int J Psych Med* 14:315–321.

25. Giannini AJ, Eighan MS & Loiselle RH, et al. (1984). Comparison of haloperidol and chlorpromazine in the treatment of phencyclidine psychosis. *J Clin Pharmacol* 24:202–204.

26. Giannini AJ, Loiselle RH & Price WA (1985). Chlorpromazine vs. meperidine in the treatment of phencyclidine psychosis. *J Clin Psych* 46:52–54.

27. Castellani S, Giannini AJ, Boeringa JA, et al. (1982). Phencyclidine intoxication: Assessment of possible antidotes. *J Toxicol Clin Toxicol* 19:313–319.

28. Giannini AJ, Black HR, Goettsche RL (1978). *Psychiatric, Psychogenic, and Somatopsychic Disorders Handbook* pp. 86–88. Garden City, NY: Medical Examination.

29. Eckardt MJ, Harford TC & Kaelber CT, et al. (1981). Health hazards associated with alcohol consumption. *JAMA* 246:648–666.

30. Perry PJ & Alexander B (1986). Sedative/hypnotic dependence: Patient stabilization, tolerance, testing and withdrawal. *Drug Intell Clin Pharm* 20:532–536.

31. Harrison M, Busto U & Naranjo CA (1984). Diazepam tapering in detoxification for high-dose benzodiazepine abuse. *Clin Pharmacol Ther* October, pp. 527–533.

32. Giannini AJ & Gold MS (1988). Cocaine abuse: Demons within. *Prim Care* 4:34–40.

33. Giannini AJ, Slaby AE & Giannini MC (1982). *Handbook of Overdose and Detoxification Emergencies* pp. 86–88. New Hyde Park, NY: Medical Examination.

34. Gold MS, Redmond DE Jr & Kleber HD (1978). Clonidine blocks acute opiate-withdrawal symptoms. *Lancet* 2(8090):599–602.

35. Warburton DM (1975). *Brain, Behavior and Drugs.* London: Wiley.

36. Jarvik ME & Henningfield JE (1988). Pharmacological treatment of tobacco dependence. *Pharmacol Biochem Behav* 30:279.

37. Cocores JA, Sinaikin P & Gold MS (1989). Scopolamine as treatment for nicotine polacrilex dependence. *Ann Clin Psych* 1:203–204.

38. Jarvik ME & Henningfield JE (1988). Pharmacological treatment of tobacco dependence. *Pharmacol Biochem Behav* 30:279.

39. Schneider N (1988). *How to Use Nicotine Gum & Other Strategies to Quit Smoking.* New York: Pocket Books.

40. Strassman RJ (1984). Adverse reactions to psychedelic drugs. A review of the literature. *J Nerv Ment Dis* 172:577–595.

41. Taylor RL, Maurer JL & Tinklenberg JR (1970). Management of "bad trips" in an evolving drug scene. *JAMA* 213:422–425.

42. Giannini AJ, Loiselle RH, DiMarzio LR & Giannini MC (1987). Augmentation of haloperidol by ascorbic acid in phencyclidine intoxication. *Am J Psych* 144:1207–1209.

24

Group Therapy

OVERVIEW

The dominant form of treatment for addiction (postdetoxification) to alcohol and other drugs is group therapy. Group therapy is found in nearly all types and models of addiction treatment such as inpatient, intensive outpatient, outpatient, and therapeutic community settings, whether private or public. This form of treatment is supported by a growing and substantial body of research demonstrating the efficacy of the group approach. Of importance is that the growth of group therapy for addiction treatment has been supported by vast clinical experience coupled with the need for a therapeutic approach that can assertively and collectively confront the addicted person's unconscious defense system, principally denial, projection, and minimization. An early model for the current form of group therapy was Alcoholics Anonymous (AA), because it illustrated the importance and utility of positive peer identification and peer support within a therapeutic group setting.

Similarly, the use of group therapy is widespread for the treatment of psychiatric disorders. Clinical experience and anecdotal evidence support the position that group therapy is an effective treatment strategy for several types of patients. Such patients include patients with psychotic disorders, schizophrenia, anxiety, depression, personality disorders, and posttraumatic stress disorder. However, patients with active and unmedicated symptoms of psychosis and mania are often poor candidates for group therapy, as are some patients with antisocial personality disorder. Group therapy is particularly valuable for patients with dual disorders.

Advantages of the Group Process

The group process teaches patients interdependence with peers rather than dependence on a psychotherapist. By so doing, the group process helps to nurture healthy social bonds in which deeply personal issues are shared with others; and participants learn to listen to the concerns of others. Important to this procedure is learning to give feedback regarding the statements of others and learning to receive feedback about one's own statements.

Central to interdependence, healthy social bonds, and feedback in the group process is that patients identify examples of denial, minimization, and projection in their peers. Patients are able to identify distorted thinking in others even when they cannot within themselves. Also, patients are often more willing to accept insights, criticisms, confrontations, and interventions from peers than from health care professionals or other authority figures who may appear judgmental.

Similarly, because addicted people have often repressed, drugged, and ignored their emotions, they are often unable to accurately identify their feelings, which are often intense, diffuse, and ill-defined. Since patients generally have suppressed their emotions and feelings with alcohol and other drugs over years of heavy use, they are often extremely uncomfortable experiencing their feelings in the absence of mood-altering drugs. The group process allows a safe opportunity for patients to identify, express, and talk about their emotions. Indeed, one of the goals of group therapy is to have patients search for and articulate their feelings, including anger, peacefulness, depression, joy, resentment, and happiness.

Addicted people usually are withdrawn from their own feelings and often have weakened emotional bonds with other people. Because addicted people listen to the fears, wishes, and experiences of others that are similar to their own, they learn that their own experiences are not unique, and are, in fact, shared by many others. This helps break down emotional isolation that is often tied to social isolation.

In addition, the group process provides an opportunity for patients in early recovery to observe and practice healthy behaviors modeled by patients with longer periods of recovery. The group process is also something of a living laboratory in which the group therapy facilitator can identify patterns of interpersonal behaviors among patients. For example, the group process allows patients to practice newly learned interpersonal skills and problem-solving techniques and is the facility of self-disclosure and self-expression. The group process also allows the facilitator to identify whether patients are able to translate learned cognitive information into active behavior.

DEFINITION

Attributes of the Group Therapy Process

There are several attributes that are characteristic of the group therapy process.[1] These attributes make group therapy uniquely suited for treating patients with addiction to alcohol and other drugs. Primary to recovery from addiction is the acceptance of addiction as a disease and establishment of a commitment to recovery.

Acceptance. Acceptance is not compliance but a surrender of emotions in concert with the cognitive realization that the individual has the disease of addiction. The group provides the means of identification with another addict to arrive at acceptance.

Commitment. The group supports and directs an individual towards commitment to recovery. This is the key ingredient to maintaining abstinence and contentment in order to make the fundamental changes to sustain recovery.

Informative. While the primary intent of group therapy is not purely didactic education, group therapy is an opportunity to obtain education and information. Through the words and behaviors of facilitators and patients, participants can learn about addiction, treatment, recovery, relapse, and other people's problem-solving experiences. The group process often provides an opportunity to dispel myths and correct misinformation. The education format of some groups is a subtle way to confront denial, i.e., get someone to think about something he or she would not normally consider.

Hope. Group therapy is an opportunity in which patients can learn to have positive expectations because their problems are not unique, problems have solutions, and unmet needs can be met. They learn that problem-solving is a positive alternative to impulsive thrashing about and alcohol and drug use.

Universality. The group process is particularly useful in helping patients learn that they are not unique with regard to their compulsions, loss of control, guilt, shame, and other overwhelming emotions. Patients learn that their addiction, response to addiction, and their strivings for recovery are more similar than different from others.

Catharsis. Patients learn that they can express and display their feelings without experiencing overwhelming anxiety, rejection, ridicule, or a fight. They learn that expressing their emotions generally results in positive feedback and emotional attachments to others. Hearing others discuss the same types of problems helps to reduce inappropriate guilt and shame.

Altruism. The group therapy process, especially when experienced in tandem with self-help groups such as AA, provides opportunities for patients to practice helping others. Experiencing reciprocal helping relationships helps to increase patients' sense of self-worth.

Imitation. The group therapy setting helps patients to identify, model, and practice problem-solving skills, coping behaviors, and healthy social skills. These help patients to acquire a new social identity as a healthy, recovering individual. (See one, do one, teach one.)

Cohesiveness. By its nature, the group process provides a sense of solidarity, cohesiveness, comradeship, and often a group identity. The group process often becomes a prototypical model for the family, in which problem-solving, mutual caring and respect, and positive change is central.

Interpersonal Learning. Often for the first time, patients in group therapy learn how they are perceived by others, and how they often cause or maintain their own problems or crises through maladaptive behaviors and misconceptions. They often learn how they can learn to become responsible for their own feelings and their own lives without using alcohol or other drugs.

In studies of group therapy participants, patients were asked to describe their perceived benefits of group therapy.[2,3] Patients value their group therapy for:

- Giving them feedback in their interpersonal behavior.
- Allowing them opportunities to express their repressed emotions.
- Allowing them to feel less isolated.
- Experiencing a sense of acceptance from other people.
- Improving their self-esteem by being able to help others.
- Helping them to discover unconscious motivations for their behaviors.
- Giving them feelings of optimism by watching others improve and leave treatment.

Group Therapy Participants

The group therapy process is built on the concept that the group is more than the sum of the parts. That is, the interpersonal interaction of group therapy participants assumes a therapeutic dynamic that can only happen when there are several participants. In fact, this dynamic generally will not occur when there are too few participants and is hindered when there are too many participants. For this reason, group therapy generally involves 6–12 patients, with the optimal number generally thought to be eight. In many settings, newly arriving patients join existing groups, allowing patients in early treatment to observe a progressive mental clearing in other patients in later stages of treatment. In other settings, all patients join the group at the same time.

Group Therapy Facilitators

Group therapy differs from self-help and other support groups by the presence of a therapist or facilitator. Group therapy may involve one facilitator or two cofacilitators. Depending upon the specific purpose, setting, and goals of the group, it may be optimal to have a male–female cofacilitator team, especially when encouraging discussion of parental, gender, and sexual themes. There are advantages of having co-facilitators as group therapists.[4] These include:

- Enhanced objectivity in assessment of patients, resulting from discussion between the therapists after group sessions.

- Potential for increased transference feelings in the group.
- Continuity of the group when one facilitator is absent due to vacation or illness.
- Better control of the group during crises.
- Facilitators learning therapeutic techniques from one another.

Group Therapy Format

There are different types and styles of group therapy formats. The dominant format of group therapy for patients who are addicted to alcohol and other drugs, and also for patients with dual disorders, is a nondirective, discussion-oriented format.

Directive group therapy involves the use of a facilitator who actively leads and guides the group process. In this format, the facilitator is an ongoing participant in the group process and exerts great control over the content being discussed, the process of the group, and the therapeutic interventions that occur.

Many facilitators who are directive-oriented run groups that share similarities with didactic educational groups. Directive groups are often best used for patients who are unable to maintain a therapeutic dynamic (such as feedback, healthy disagreement, peer confrontation, and problem solving).

In contrast, a nondirective format involves a facilitator who plays an active role in the group process during those times when the group therapy dynamic is subdued, but allows the group process to be primarily governed by the patients. Nondirective groups promote the active participation of group members and a more likely and therapeutic interplay among participants.

Nondirective facilitators do not merely watch and listen, but do not exert an overwhelming control over the proceedings. Rather, they help to "get the session started," often by asking each participant to "check in" and mention at least a few words about their current emotional state. Facilitators help to elicit from participants, especially reluctant patients, their feelings, opinions, and concerns about the discussion. While they help to support patients to therapeutically confront one another about perceived evidence of denial, minimization, and projection, facilitators help to prevent patients from hurting one another.

While there are numerous, complex philosophical approaches to group therapy (such as psychoanalytic, existential, and behavior), the most common focus is a "here-and-now approach." While some forms of individual psychotherapy frequently focus on intrapsychic problems that were developed because of trauma during early developmental phases, group therapy in addiction treatment settings generally focuses on the "here-and-now."

While the therapeutic goals of most types of group therapy include the relief of symptoms and resolution of intrapsychic and interpersonal problems, they are often achieved by focusing on behaviors and attitudes that emerge during the group process itself.

The group therapy facilitator can utilize different techniques to foster the treatment and recovery process. Some of these techniques include specific discussion topics, role-play exercises, and group confrontation of individual participants.

FOCUS

Group Dynamics and Development

As mentioned above, group therapy is based on the assumption that a group of people create a dynamic that goes beyond the dynamic seen in couples and triads. These collective forces can be positive or negative, and one of the facilitator's role is to maximize the positive, therapeutic forces, and to minimize the negative, nontherapeutic forces.

For example, by eliciting and encouraging the free expression of feelings, ideas, and opinions, patients learn the importance of healthy expression of honest feelings. Conversely, if the facilitator does not allow such expressions, the group members will participate only superficially and will be unlikely to express feelings in a healthy fashion outside of the group.

Facilitators can influence the group dynamic by pointing out specific characteristics of a given group. For example, the facilitator can mention that group members seemed especially quiet in therapy after one of their peers left the program against medical advice. Such process comments are made with the intention of providing the patients with opportunities for insight into psychodynamic or interpersonal issues. They are also made for the purpose of minimizing group resistance to a specific topic.

Three Phases of Group Development

Regardless of the setting, purpose, or type of group therapy, the group dynamics change over time. The following phases of group development are related to the dynamics of groups as they are related to clinical and therapeutic issues.

The First Phase of Group Development. The initial phase of the development of the group is characterized by reluctant or hesitant participation followed by the creation of group norms. Initially, group therapy participants rely upon the facilitator for approval and guidance. Patients should understand why they are participating in the group therapy, understand the goals of the group, and be able to state their own personal treatment goals. During this phase the facilitator helps to promote the creation of bonds among group therapy participants.

The Second Phase of Group Development. At some point, the group dynamics change and are often characterized by open conflict, struggles for dominance, and the development of a type of hierarchy among patients. The facilitator often becomes a favored target for rebellion, criticism, and verbal attack. Similarly, a group of patients may express their dislike for another patient and attempt to make that patient the "scapegoat" for the group. This is often done to divert attention away from their own concerns, worries, and fear of change. During this phase, the facilitator helps patients to deal with such aggressive tendencies in a healthy fashion, and helps patients to gain insight into their faulty thinking.

The Third Phase of Group Development. Ultimately, the group establishes a cohesiveness and a therapeutic bond. While there may be differences of opinion and conflicts, the group can establish a sense of identification, intimacy, mutual affection, and interdependence with one another. During this phase, participants are more willing to share intimate details of their lives that would have been threatening previously. They become more willing to say and do things that they would have previously felt would make them vulnerable to the attacks and ridicule of others. This allows integration of the new ideas, skills, and behaviors.

TREATMENT

During the course of treatment and recovery, the same group therapy will have different purposes for the same patient, just as different group therapy sessions will have different goals and objectives. While all sessions will ultimately support the establishment and maintenance of sobriety, there will be different approaches to meet these goals. For example, some of the goals of group therapy include:

- Learning about the nature of addictive disease.
- Helping patients to make a self-diagnosis of addiction.
- Teach addicted and dually-diagnosed patients how to successfully manage their disorders.
- To encourage patients to assume personal responsibility for continuing recovery.[5]

While the phases of group development describe the general and normal evolution of the group dynamics, there are also stages that specifically relate to the goals and objectives of group therapy for patients who are addicted to alcohol and other drugs.

The stages of group therapy with addicted and dually disordered patients can be divided into three stages. Each stage of treatment involves specific tasks and objectives: 1) establishing abstinence and sobriety, 2) developing a contented, drug-free lifestyle, and 3) dealing with issues of arrested maturity and delayed maturity.[6]

Passage through these stages of treatment is not necessarily done in sequence. Rather, group therapy for addiction is best designed to include patients who are in various stages of treatment and recovery and who have different levels of treatment acceptance or resistance, motivation, drugs of abuse, and perspectives. In this way patients are struggling with establishing abstinence are participating in group therapy with patients who have been drug-free for longer periods of time and are dealing with drug-free lifestyle issues.

The interplay between the newly arrived patients and those who have been in treatment longer works both ways. For instance, newly arrived patients in early treatment can gain several types of insights from people who are in later stages of treatment or recovery: learning that they are not alone or unique in their addiction, learning that treatment works, hearing others speak openly about how withdrawal symptoms diminish over time, and learning how the self-help, twelve-step programs can be incorporated into an abstinent lifestyle.

But people in later stages of treatment or recovery can benefit by having people in early recovery in the same group. For example, people who have been abstinent for several months may have denial returning and selective memory or euphoric recall regarding their use of cocaine. Because their physical health may be returning to normal and they are beginning to feel better, they may begin to wonder if they now have the ability to control their alcohol or other drug use. Addicted people who experience euphoric recall or delusions of controlled drug use often benefit from listening to the experiences of patients who only recently experienced intense craving, compulsions, loss of control, and adverse consequences.

Initiating and Maintaining Abstinence

An initial task in group therapy for addicted patients relates to self-diagnosis of their addictive disease. In other words, by identifying with others, patients will understand that their use of alcohol and other drugs qualifies for the diagnosis of addiction, and accept their addiction. The interaction with other patients in a group setting increases the likelihood that they will be therapeutically confronted by their peers when they attempt to deny their addiction, minimize the seriousness of their addiction, or deny the adverse consequences of their addiction.

Patients also need to learn that, because they are addicted, they experience compulsions, cravings, urges, and hunger for their drug(s) of choice. Patients must learn that ignoring, denying, minimizing, or repressing these feelings tends to distance people from their feelings.

The group therapy setting provides an opportunity to openly discuss these desires and the emotions that accompany them. They learn that talking about these feelings helps to diminish the power of the desires, which are often endured in silence, fear, and shame. Learning to talk openly about cravings increases the likelihood that they will locate and speak with someone when experiencing cravings during nontreatment hours.

In much the same way, patients must learn about those things in their lives that precipitate drug urges or desires into a relapse. These precipitants include such things as environmental events, emotional states, social situations, and specific people. Relapse is not a single event but a process. For most people the process of relapse involves a progression from a loss of commitment to abstinence to relapse. Most often the urges or thoughts about using drugs or alcohol are not conscious. The precipitants are usually the last step in relapse. This process can be described as having four steps.[7]

Step 1—Precipitants. Precipitants are those people, places, and things that remind addicted people about their drug-using experiences. They automatically make people think about alcohol or other drugs, sometimes consciously, sometimes unconsciously. Some precipitants can be avoided and some can be minimized by leaving the situation rapidly.

Step 2—Thoughts. Precipitants may automatically remind people of drug-using experiences, but the individual decides whether to continue thinking about those experiences. Being in high-risk situations prompts people to think excessively about using alcohol and other drugs. However, patients can learn to interrupt these thoughts.

Step 3—Urges. When patients remain in high-risk situations, it often leads to obsessional thoughts about drugs or alcohol. Obsessional thoughts that are not interrupted may lead to drug hunger and desire, which includes both physical and psychological symptoms.

Step 4—Relapse. Precipitants and thoughts can be interrupted much more easily than urges. Preventing relapse is easiest before precipitants and thoughts lead to urges.

As patients learn that they can interrupt the process of precipitants leading to urge and relapse, they can learn to develop specific action plans regarding the avoidance of precipitants and diminishing the effect of unavoidable precipitants. The group therapy setting is excellent for patients to share the positive experiences of avoiding and interrupting precipitants: stress reduction techniques, aerobic exercise, improved diet, participation in twelve-step meetings, and the utilization of a twelve-step group sensor. Within the group therapy session, patients can:

- Learn to identify their personal precipitants for drug urge.
- Learn ways to avoid those precipitants that can be avoided.
- Learn to minimize the exposure to precipitants that cannot be avoided.
- Learn to interrupt precipitants and stop them from leading to obsessional thoughts, urges, and relapse.

Patients in early stages of treatment often have great reluctance to give up their other drugs of addiction. For instance, someone who is addicted to cocaine but also uses alcohol and marijuana may be reluctant to discontinue using alcohol and marijuana. They may perceive that they had a problem with cocaine but not with other drugs. In group therapy, patients in later recovery often describe their experiences in which the use of other drugs of addiction led them back to compulsive, addictive patterns. In so doing, the other patients benefit because it serves to remind them that their reluctance to stop using all drugs of addiction, and their delusions of controlled use of alcohol and other drugs, is a part of the distortions in thinking caused by addiction.

Creating a Lifestyle of Sobriety

Within addiction treatment, the term "abstinence" describes the lack of use of mood-altering drugs such as alcohol and other drugs of addiction. Thus, an abstinent person is someone who, at a given time, has not had a drink or used a drug. Similarly, an abstinence syndrome simply refers to the biopsychological processes that occur when alcohol or other drug use has ceased or is withdrawn.

In contrast, the term "sobriety" refers to a quality of life that is characterized by an ongoing abstinence, growth, and maturity from a recovery program such as AA. In other words, sobriety is a lifestyle that includes the avoidance of alcohol and other drugs—generally a mature lifestyle.

Thus, while the task of the first stage of group therapy is establishing abstinence, the task of the second phase of group therapy is establishing a lifestyle of sobriety. To achieve this task, patients must deepen their commitment to such a lifestyle that includes abstinence from all drugs of addiction. Similarly, patients must confront the problems that are caused by their addiction (many of which remain despite abstinence).

Group members provide support to one another in their efforts to identify those facets of their behavior and those patterns in their interpersonal relationships that cause pain for themselves and others. Group members support each other in finding ways to establish healthy alternatives to their dysfunctional interpersonal patterns. During such processes, patients often explore ways to make amends to those people whom they hurt during active addiction.

Central to the creation of a lifestyle of sobriety is the establishment of mature friendships. Addiction often causes people to become emotionally isolated and distant, and have relationships that are shallow, superficial, and often centered around the use of alcohol and other drugs. Thus, an essential task of establishing and maintaining sobriety is having relationships that support and do not jeopardize sobriety. Active involvement in the twelve-step programs is central to achieving this task.

The group therapy sessions are opportunities for patients to discuss their ambivalence and frustrations with sobriety and with participation in the twelve-step programs. It allows patients the occasion to cathartically vent their frustrations about participation, especially during those times when it feels as if it isn't productive. It also allows patients to remind others that such frustrations are a normal part of living, and to assess whether such frustrations are in isolation or are part of the distorted thinking of a prerelapse syndrome.

Indeed, learning to identify and accept the entire spectrum of one's feelings and emotional states is an indispensable aspect of treatment and recovery. Patients must learn to understand the difference between *sitting on feelings* (repression, avoidance, or denial) and *sitting with feelings* (acceptance and surrender).[8] Patients' awareness of these differences will be illustrated and practiced within group therapy. For example, awareness of these perceptions are exhibited when patients are willing to take responsibility for their feelings and replace negative feelings with positive ones, instead of chronic wallowing in the dysfunctional patterns of guilt, blame, resentment, and anger. Responsibility for one's feelings often implies the ability to identify emotional states, recognize and admit that these emotional states are one's own, take action so that the feelings do not cause harm to oneself or another, and be willing to respond in a productive way.

Subacute Withdrawal and Arrested Maturity

Although the addiction-recovery process can be considered a lifelong process of emotional growth, personal maturation, and spiritual development, the treatment process is time-limited. While there are differences of opinion regarding the length of treatment, and treatment length should be driven by individualized treatment needs; patients should remain in some aspect of treatment for 1 year to 18 months.

For many, this means a brief stay in a medically managed inpatient program for detoxification, several weeks or months in an intensive inpatient and/or outpatient treatment program, followed by several months participating in outpatient services such as group therapy. The importance of a lengthy treatment cycle relates directly to subacute withdrawal, precipitants, urges, and relapses. Overall, the reeducation and development of maturity for recovery require extended periods.

The group therapy setting is particularly valuable as a way for patients to learn about the expected course of their treatment and recovery. When enduring noxious withdrawal symptoms such as anxiety, agitation, and depression, patients often fear that these symptoms are permanent. For this reason, patients benefit greatly by hearing others talk about the course of their symptomatology and how it faded over time. This is true for acute and subacute withdrawal syndromes. Thus, if patients understand that their withdrawal symptoms are an expected part of the recovery process that are often easily managed with nonpsychoactive pharmacotherapy and non-drug treatments, their ability to tolerate the withdrawal episodes is much greater. By so doing, such patients are less likely to relapse at the first sign of noxious symptoms.

Clinicians should understand that relapse is an unfortunate character-istic of addiction. Relapse does not signify that the treatment has failed. Rather, it is a sign that the patient's treatment plan needs to be strengthened and adjusted. Although they should be strenuously avoided and prevented, when relapses occur, they can be used as opportunities for patients to help identify weaknesses in their treatment and recovery plan. For example, relapses are frequently opportunities for patients to begin practicing certain behaviors that were learned but not used.

Patients who describe their relapse experiences in group therapy help themselves and others. By describing the course of events that led to their relapse, patients help others understand that relapse is a process, not an event, that often begins with the resumption of distorted thinking, the ignoring of precipitants, the disregard of feelings, and the reemergence of unconscious defense mechanisms such as denial, projection, and minimi-zation.

Group therapy has particular value because the use of defense mecha-nisms such as denial and minimization often precede the actual use of drugs, and group therapy participants become quite adept at identifying these early warning signs of relapse.

An important concern of later stages of recovery relates to the concept of arrested maturity.[9] While other people generally develop a wide range of psychosocial tools, addicted people often fail to do so. While the emotional maturity of addicted people often becomes arrested during their active addiction (typically with a focus on primitive defense mechanisms such as denial), most nonaddicted people develop self-awareness, self-esteem, the capacity for intimacy, and a sense of empathy for others.

The therapeutic task for addicted people is often to resume personal and interpersonal growth and development. In order to learn skills that will support emotional growth, patients often must learn to identify and address repressed feelings and begin to confront unresolved conflicts. The group therapy process is an ideal setting in which to do so.

REFERENCES

1. Yalom ID (1985). *The Theory and Practice of Group Psychotherapy* 3rd ed. New York: Basic Books.
2. Maximen JS (1973). Group therapy as viewed by hospitalized patients. *Arch Gen Psych* 28:404.
3. Yalom ID (1975). *The Theory and Practice of Group Psychotherapy* 2nd ed. New York: Basic Books.
4. Kanas NK & Farrell D (1988). Group Psychotherapy. In: Goldman HH (ed.), *Review of General Psychiatry* 2nd ed. Norwalk, Connecticut: Appleton & Lange.
5. Rogers RL & McMillin CS (1989). *Don't Help: A Positive Guide to Working With the Alcoholic.* New York: Bantam.
6. Ehrlich P & McGeehan M (1985). Cocaine recovery support groups and the language of recovery. *J Psychoact Drugs* 17(1):11–17.
7. The Koba Institute (1991). *Living in Balance Counselor Manual.* Washington, DC: Koba Institute.
8. Ehrlich P & McGeehan M (1985). Cocaine recovery support groups and the language of recovery. *J Psychoact Drugs* 17(1):11–17.
9. Milam J (1981). *Under the Influence: A Guide to the Myths and Realities of Alcoholism.* Seattle, WA: Madrona.

25

Psychotherapy

OVERVIEW

The psychotherapeutic interventions for patients who have coexisting psychiatric and substance-use disorders consist of achieving sobriety, maintaining abstinence and early recovery, and advancing recovery.[1] Some of the tasks that must be achieved during this initial phase of therapy include: 1) assessing psychopathology; 2) assessing the extent and consequences of addiction; 3) developing methods to establish and maintain a drug-free state; 4) diagnosing and beginning treatment of concomitant disorders; 5) enlisting participation of significant others; and 6) developing a therapeutic contract.

The phase of early recovery involves a supportive, directive, educational, and psychotherapeutic approach that focuses on the individual's acceptance of the disease of addiction and establishing a commitment to abstinence in addition to treatment for any existing concomitant psychiatric disorders. In this phase, defenses are redirected and psychotherapy is used mainly to reinforce methods of maintaining abstinence.

During maintenance and early recovery, therapy is directed towards assisting patients to recognize the consequences of a relapse to alcohol and other drug use, promoting medication compliance, and assisting patients to understand the interrelationships between the use of alcohol and other drugs and psychiatric symptoms and disorders.

During the advanced recovery phase, therapy involves a more traditional reconstructive psychotherapeutic approach that explores underlying issues.[2] This is especially true with nonpsychotic patients. When the psychiatric diagnosis is a major psychotic illness such as schizophrenia or bipolar disease, therapy is directed more toward prevention of recurrence of psychosis through understanding of psychosocial stressors, facilitating medication compliance, and family education. With personality disorders and anxiety disorders, the goal is insight and personality change using an integration of psychodynamic psychotherapy and cognitive behavioral methods. Defenses and underlying issues are explored while insisting on supporting abstinence from drug addiction.

TREATMENT

Achieving Sobriety

Addiction to Alcohol and Other Drugs. The initial phase of therapy requires an assessment of the nature and extent of addiction to alcohol and other drugs, and its physical, psychiatric, emotional, social, vocational, and familial consequences. Medical examination for the specific physical effects of the alcohol and other drugs involves may be indicated. The consequences of alcohol and other drug addiction pervade all biopsychosocial spheres. Assessment should include the behaviors that are the consequences of the addiction and related directly and indirectly to addictive use of drugs and alcohol. The disease is given a specific name, such as the disease of alcoholism or, depending on therapeutic context, drug addiction. This early approach emphasizes the disease as the problem, not the person. This reduces the guilt, shame, and stigma associated with drug and alcohol addiction.

A modified approach may be necessary when assessing alcohol or drug addiction in psychiatric patients. If the diagnosis of addiction is already well established, particularly if they are hospitalized, the approach can be direct and focus on addiction. Previously undiagnosed addiction in psychiatric patients may have to be elicited cautiously and without confrontation or judgment. Intervention techniques can only be used with caution and skill in severely mentally ill patients.

Assessment of Psychopathology

In a careful evaluation of psychopathology, specific attention must be paid to determining whether signs and symptoms of mental illness are primary or induced by alcohol and drug use. Essentially all addicted patients have some transient psychopathology from acute and chronic use of alcohol and drugs.

Although the final determination and diagnosis of psychopathology should be postponed for an extended period (weeks to months) after detoxification, assessment should begin in the initial evaluation. Postponement is necessary because so many addicts present with psychopathology that is secondary to addiction that dissipates as drug and alcohol addiction is treated. These common symptoms of mental illness include depression/anxiety, which are very common in the first week after detoxification, hallucinations/delusions, cognitive dysfunction, and personality disturbances. Alcohol and drug induced hallucinations/delusions resolve in days. Most cognitive dysfunction resolves in the first three weeks after detoxification, but lingering dysfunction persists and only resolves slowly after two to three years of sobriety.[3] Personality disturbances from addictive illness recede more gradually and more definitively with treatment.

Family Assessment

The therapist should insist that the entire family participate in the diagnostic assessment. The patient may or may not be more honest about use and addiction in the presence of the family, and family members can often provide information that would otherwise be denied or minimized. The family's pattern of reactivity to drug use and psychopathology should be observed as well as discussed.

Family members and the entire family system are evaluated for their conscious or unconscious enabling through participation or support of the patient's use of alcohol and other drugs and related behaviors as well as their own alcohol and other drug addiction and psychopathology. While the person who is addicted to alcohol and other drugs is ultimately responsible for all drug use and related behaviors, it is important to examine the role of the family's interactional patterns regarding alcohol and other drug use and addiction.

For instance, it is important to examine the family's dynamic to maintain the addicted person's behavior in order, for example, to create excitement, triangulate conflicts, avoid intimacy, or keep an eternal, pseu-doindividuated baby in the household forever. It is critical to evaluate active addiction in other family members as well as their enabling be-haviors and the extent of their own suffering and maladaptive behavior as a result of the addict's problems (codependency). Family assessment, if possible, is directed toward a treatment plan that involves each family member in the effort to achieve new behaviors that help not only the addicted person but the family members as well.

Detoxification

The method employed for detoxification will depend on the severity and duration of dependence as well as on the existence of concomitant dis-orders, including polydrug addiction, medical conditions, and psychiatric disorders. Patients with severe problems in the above three areas may require pharmacological detoxification in inpatient or outpatient settings.

Therapist Countertransferase

The psychic state of countertransferase is a complex, multidetermined phenomena occurring in therapists who treat patients who are addicted or with those who are mentally ill. When one individual carries both diag-noses, countertransference feelings become even more complicated. The initial definitions of countertransference in psychoanalytic psychotherapy focused on the therapist's transference, particularly those caused by re-acting to the patient as if he or she were an important figure from the therapist's own past.

The concept of countertransference has been broadened to include the therapist's uncontrolled reactions to who the patient is as a person[7] (angry, depressed, paranoid, competitive), the type of material the patient is deal-ing with (incest, violence, greed, victimization), or the concept of the superiority of the therapist over the patient.

When the therapist cannot recognize or will not acknowledge his or her own role in producing or provoking behavior in the patient, countertrans-ference is often relabeled as therapist codependency or enabling and is one of the most frequent causes of "burnout."

Codependency covers only a minority of countertransference reactions, and a focus only on it can blind therapists to looking for other types of unconsciously determined personal reactions. On the other hand, the concept of codependency can greatly enhance our understanding of many different forms of countertransference. The concept of codependency gives the therapist a frame of reference for changing his or her antitherapeutic countertransference reactions; for example, the overprotective, overcontrolling, or overinvolved therapist can relate these behaviors to codependency and change them through self-knowledge as well as through Al-Anon, or where appropriate, Adult Children of Alcoholics group.

Addicted patients tend to evoke strong emphasis in therapists, either of overinvolvement/rescuing or of distancing/rejection. Some therapists may alternate between the two depending, respectively, on the patient's compliance or defiance. These therapist behaviors are intensified in dually diagnosed patients, particularly in patients with borderline, histrionic, or passive–aggressive personalities, or with manic–depressive disease, all of whom invariably also provoke a great deal of therapist overinvolvement and/or rejection.

However, patients with antisocial personalities may be very successful at seducing a therapist for personal gain; depressive patients may foster the therapists' sense of powerful healing omnipotence; and obsessive–compulsives may evoke the therapists' anxiety, competitiveness, boredom, or rejection.

Countertransference includes the therapist's awareness of his or her own unconscious feelings and fantasies about patients in order to learn aspects of the patient's behavior that are not consciously obvious. The more the therapist is aware of his or her own underlying feelings, the less they will be acted out in a manner that is harmful to the patient. Thus a therapist can learn by knowing and accepting his or her own positive or negative feelings that the patient is provoking loving or angry feelings.

Self-knowledge permits the therapist to emotionally understand what the patient is experiencing. As therapists understand their own feeling states, they will identify patients' conflicts and feelings before they become overt. Thus the therapist uses countertransference in this context as an extremely effective tool.

Countertransference feelings are often strongly provoked in the early phases of therapy as the dually diagnosed addict resists, tests, fuses with, and rejects the therapist. In beginning therapy, the therapist may not share the majority of countertransference feelings with dually diagnosed patients. In later stages of therapy, the therapist can share certain countertransference responses as a way of facilitating, uncovering, and enhancing the patient's self-knowledge.

Self-Help Groups

A plan for maintaining abstinence is made a condition of the psychotherapeutic contract. The therapist engages in psychotherapy only if the patient has chosen to participate in a program for staying drug-free. Patients attending AA (or related meetings) may have to try different groups for the type of meeting most suitable to them.

Initially, patients may find that larger, passive meetings with speakers are more comfortable and provide successful models for identification. Once a patient engages with a program, smaller twelve-step study groups and male or female groups, requiring a more active role by participants, are often extremely beneficial. Patients are also encouraged to obtain a sponsor.

For those patients who require psychotropic medication, it is essential that the patient find a sponsor who is supportive of such treatment and of the psychiatrist who prescribes the medication. AA takes no position on outside issues such as medications, according to traditions. However, many AA members have opinions about psychotropic medication because so many nonpsychotic members have been prescribed addicting medications by physicians unskilled and skilled in addiction treatment.

It is of importance that over the past 10 years most psychotherapists working with addicted patients have become increasingly more insistent on maintenance of abstinence as a *prerequisite* for psychotherapy. Each provides different psychodynamic justifications for this practice. Bean-Bayog,[1] Brown,[4] Khantzian and Schneider,[5] Kaufman,[6] and MacKinnon and Michels[7] all agree on this requirement.

Treatment Contract

In the final phase of the assessment, the following are suggested:

- Agreement on method of detoxification and completion of same.
- Commitment to abstinence and recovery.
- Commitment to a comprehensive method for continuing abstinence after or instead of hospitalization including:
    The number of weekly twelve-step meetings (2–7).
    The number of weekly educational meetings (1–2).
    The number of weekly group therapy sessions (1–2).

The extent of modification of diet, exercise, and relaxation techniques.

Weekly family and couple therapy.

Testing of urine and/or breath for alcohol or other drug use.

- Commitment by each family member to a comprehensive family program including specifying number of self-help support groups such as Al-Anon, Cocanon, etc., significant-other groups, couple and family therapy, adolescent peer groups, and ACA groups (1–7 weekly).
- When there is major psychiatric illness requiring medication such as lithium, major tranquilizers or antidepressants, the patient agrees to take the medication as prescribed.
- The therapist may choose to list his or her desired therapeutic behaviors as part of the contract, e.g., listen carefully not act as a critical judge, avoid enabling behaviors, etc.
- Regular or random urine analysis or breathalyzer checks for alcohol and other drugs as part of treatment also may be extremely helpful to some individuals in maintaining early abstinence.

If the patient or his family do not follow the contract and the patient continues to use alcohol and other drugs, it may be best to terminate treatment until the patient either enters hospital or shows evidence of reimplementing the required behaviors as specified in the contract. Many patients and families who do not commit to workable contracts and who are asked to leave therapy return in the future agreeing to participate in a workable therapeutic program.

Early Recovery

Initial treatment in early recovery focuses on maintaining abstinence from drugs and alcohol. The initial 6 months to 2 years of psychotherapy should be supportive and utilize more directive therapies such as cognitive–behavioral. Maintaining sobriety is still the goal of therapy in early recovery. Interventions are directed at the cognitive and behavioral aspects of alcohol and other drug abuse.

The focus should be on "how" the patient abuses alcohol and other drugs, not on "why," when reviewing the history or immediate stressors. Examining "how" (behavioral causes and effects) allows the suggestion of alternative behaviors that can avoid precipitating relapse. Encouraging and presenting opportunities to practice drug-free behavior provides coping strategies for the sober patient. Focusing on "why" should only be done when it facilitates rapid abandonment of destructive behaviors. "Why" questions should be avoided when they provoke excuses and the need to defend oneself as a good person.

Replacing maladaptive and dysfunctional activities with behavior that maintains sobriety is a treatment goal of early recovery. Healthy substitute objects and behaviors of all kinds are useful. The therapist may encourage active alternatives such as regular exercise or education. Object substitution may also prevent or at least lessen the grieving that addicts sometimes experience while mourning the loss of the drug with its associated activities and people.

Psychotherapy during early recovery does not confront defenses too vigorously or remove them prematurely. These defense mechanisms are instead redirected and supported to promote abstinence and continued treatment. If long-term sobriety is to be maintained, defenses must ultimately be removed, but only gradually over periods of time often ranging from 2 to 5 years of abstinence. Therapy is a time-dependent process. Therapeutic interventions indicated later may be useful during early sobriety.[7]

Denial is a prominent unconscious defense mechanism in addictive illness that can serve the purpose of supporting and continuing addictive behavior. However, denial should not always be confronted early in therapy. Denial used as a mechanism for integrating the depths of reality and its uncontrollable dangers are essential to preserve. In the addict, increments of self-awareness and disclosure are often associated with increased anxiety and depression. Premature reduction of denial hinders defenses against this anxiety, which may result in a flooding of anxiety and rebound increase in denial. Denial should be worked gradually, titrating any anxieties and depression that arise from confronting it and that threaten a return to alcohol and other drug addiction.[7]

Inherent in addictive illness are projection and rationalization as mechanisms to defend against anxiety and depression. Uncomfortable and undesirable feelings and cognitive states are attributed to others. Blaming others arouses resentment in the addict, which can precipitate a relapse or continued alcohol and other drug use. Addicts can find themselves in cycles between two equally untherapeutic psychological alternatives (e.g., self-blame versus blaming others).[7] Self-blaming by the addict can lead to a relapse as well. Projection and rationalization are shifted in psychotherapy from the addiction to productive maintenance of abstinence. Previous dysfunctional behavior is attributed (by projection and rationalization) to the disease rather than to others or the self.

Therapeutically, this preferred defense allows identification by alcoholics with their alcoholism, enabling the patient to explain past behavior and to learn the new behavior of sobriety through identification with sober alcoholics. Later, after prolonged sobriety, the patient has a lifetime to recognize that not all difficulties can be explained by alcoholism.[7] Staying sober can be justification for avoiding stressful situations and emotional cues that previously precipitated drinking.

The therapist should recognize and therapeutically redirect defenses to help accomplish the primary goal of early recovery: staying sober. Prematurely reducing or removing preferred and effective means of coping with anxiety and depression can result in relapse of the addict or in the patient's terminating therapy. Confronting and interpreting defenses, as well as increasing responsibility by the patient for their intrapsychic state, comes later in successful psychotherapy of alcohol and other drug addicts.

At least partial resolution of certain intrapsychic conflicts is useful in reinforcing the principles of Alcoholics Anonymous or other twelve-step groups. For example, unresolved omnipotence, narcissistic entitlement, and power/dependency conflicts may prevent a patient from obtaining a sponsor or using AA fully, or may result in the patient's continuing patterns of grossly unsatisfying relationships. Psychodynamic therapy of such conflicts may help the patient to accept the principles of AA and to build more mutually satisfying relationships. However, intimate relationships are fraught with danger at this phase and should be discouraged.

Psychotherapy can be integrated with Alcoholics Anonymous. The period of early sobriety is characterized by extreme dependency and a corresponding need and reliance on external structure and support.[4] Alcohol (or drugs) becomes the primary object to the addict, providing constant stimulation without disappointment, for the addict thinks this object is under his control. This object cannot be relinquished without primitive object replacements, such as AA, cigarettes, coffee, food, soft drinks, and temporary relationships. A selection of these should be permitted to each addict, as they will evolve out of this dependent phase over time[5] and give up these objects only very gradually.

Addicted people are especially conflicted in regard to interpersonal dependency. Addicts alternate between distance, grandiose postures or self-sufficiency, and self-destructive dependency.[5] Transference manifestations of intolerable anxiety about dependency feelings could easily be misinterpreted as resistance to the therapy. Defenses against this anxiety should not be confronted as resistance, but supported as allowing the patient to continue in treatment. The conflicts about dependency that threaten to end treatment prematurely should be addressed directly.[4]

Other substitutes for the lost object should include active replacement with a new repertoire of patterns and behaviors. In this phase, identification with AA, NA, etc., helps addicts develop a means of establishing control. As they deal with and grasp their dependency, these patients need to feel some sense of control over their environment. They can be given control over the therapeutic hours (time of meetings, content of sessions) as well as their input into how many, what kind, and where and when they attend AA meetings.[4] It is suggested often that the alcoholic attend 90 meetings in 90 days initially. After this period, the number of meetings can be reduced according to the alcoholic and therapist.

In this phase, addicted people are coached and supported in moving out of friendships, patterns, and environments that were precipitants for alcohol and other drug addiction. A suggestion from AA members is that newly sober members stay away from slippery places if they are to avoid slipping (relapse). A new environment that does not contain cues to alcohol and other drug use provides a sense of safety, if the anxiety about the newness of it can be overcome.[4]

This phase also requires a dual shift for the average therapist (e.g., from confronter of denial and motivator of the addict into treatment, the therapist shifts to the supporter; from nondirective listener, to active teacher of new strategies and coping behaviors.[4]

Long-Term Recovery

Long-term recovery involves more traditional in-depth psychotherapy that gradually shifts from supportive to reconstructive. Patients with personality and anxiety disorders, but rarely those with psychoses, will respond to more dynamic forms of psychotherapy. The therapist can assist the patient in understanding noticeable changes in the therapy. The therapist will at this point interpret transference more, structure the therapy around psychodynamic themes, and examine dreams in more detail and depth.

Once the core identity as an alcoholic is firmly in place, a shift occurs from external behavioral control to internalization of control through identification, expansion of focus, and the use of uncovering psychotherapy.[4] This is a difficult time for patients, because they must simultaneously maintain an alcoholic/addict identity, apply cognitive–behavioral controls over addiction, and explore underlying issues relating to the recovery from alcoholism or hindering a satisfying sobriety.

Intense anxiety or anger often erupts as defenses are lowered and uncovering psychotherapy continues. For the patient to tolerate the anxiety necessary for insight, his or her identity and acceptance as an alcoholic or drug addict must first be solid. Personal controls on alcohol and other drug addiction must be intact in the addict.

Throughout therapy the patient and therapist must be constantly aware of the centrality of drugs and alcohol. Specific precipitants can be identified and explored in therapy and the focus can be shifted to underlying issues. Desires to use alcohol and other drugs may be warning signals to stop uncovering or, when interpreted as such, may permit the reconstructive psychotherapy to continue.

A critical area in implementing full recovery is the capacity to tolerate meaningful intimacy. Because many of these patients have not developed adolescent and young adult maturational relationship patterns, they must begin from the beginning in forming adult relationships. Thus, they may not be capable of even beginning to deal with meaningful intimacy until several years into this phase of long-term recovery. The incorporation of the therapist as capable of intimacy facilitates this process, but the development of intimacy also depends on a good deal of practice. During this time, the therapist should be supportive of continued relationship trials while exploring the underlying fears and should maintain a continued role as teacher of the gradual steps and frustrations of achieving intimacy.

The final step in psychotherapy during recovery is working through termination. This step is not done with finality in alcohol and other drug addicts, because the door should always be left open for their return. In addition, they are encouraged to continue in a twelve-step group at varying levels of intensity as needed for the rest of their lives.

REFERENCES

1. Bean-Bayog M (1986). Psychopathology produced by alcoholism. In: Meyer RE (ed.), *Psychopathology and Addictive Disorders*. New York: Guilford.

2. Kaufman E & Reoux J (1988). Guidelines for the successful psychotherapy of substance abusers. *Am J Drug Alc Abuse* 14:199–209.

3. Grant I & Reed R (1985). Neuropsychology of alcohol and drug abuse. In: Alterman A (ed.), *Substance Abuse and Psychopathology.* New York: Plenum.

4. Brown S (1985). *Treating the Alcoholic, a Developmental Model of Recovery.* New York: Wiley.

5. Khantzian EJ & Schneider RJ (1986). Treatment implications of psychodynamic understanding of opioid addicts. In Meyer RE (ed.), *Psychopathology and Addictive Disorders.* New York: Guilford.

6. Kaufman E (1989). The psychotherapy of dually diagnosed patients. *J Subst Abuse Treat* 6:9–18.

7. MacKinnon RA & Michels R (1971). *The Psychiatric Interview in Clinical Practice.* Philadelphia: Saunders.

PART VII

Prevention

26

The Prevention of Abuse and Addiction to Alcohol and Drugs

OVERVIEW

Addiction to alcohol and other drugs is a consummate example of a preventable disorder. Physicians can play a valuable role in the prevention of addiction as well as intervene in the early stages of the disorder—thus preventing its progression. As with other disorders, if a fraction of the effort and money that is expended for sequela of these illnesses and for their treatment was devoted to prevention, there would be astonishing savings in cost, suffering, and lives. Many physicians could play decisive roles in the battle against the onset of these illnesses.

Many physicians feel compelled to "go all out" to save lives almost irrespective of age and cost once the illness has been established. Their attitude is against weighing the cost versus benefit except in extremely obvious cases once the illness has developed.

Prevention is not ordinarily aggressively pursued except in large-scale, community-based operations such as for vaccinations and detection campaigns that may identify a patient population for diagnosis and treatment of an illness, and less so to prevent one. Perhaps prevention is so little regarded, paradoxically, because of the high cost–effectiveness ratio. Furthermore, physicians are not well trained in prevention in medical school and specialty training.

Addiction is an area of medicine that heretofore has received little time and attention in medical school curricula. Addiction has only recently gained acceptance as an illness or a disease. Other psychiatric illnesses have much longer had such regard. However, some physicians still debate whether or not addiction or other psychiatric illnesses are diseases. Others talk about "the disease *concept* of addiction" rather than simply "addictive disease" or "the disease of addiction"—finding it necessary to think in conceptual terms, instead of actual disease processes.[1] Other psychiatric illnesses have gained a more favorable attitude.

The physician is not alone in the poor recognition of addiction as a disease. For example, alcoholism is still popularly regarded as an accepted consequence of some other problem, whether psychiatric, emotional, social, or cultural. Excessive or problem drinking is still denied on an individual or institutional basis ("we don't have those kinds of problems in this hospital"). Addiction to nicotine, alcohol, and other drugs constitute the most significant and preventable health problem in America. Yet the American public maintains attitudes condoning the acceptance of widespread alcohol consumption. It remains perplexing that our society allows pervasive and intrusive advertising and permissive access to alcohol. The country is currently preoccupied with a "drug problem," i.e., cocaine, but appears less concerned about the alcohol problem, which causes death and destruction at rates exceeding all other drugs combined.

It is impossible to watch a sporting event on television without seeing forceful enticements to drink beer, and to drink more beer. The young of today must know as much about beer as they do about their favorite star athletes. Athletes themselves are participants in the advertisements. The heroes of modern America are rallying the young and old to drink more and more beer.

INTERACTIONS

If we take the universe of those with the diagnoses of alcohol and drug addiction, the rates for other psychiatric disorders are not greatly elevated above those rates in the general population. However, if we take psychiatric disorders as the index diagnosis, the rates for addictive disorders are elevated above the general population, particularly, for schizophrenia and antisocial personality disorder (ASP). Fifty percent of schizophrenics and 80% of those with ASP have a diagnosable addictive disorder.

We do not know by schizophrenics are at such great risk for addictive disorders. Perhaps a biochemical explanation of a shared "dopamine hypothesis" is a beginning. We believe excessive dopamine transmission is important in the generation of psychotic symptoms in schizophrenia and also underlies reinforcement in the self-administration in addictive use of alcohol and drugs. More research is needed to develop prevention and intervention in this vulnerable population.

We have speculated that sociopaths seek excitement and exhibit many behaviors of excess, particularly those that enhance danger and risk. Also, the profit factor of the drug trade places them at higher risk to be exposed to addicting drugs. For reasons not entirely understood, the lifestyle of those with ASP frequently involves alcohol and other drugs. The increased exposure from whatever origins appears to play a significant role in the development of ASP. Future research is needed to develop prevention and intervention in this significant population.

FOCUS

According to surveys, youngsters today know more names of beer and other forms of alcohol than Presidents and States. Children's minds are permeated with clever and powerful advertisements programmed by the genius of Madison Avenue. These innocent citizens are being hit with themes and acts that are designed to get people (and them) to drink.

The older children and adults who read magazines of all kinds, including the literary ones, are subjected to persistent and often sexy illustrations of compelling reasons to drink, i.e., high society, success, companionship, intimacy, and power. The back page of the New Yorker frequently has an advertisement for a liquor. The program for the New York Philharmonic frequently contains advertisements for liquor as well. Young people who are encouraged to learn about and experience higher culture are repeatedly subjected to exhortations to drink to be more advanced.

There are many more examples in all aspects of American society in which alcohol, and more than informative exposure to alcohol, is everywhere, in fully acceptable and unqualified endorsements by those who use the proceeds for financial support. Unfortunately, little consideration and restraint are given to the wide exposure and use of alcohol by all ages.

A useful, pragmatic, conceptual approach for understanding the prevalence rates for addiction is a simple equation that *addiction* to alcohol and other drugs equals *vulnerability* plus *exposure*. The most difficult part of the equation, and the first step, is to recognize that the problem exists and to what magnitude. Without an accurate assessment of *addiction,* the solutions are vague and understandably inept.[1,2]

The identification of addiction is explored elsewhere in this book and mostly involves some education and an honest appraisal of the problem. The behaviors associated with addiction include preoccupation with the acquisition and use of alcohol or other drugs, compulsive or continued use despite adverse consequences, and a pattern of relapse or return to alcohol and drugs in spite of adverse consequences.

The vulnerability to the development of addiction has been demonstrated to be genetic, at least, in part. As presented in another chapter, twin and adoption studies, and familial and high-risk studies have confirmed that a genetic component is implicated in the transmission of alcoholism and drug addiction. The exact nature of this genetic vulnerability has not been identified, although the studies in high-risk individuals strongly suggest that it has a physical basis. Alcoholics and high-risk individuals appear to have enhanced tolerance to alcohol, manifested subjectively and objectively, and attributable to central nervous system functions, namely, brain and brain stem.[1,2] Some familial studies have found that alcoholism is prevalent in the families of cocaine and cannabis addicts, suggesting a genetic link between vulnerability to develop addiction to these drugs and alcohol.

However, the *vulnerability* portion of the question does not lend itself to easy manipulation. The genetic vulnerability to alcoholism or drug addiction is changed only after generations of mating, perhaps, and no ready and quick solution to altering the genes is currently available—or perhaps desirable. Education and genetic counseling may have an impact on assortative mating of alcoholics, although this has not been attempted on a large scale. It is not clear that it has been advocated by very many, or should be.

However, the exposure portion of the equation is subject to manipulation, although not easily, because of recognizable resistance. *Exposure* is inclusive and covers all the various factors that contribute to the eventual use of the drug or alcohol, particularly by those who are susceptible and vulnerable to addiction. Exposure is determined by a large number of influences, although these may be categorized under attitudes and practices regarding alcohol and drugs.[3,4]

The attitudes towards the use of alcohol are reflected in virtually every aspect of America's way of life, because alcohol consumption is a firmly rooted institution. The permissive attitude towards the use of alcohol is evident in everyday life. It is difficult to describe a drinking behavior or event without some attachment of frivolity and humor. Drinking, even to the extreme, is generally considered entertaining. Alcohol is served in many public places, at the White House, most weddings and funerals, and other social gatherings. In fact, it is the exception to not have alcohol available as part of the event. The public pressure to have alcohol as part of a social event is as great as is the pressure to use alcohol by those attending.

The peer pressure on children in and out of school is intolerable. Children must endure tremendous and often insurmountable pressures from their peers to drink and use drugs. Alcohol is the drug first introduced to the child and is frequently the most often used. Childhood and adolescent alcoholism is common, unfortunately; as many as 25–50% of the alcoholics in the U.S. had the onset of their alcoholism in their teenage years. The combination of peer pressure and widespread exposure to alcohol in advertisements and practices results in the majority of young Americans being exposed often and in large doses to alcohol.

Other commonly expressed factors in exposure are the psychosocial factors. The exposure to alcohol does not depend on psychosocial factors that are distinctive, except for some notable conditions. Sociopathic males appear to be more likely to be exposed to alcohol, probably for obvious reasons. Sociopaths appear to be high consumers of alcohol and have high rates of alcoholism. As many as 90% of those incarcerated in prisons are alcoholic and 80% of homicides involve alcohol use. Over 75% of the cases of domestic violence involve the use of alcohol in states of intoxication.[3]

The states of deprivation in economic and social conditions do not seem to be distinguishing "psychosocial factors" in the development of alcoholism and most drug addiction. These psychosocial factors may be more important in the origin of illicit drug use and trade, where profit for drug dealing is present and represents an additional motivation for propagation of drug use.

It is also important to recognize that alcohol is a gateway drug for the use and development of addiction to other drugs. Most cocaine and cannabis addicts use and become addicted to alcohol before cocaine and cannabis are tried. It seems that the introduction to drugs other than alcohol is somehow dependent on alcohol. In some ways alcohol is a conduit to other drug use and addiction. The reasons may lie somewhere in the realization that alcohol is a drug and has similar drug effects to the illicit drugs.

The sharp demarcation between alcohol and other drugs is not readily possible on pharmacological and pathophysiological grounds. The distinction between alcohol and other drugs is a legal and social and subject to considerable error in conferring greater safety for alcohol over some other drugs.

TREATMENT

The manipulation of the *exposure* portion of the equation is possible and could result in the dramatic reduction in the onset of alcoholism and drug addiction. The current changes in attitudes and practices towards cigarette smoking provide a model to use for alcohol and other drugs. Public awareness and attitudes changed sufficiently to finally allow the government to acknowledge that nicotine contained in cigarettes is addicting. Heretofore, public opinion and successful lobbying efforts by the tobacco industry prohibited a realistic appraisal of the magnitude of the health problem from cigarette smoking. Finally, public sentiment was reflected in new city, state, and federal laws regarding the use and sale of cigarettes.

Some of the more dramatic and effective legislation forbids cigarette advertisement on television, restricts smoking in public places, and warns the public of the hazards of cigarette smoking. These and other measures have resulted in significant reductions in the exposure to cigarettes. As a consequence, the use of tobacco has dropped considerably in recent times. A gratifying, corresponding reduction in the adverse consequences of cigarette smoking will certainly follow with the lower rate of addiction to cigarettes.

The same paradigm can be applied to alcohol consumption. Public awareness and attitudes toward alcohol can result in a change in practices regarding the sale and consumption of alcohol. The type and amount of advertisement of alcoholic beverages can be modified to sane proportions, and perhaps eliminated altogether, at least on television. Restricting the places and hours where alcohol can be purchased and used would reduce consumption rates dramatically. These changes could be brought about by legislation prompted by the public—lawmakers would never venture such decisions regarding alcohol without a directive from the public.[5]

The lowered exposure would likely result in a reduction of consumption and a subsequent lowering of the prevalence rates for alcoholism and drug addiction. This in turn might lead to a reduction in the exposure to illicit drugs, without alcohol as a gateway to their use. The adverse consequences of alcoholism and drug addiction would be fewer and less compelling with a reduction in their prevalence.

REFERENCES

1. Schuckit MA (1987). Biological vulnerability to alcoholism. *J Consulting & Clinical Psychology* 55:301–309.
2. Monteiro MG & Schuckit MA (In press). Populations at high risk—Recent Findings. *J Clin Psych.*
3. Proceedings of the National Conference on Alcohol and Drug Abuse Prevention (August 3–6, 1986). *Sharing Knowledge for Action.* U.S. Dept of Health and Human Services, PHS: ADAMHA.
4. Smart RG (1986). The impact on consumption of selling wine in grocery stores. *Alc Alcoholism* 21:233–236.
5. Gerstein D (1984). Alcohol Policy: Preventative options. In: Grinspoon L (ed.), *Psychiatry Update III* pp. 359–371. Washington, DC: American Psychiatry Association.

Index